DIVERSITY CONSCIOUSNESS

Opening Our Minds to People, Cultures, and Opportunities

DIVERSITY CONSCIOUSNESS

OPENING OUR MINDS TO PEOPLE, CULTURES, AND OPPORTUNITIES

RICHARD D. BUCHER

Baltimore City Community College

PRENTICE HALL
Upper Saddle River, New Jersey 07458

Library of Congress Catologing-in-Publication Data
Bucher, Richard D., 1949–
    Diversity Consciousness: opening our minds to people, cultures,
and opportunities / Richard D. Bucher
      p.   cm.
    Includes bibliographical references and index.
    ISBN 0-13-080338-3
    1. Diversity in the workplace   2. Multiculturalism. I. Title.
HF5549.5.M5B83 1999
331.13'3—dc21   99-42489
                                                       CIP

Production Supervision: *Kathryn Kasturas*
Managing Editor: *Mary Carnis*
Director of Production and Manufacturing: *Bruce Johnson*
Manufacturing Manager: *Marc Bove*
Acquisitions Editor: *Sande Johnson*
Editorial Assistant: *Michelle Williams*
Marketing Manager: *Jeff McIlroy*
Interior Design and Page Layout: *Kathryn Kasturas*
Cover Design: *Joe Sengotta*
Cover Photo: *Izzy Schwartz*

©2000 by Prentice-Hall, Inc.
Upper Saddle River, New Jersey 07458

Printed in the United States of America

10 9 8 7 6

ISBN 0-13-080338-3

Prentice-Hall International (UK) Limited, *London*
Prentice-Hall of Australia Pty. Limited, *Sydney*
Prentice-Hall Canada, Inc., *Toronto*
Prentice-Hall Hispanoamericana, S.A., *Mexico*
Prentice-Hall of India Private Limited, *New Delhi*
Prentice-Hall of Japan, Inc., *Tokyo*
Pearson Education Asia Pte. Ltd., *Singapore*
Editora Prentice-Hall do Brasil, Ltda., *Rio de Janeiro*

CONTENTS

Foreword *ix*

Preface *xi*

About the Student Editors *xv*

In Appreciation *xvii*

Chapter 1   Diversity: An Overview 1

Chapter Objectives *1*
Our Changing Cultural Landscape *2*
Views of Diversity: Assimilation and Pluralism *10*
Dimensions of Diversity *13*
Diversity between and within Groups *17*
Diversity Myths *18*
What Is Diversity Consciousness? *20*
Diversity Education *21*
Exercises *23*

Chapter 2   Diversity Skills and Success 26

Chapter Objectives *26*
Definitions of Success *27*
Sociocultural Theory and Success *30*
Why Diversity Skills Are Important *32*
Diversity Skills and Individual/Organizational Benefits *45*
The Costs of Inadequate Diversity Skills *50*
Exercises *52*

v

Chapter 3   Personal and Social Barriers to Success 57

Chapter Objectives 57
Six Barriers to Success 59
Acknowledging and Overcoming Diversity Barriers 83
Exercises 89

Chapter 4   Developing Diversity Consciousness 94

Chapter Objectives 94
Diversity Consciousness 95
Isolation 96
Six Areas of Development 101
Strategies for Developing Diversity Consciousness 118
A Continuing Process 122
Exercises 123

Chapter 5   Communicating in a Diverse World 127

Chapter Objectives 127
Communication and Culture 128
Electronic Communication 132
Diversity Consciousness and Communication 134
The Importance of Communication 142
Barriers to Effective Communication 144
Hot Buttons 146
Difficult Dialogues 149
Communicating Inclusively 151
Exercises 154

Chapter 6   Teamwork 158

Chapter Objectives 158
Teams Today 159
Developing Teamwork Skills 167
Diversity Consciousness and Teaming 168
Team Leadership 170
High-Performance Teams 173
Obstacles to Teamwork 177
Conflict 179
Exercises 187

Chapter 7 Conclusion *192*

Chapter Objectives *192*
Opening Your Mind to Opportunities *194*
Future Challenges *196*
Exercises *204*

Bibliography *209*

Suggested Readings *221*

Index *227*

FOREWORD

By the year 2050, almost 50% of the population will be minorities and 50% will be women. These U.S. Bureau of Labor statistics paint a very clear and convincing picture of why diversity must be viewed for what it truly is: a core corporate strategic initiative that directly affects the bottom line, not the latest human resources initiative or fad.

In order to compete in today's highly competitive labor market for skilled, creative, dedicated employees, leaders must achieve a diverse work force at all levels of their organization. They must also create a corporate culture that will effectively utilize and retain the diverse talents they bring into their organizations.

At Fannie Mae, we made a serious long-term commitment to "look like America." We have discovered that when you broaden your employee base, then utilize that expanded pool of talent, experience, and insight, you let loose in your business a tremendous force for the creation of innovation and change. Our experience is that this leads to competitive advantages. In essence, diversity becomes a powerful tool you can use to create a positive impact on your markets and better capitalize on business opportunities. We know that our unwavering commitment to diversity is one of the key elements that has made it possible for Fannie Mae to achieve twelve consecutive years of double digit earnings.

The cornerstone of any successful diversity initiative must establish and create a core culture and environment in which:

- employees are treated fairly
- employees are recognized and rewarded based on ability and merit for their contributions
- employees have equal access to opportunity for growth and advancement
- employees respect each other and are free from harassment, discrimination, and intolerance
- the diversity of American society is represented at all levels throughout the company
- the management and development of employees is viewed as crucial to the success of the business.

On an individual level, developing a high level of diversity consciousness is an absolutely essential part of a student's preparation for entering the workplace. Students who hone these skills will find they have a distinct advantage when they look for jobs or seek advancement.

The single most essential element necessary to creating an environment in which diversity will thrive, is the unwavering commitment and active, visible involvement of senior management, starting from the very top of the organization. Like any successful corporate initiative that affects the profitability and survival of an organization, diversity must be interwoven into every aspect of the organization. Results cannot be achieved overnight. There is no quick fix or panacea. It is hard work that pays big dividends.

The way America will be able to excel in the increasingly competitive world market of the twenty-first century is to utilize the incredible wealth of untapped, diverse talent in this country. Those companies that maximize their utilization of our greatest natural resource will be the ones who emerge as the global leaders of the next millennium. Diversity is an essential fact of life for everyone, everyday in America. It is an issue that will never go away.

Richard Bucher's work makes a major contribution to a clearer understanding of how and why diversity is crucial to the basic prosperity and future survival of our country.

Franklin D. Raines
Chairman and CEO, Fannie Mae

Franklin D. Raines is Chairman and Chief Executive Officer of Fannie Mae, a New York Stock Exchange company and the largest non-bank financial services company in the world. Fannie Mae is the nation's largest source of financing for home mortgages. He became Chairman and Chief Executive Officer on January 1, 1999. He is the first African-American to head a Fortune 50 firm.

Raines serves as a member of the congressionally-mandated Commission on Roles and Missions of the Armed Forces. He has also served on a number of federal and state public policy advisory groups regarding tax equity, education, poverty, and welfare reform.

Raines was elected a Fellow of the American Academy of Social Insurance, and the Council on Foreign Relations.

Raines was graduated magna cum laude with a B.A. degree from Harvard College. He was graduated cum laude with a J.D. from Harvard Law School. He also attended Magdalen College, Oxford University as a Rhodes Scholar.

PREFACE

I recently happened to pick up a magazine that featured this advertisement: "Life without technology isn't an option." As we begin the next century, it is becoming increasingly apparent that life without diversity is not an option either. Our personal worlds are expanding as people and cultures throughout the world become more and more interconnected. Human diversity, in its many shapes, forms, and colors, is an integral part of our everyday life. As a result, each of us desperately needs to develop our *diversity consciousness*: our awareness, understanding, and skills in the area of diversity.

Diversity consciousness is important for a number of reasons. It allows us to appreciate and enjoy the infinite variety of people and lifestyles that are part of our expanding social world. More specifically, we will increase our knowledge and stretch our thinking. By learning to interpret events through different cultural lenses, we will be able to think critically and adapt to a large variety of situations. Because of our ability to communicate and team with different kinds of people, we will be more successful at work, school, and in other realms of life.

This book is an outgrowth of my personal and professional experiences during the past thirty years. From the beginning, I have wrestled with the subject of diversity intellectually and emotionally. I attended Howard University, a historically black institution, to pursue my studies in the area of race and ethnic relations and earn my doctorate degree. As a white male, this experience radically altered my thinking about diversity. My experiences as a college professor have also been invaluable. For the past twenty-five years, I have taught students from a rich variety of cultures and backgrounds at Baltimore City Community College (BCCC). More than anything, this experience has taught me the importance of listening to my students and appreciating their diversity. It has also made me look inward, into my own thoughts, feelings, and behavior. In addition to my teaching, I served as the first Director of BCCC's Institute for InterCultural Understanding (IIU). Nationally recognized for its work in diversity education, the IIU nourishes an inclusive, international learning community of students, faculty, staff, and community members. On a more personal level, my work with the IIU makes me more aware of the difficulty and importance of making students as well as educators more conscious of diversity and its central place in a high-quality education.

Another extremely important dimension of my own diversity is my status as the parent of a son who has a disability called autism. My son, as well as the rest of my family, provides me with daily reminders of the joys and challenges of diversity. Jimmy has enriched our lives and brought our family closer together. Because of Jimmy, my family and I see and experience life differently. My daughter Katie, who is in college, was recently asked to write about someone who has influenced her life. She wrote about Jimmy. "Growing up with my autistic brother, I have discovered more and more about myself and other people. He has shown me that not everything wonderful seems wonderful at first sight. When you have someone so different that is so close to you, you develop an uncommon compassion for others."

The aim of this book is two-dimensional. First, it examines the relationship between a person's success and his or her ability to understand, respect, and value diversity. Success, as defined in this book, means to achieve your goals. A second aim is to explore how people can develop diversity consciousness. Subjects such as teamwork, conflict management, communication, and flexible thinking are discussed in a style that promotes self-reflection and dialogue. A wide variety of real-life student experiences and perspectives appear throughout. Finally, this book addresses critically important subjects often missing in the curriculum and avoided in the classroom.

Diversity Consciousness introduces a perspective that is largely absent in college courses. Many of these courses avoid diversity issues or treat them as an afterthought. For example, it is a common assumption that students share the same perspectives and life experiences. Some instructors assume that students will learn about diversity "on the side" or "on their own." Unfortunately, students may interpret this to mean that diversity is not central to their education or their success. This interpretation is not borne out by numerous studies in the fields of education and business. These studies, which are cited throughout the book, reveal that a wide range of diversity skills, such as teaming, communication, and conflict resolution, are directly related to success in college and beyond.

Throughout the book, I have used different terminology to refer to certain groups of people. For instance, I use the term Black as well as African-American; Latino as well as Hispanic. Using a variety of terms is one way of acknowledging that we do not all agree regarding the labels we attach to human differences.

Diversity Consciousness: Opening Our Minds to People, Cultures, and Opportunities possesses five key features that make it relevant and meaningful to students. This book is:

1. *Student-Oriented.* It is infused with genuine anecdotes and perspectives from a very diverse population of students. Too often,

educators do not really listen to students when we teach and write. We do not actively collaborate with students in the process of learning and sharing. This book provides a sounding board for a large number of college students from a wide variety of educational, social, and ethnic backgrounds. One distinguishing feature is the integration of real-life "student perspectives" throughout each chapter. They provide a wealth of insight that we need to digest and share. As you read this book, you will recognize everyday struggles, stories, and achievements.

2. *Success-Oriented.* More and more employers are realizing that diversity awareness and skills are crucial because they result in greater teamwork, creativity, productivity, and profit. Students who have a solid grounding in the area of diversity have more to offer their employers. Research shows that diversity is not some feel-good issue. Only now are we beginning to realize that education in the area of diversity relates strongly to success.

3. *Focused on Personal Growth and Empowerment.* The book emphasizes the importance of educating oneself in the area of diversity. The process begins with one's own background and culture and then extends to others. In addition, the book views diversity education as an ongoing process rather than an event—a process that requires self-reflection and evaluation, patience, and commitment. Although education of this nature is hard work, it pays off regardless of who you are or where you come from.

4. *Grounded in Research.* A growing number of studies have examined the impact of education or training in the area of diversity. For example, a number of studies indicate that college students who are exposed to diversity issues are more apt to be culturally sensitive and satisfied with college life. Similarly, a number of companies report that diversity education programs are making a measurable difference in worker creativity and productivity. These kinds of studies are important because they move us beyond anecdotal evidence. Research can help us evaluate the impact of educational strategies and plan for the future.

5. *Oriented Toward the Value of Diversity.* Throughout our lives, we have been taught that diversity is a problem rather than a valuable resource. Traditionally, the focus has been on minimizing or denying differences rather than rethinking how we approach differences. To be successful we need to develop a new kind of thinking that enables us to appreciate diversity and use it to benefit ourselves and others.

As you read the book, remember that it is designed to help you do more than just learn about diversity. Regardless of your feelings about diversity, try to approach the book with an open mind. Rather than simply taking in what you read, get involved and stretch yourself intellectually and emotionally. One way to do this is to respond to journal questions. Whenever you see ✎ or any time you feel a need to record something in writing, place an entry in your journal. Writing in a journal reinforces your learning, provides you with a record of your thoughts, and provides a basis for further reflection.

Try to open your thinking to different points of view. Take time to reflect on what you read and how it relates to you. Imagine how the world might be viewed by people who do not look, think, and act like you. Wrestle with the subject matter. If what you read makes you feel uncomfortable, that is OK. It is an inevitable part of the learning process. Finally, share your thoughts and feelings *and* learn to listen carefully and respectfully to others—even when it is difficult.

I welcome feedback from students, faculty, employees and employers, or anyone else who might read this book. You may e-mail your comments to me at rdbucher@aol.com; or write me at Baltimore City Community College, 2901 Liberty Heights Avenue, Baltimore, MD 21215.

ABOUT
THE STUDENT
EDITORS

Kyra Capen graduated from the University of Maryland at College Park (UMCP) in 1998. She received a B.A. degree in government and politics and earned a university honors citation. For two years, Kyra taught a freshmen honors course designed to introduce students to a liberal arts education and how diversity affects that education. Kyra is currently the academic advisor for the Department of Government and Politics at UMCP.

Stephanie Freeman is finishing her studies at Baltimore City Community College. Upon graduation, she will be leaving with an Associate of Arts degree in general education. She intends to "pursue her heart" by entering the undergraduate program at the University of Baltimore and majoring in English. Stephanie is an aspiring author, currently hard at work on two novels with the hope that both will be published in the not too distant future. According to Stephanie, the book *Diversity Consciousness: Opening Our Minds to People, Cultures, and Opportunities* "is a long time coming." She continues: "As a student, I have never seen anything like this book out there. It is good to see that someone else has an interest in this besides me."

IN
APPRECIATION

This book has been a true team effort, from its inception to the final product. I am indebted to so many people.

First, I want to thank all the students from many different colleges and universities who have taught me so much and are such a big part of this book. In particular, I would like to acknowledge the valuable contributions of students I have taught at Baltimore City Community College (BCCC) for the past twenty-five years. I would be remiss if I did not mention my two wonderful student editors, Stephanie Freeman of the University of Baltimore and Kyra Capen of the University of Maryland.

In addition, the help of my colleagues has been invaluable. These people include a great number of faculty, administrators, and staff at BCCC. Particularly, I am indebted to President James Tshchechtelin, Vice-President Wilfredo Nieves, and faculty as well as staff: Walter Dean, Karen McClaskey, Schuzan Yang, Sukuntella Dhanesar, Meintje Westerbeek, Betsy Mackey, and Charlie McMartin.

My job has been made that much easier by an extremely strong, supportive team at Prentice Hall. While I cannot name everyone, there are a number of people to whom I am deeply indebted. They are Carol Carter, Publisher; Sande Johnson, Acquisitions Editor; Mary Carnis, Managing Editor; Kathryn Kasturas, Production Editor; Bruce Johnson, Director of Manufacturing; Jeff McIlroy, Marketing Manager; Barbara Rosenberg, Marketing Assistant; Marc Bove, Manufacturing Buyer; Jane Conte, Cover Director; Joe Sengatta, Cover Design; Izzy Schwartz, Cover Photo; Michelle Williams, Editorial Assistant; Alice Barr, Senior Sales Representative; and Todd Russell, Senior Marketing Manager/Product Specialist. Each member of this team has given me the encouragement and guidance I needed, but also the freedom to explore and create. For that, I am extremely appreciative.

As a writer, I have had the luxury of working with a very diverse and knowledgeable group of reviewers. They have put in countless hours and their input has been invaluable. The reviewers include Jim Cebulski, University of South Florida; Kathy York, Community College of Denver; Patricia Terrell, Utah

State University; Kim Wells, Northern Virginia Community College; Adrienne Conover-Williams and Janice Pressey, Baltimore City Community College; Chris Tucker, Watkins Mill High School in Gaithersburg, Maryland; and Sarah Lyman Kravits, an author who resides in San Francisco.

A number of other people have also made significant contributions. Regina Bryan, an accomplished photographer, provided advice and contributed two of her photographs. Kathy Calderazzi, a lawyer based in Virginia, has shared her expertise regarding a number of questions dealing with diversity and its relation to conflict resolution and the law. Additionally, I have corresponded with a large number of educators and businesspersons throughout the country. Their insight was extremely helpful, and in some cases their comments appear in the book.

Finally and most important, I would like to express my deep gratitude to members of my family. Every day they teach me something new and different about diversity. My son, Jimmy, and my daughters, Katie and Suzy, help me laugh at myself and keep my priorities in order. My mother, who is living in the San Diego area, and my late father, a teacher as well as a prolific writer, provided me with my first lessons in valuing diversity. Finally, my wife, Pat, has been the person who has supported me the most. Pat is an experienced, highly innovative educator. In addition to teaching, she trains other teachers, develops curriculum, and speaks at conferences. While writing this book I have continually asked questions of her. Somehow she always found the time to help, whether it was providing another perspective, helping me with a computer question, or pushing me to probe deeper. Without Pat's help, this book would never have been written.

Richard D. Bucher

DIVERSITY CONSCIOUSNESS

OPENING OUR MINDS TO PEOPLE, CULTURES, AND OPPORTUNITIES

1

DIVERSITY: AN OVERVIEW

Upon completion of this chapter, you will be able to:

○ Define **diversity**.

○ Explain what is meant by our *changing cultural landscape*.

○ Describe and give examples of demographic, social, and cultural changes that are responsible for the growing importance of diversity.

○ Contrast **assimilation** and **pluralism** and give an example of each.

○ List at least four characteristics of diversity.

○ List and explain five diversity myths.

○ Define **diversity consciousness**.

○ Define **diversity education**.

> *Many cultures contribute to the richness of our world community. Just as every culture has time honored traditions that make its heritage unique, each of us has individual qualities and characteristics that make us special. Let us learn more of one another...in knowledge there is understanding; in understanding there is respect; and where there is respect, growth is possible.*[1]

Diversity is defined in the dictionary as "a state of unlikeness" or "the condition of being different." Diversity can be viewed and defined in many different ways. In this book, **diversity** refers to *all* of the ways in which people are different. This includes individual, group, and cultural differences.

Today, diversity is getting a great deal of attention. We don't have to look far to see why. Imagine a group of employees at work or a class of students at college. Then imagine how that same group might have looked, thought, and acted differently two or three decades ago. Now picture how this same group might change by the year 2050.

◼◼◼ OUR CHANGING CULTURAL LANDSCAPE

Traditionally, the concept of diversity is most often used in relation to culture. **Culture** refers to our way of life, including everything that is learned, shared, and transmitted from one generation to the next. Language, values, rules, beliefs, and even the material things we create are all part of one's culture. *Landscape* means a scene or a setting. When we talk about **cultural landscape**, we are referring to the different lifestyles, traditions, and perspectives that can be found in the United States and throughout the world. Our cultural landscape is changing constantly.

Demographic Changes in the United States

Diversity is not a new phenomenon. If we look back at the first U.S. Census in 1790, we see some interesting differences and similarities with today's society (see Fig. 1.1). The first U.S. Census revealed our rural character. Only 3 percent of the population lived in settlements of 8000 or more.[2] In 1790, almost one out of five residents (about 19 percent) was African-American. It is interesting to

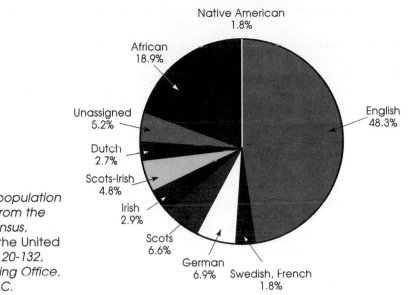

Figure 1.1: *Total U.S. population distribution in 1970. (From the U.S. Bureau of the Census,* Historical Statistics of the United States, *Part II, Series Z 20-132, U.S. Government Printing Office, 1976.) Washington, D.C.*

note the cultural diversity among Whites at that time. About 75 percent of the white population were White Anglo-Saxon Protestant (English, Scots, Scots-Irish); 25 percent were mainly Dutch, French, German, Irish, and Swedish.[3] These statistics show that early inhabitants of this country were not monocultural. In other words, they were not all culturally alike.

Since 1790, the cultural landscape of the United States has continued to change. We are no longer a rural society. Approximately 75 percent of our population lives in urban areas.[4] Our racial and ethnic mix has a different look as well. The percentage of African-Americans has declined from approximately 19 percent in 1790 to slightly more than 12 percent today. Asians and Pacific Islanders have steadily increased in numbers since they were first counted in the 1860 Census. This population is one of the fastest-growing ethnic groups in the United States. Census Bureau projections indicate that Hispanics, another rapidly growing population, will outnumber African-Americans in the near future. Currently, there are more Hispanic than African-American children in the United States. The percentage of Whites peaked in 1940 at approximately 90 percent, and the figure is now closer to 74 percent. The U.S. Census Bureau estimates that by the year 2050, racial and ethnic minorities will account for 47 percent of the nation's population (see Fig. 1.2). From now until that time, the percentage of Whites who are not Hispanic (Hispanics can be of any race) will shrink noticeably to 52.8 percent).

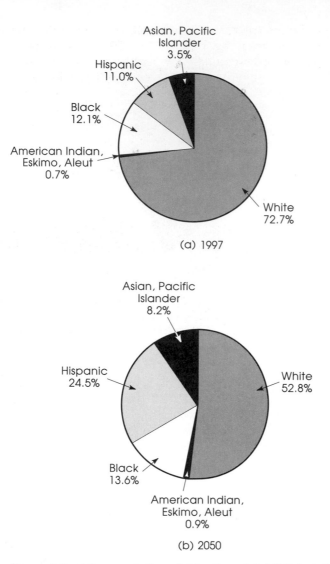

Asian, Pacific
Islander
3.5%

Hispanic
11.0%

Black
12.1%

American Indian,
Eskimo, Aleut
0.7%

White
72.7%

(a) 1997

Asian, Pacific
Islander
8.2%

Hispanic
24.5%

White
52.8%

Black
13.6%

American Indian,
Eskimo, Aleut
0.9%

(b) 2050

Figure 1.2: *U.S. population distribution: (a) 1997 (total population = 267.6 million); (b) 2050 (projected; total population = 393.9 million). Data from the U.S. Census Bureau makes it possible to compare today's population by racial and ethnic distribution with projected figures for the year 2050. Projections are based on estimates of future birthrate and immigration trends. ((a) From U.S. Bureau of the Census,* Statistical Abstract of the United States, 1998, *118th ed., Washington, D.C., 1998; (b) from U.S. Bureau of the Census,* Current Population Reports, Series P25-1092 *(U.S. Government Printing Office, Washington, D.C., 1992), and* Statistical Abstract of the United States, 1994, *(U.S. Government Printing Office, Washington, D.C., 1994.))*

Census data must be interpreted cautiously. Different groupings have been used since the first Census. In 1870, for instance, the terms *quadroon* (one-fourth Black, or having one black grandparent) and *octoroon* (one-eighth black, or having one black great-grandparent) were used to indicate the exact amount of a person's black heritage.

In recent years, racial categories have been added and an increasing number of people have chosen to identify themselves as "other." Many people do not feel that they belong in a single category, and others do not want to be categorized at all. One student, who refuses to select any category, explains, "I'm not White, I'm not Black, and I sure don't want to be an *other*."

▣ DON'T BOX ME IN

An increasing number of people are resisting the pressure to be boxed in by color. Tiger Woods, for example, has made it known that he objects to being called African-American. Rather, he prefers "Cablinasian," a term he made up that combines his Caucasian, Black, Indian, and Asian ancestry. Other well-known people who have affirmed their mixed ancestry are Keanu Reeves (Hawaiian, Chinese, Caucasian), Mariah Carey (Black, Venezuelan, Caucasian), and Johnny Depp (Cherokee, Caucasian). Groups such as Wesleyan University's Interracial Students Organization are becoming more common on college campuses. This trend will probably continue as interracial marriages become more common and society becomes more comfortable with different and new ways of defining one's heritage.

The racial options of the 2000 census have been modified to accommodate those who want to express their multiracial heritage. For the first time, Americans may choose more than one racial category when describing themselves. Consequently, "other" is no longer included as a choice. Other changes in the 2000 census include:

○ Black reads "Black or African-American."
○ Respondents are now given the choice Hispanic or Latino rather than just Hispanic. This change is based on research showing that Latino is a more popular term in the western United States.
○ The old category "Asian or Pacific Islander" is now divided. Asian is one category and Native Hawaiian or other Pacific Islander is another.

I was born in 1959 and I was "black." I did not challenge forms when I was younger, because I did not realize then how important the information those forms requested would become to me. If the form asked me to check "negro," I did. I don't remember there being racial categories other than black/negro or white.

As I grew older and learned through family conversation that there was another culture that was part of me, I began a hesitant journey of uncovering who I am as a complete person. This began with acknowledgment that my Native American heritage is as important to me as being Black. My first acknowledgment of my racial completeness was to check "other." Checking "other" was one of the most difficult things I have ever done. With that act came extreme guilt at the thought of abandoning my given culture and race.

I soon discovered that the guilt came from a sense of having banished myself to neutrality. "Other" meant recognizing no race at all. I went back to checking "Black," which once again made me comfortable but incomplete. I have now settled on checking both "Native American" and "Black."

—A student's perspective

THINKING THROUGH DIVERSITY:

journal entry

Would you describe yourself as multiracial, or do you see yourself as belonging to a single race?

It is clear that our nation's schools and workforce will feel the effects of growing diversity for some time. Demographic data indicates that

- Women, minorities, and people with disabilities will continue to account for the vast majority of new entries in the workforce.
- The nation's population of college students will grow increasingly diverse. Data from the U.S. Department of Education reveals that college students have become increasingly heterogeneous during the last two decades. This trend will continue as elementary and secondary students become even more racially and ethnically diverse in the future.
- The international student population in the United States is growing. The Institute of International Education estimates that there are 450,000 international students in the United States.[5] Most of these students come from Asian and Latin American countries.

What if the entire population of elementary and secondary schools in the United States were shrunk into one class of 30 students? What would it look like? According to the National Center for Research on Cultural Diversity and Second Language Learning, 10 of the 30 students would come from racial or ethnic minority groups. Of these 10, six would come from homes in which languages other than English are spoken, and two would be from immigrant families. Of the six students who spoke another language, four would speak Spanish, one would speak an Asian language, and the other student would speak any one of more than 100 languages. Ten students, one-third of the class, would be poor.[6]

Technological and Social Changes

A number of social and technological changes have also altered the cultural landscape in recent years.

Globalization and Technology

Peoples and cultures throughout the world meet each day. Several forces make this possible, one being the growing interdependence of economies in various countries. Another is the speed and ease of modern transportation. Technological advances have transformed our social world into what Marshall McLuhan termed a *global village*.[7] In other words, increasingly we need to think of the entire world when we talk about our social environment. Computers, satellites, and communication technology have brought the world closer together and made cross-cultural encounters an everyday occurrence.

I am a citizen, not of Athens or Greece, but of the world.

—Socrates

Heightened Awareness of Diversity

Stories about diversity appear in the news each day. These stories deal with such issues as affirmative action, discrimination, social conflict, global education, and religious as well as language differences. Scholarship on the subject of diversity has mushroomed in recent years. Diversity itself has become a thriving industry. Books, Web sites, diversity consultants, courses, workshops, and conferences have proliferated as more and more money is spent in this area.

In the United States, globalization is part of our daily lives. It is evident from the time we get up to the time we go to sleep. Take an ordinary person such as Millie Jones. She attends school part-time and works full-time. A typical day in her life connects her with many different parts of the world.

Ms. Jones wakes up and brews coffee shipped from Brazil. After a quick breakfast, she has a few minutes to read the morning newspaper. Her eye catches articles about political unrest in the Middle East, the spread of AIDS in parts of Africa, and preparations for the Olympic Games in Athens, Greece.

Millie then drives her sports car to work. The car was assembled in Germany, with parts from all over the world. She arrives at work. Her employer is a large, multinational company that manufactures and markets computer software throughout the world. After checking her e-mail, she gets on the Internet. Millie checks the financial markets in Hong Kong, Paris, Sydney, and other parts of the world.

She leaves work early to attend two evening classes at a nearby community college. On the way to school, she picks up a late lunch at her favorite Mexican restaurant.

At school, Millie listens to a lecture by an Iranian professor in an advanced statistics class. On the way to the next class, she chats with two Nigerian students. In biology, she uses the Internet to get the latest research on *Loa loa*, a worm that infects the human eye and is found in African rain forests.

After school, she drives home, eats some leftovers, and turns on the computer. She spends some time on her online service's "International Chat Room." Before going to bed, Millie turns on a CD player made in Japan and listens to music performed by a rock group from Ireland.

Pride in our cultural roots is championed by popular music, movies, ethnic festivals, and cultural exhibits. As diversity has become more visible in everyday life, it is more apt to become an issue that is addressed, discussed, and debated publicly and privately.

Continued Cultural Separation in the Midst of Diversity

Although some parts of our cultural landscape are becoming more diverse, other parts show little of this change. Sociologists refer to this as **cultural lag**, a condition in which one part of culture is not keeping pace with another part. This lag or gap is becoming increasingly evident when we look at where we live, worship, go to school, and work. Consider the following examples.

1. Many residents of the United States continue to live in neighborhoods that are separated along racial, ethnic, and economic lines. The upper, middle, and lower social classes gravitate to separate communities. Hispanic barrios, Little Japans, Little Italys, and Chinatowns are commonplace. So too are "chocolate cities and vanilla suburbs," a phrase used by musical artist George Clinton. William Frey, in his analysis of recent population estimates from the Census Bureau, concludes that most communities in the United States lack significant racial and ethnic diversity. According to Frey, Asians, Hispanics, and to a lesser extent African-Americans continue to be concentrated in specific regions of the country and a handful of metropolitan areas.[8]

2. According to the U.S. Labor Department's Federal Glass Ceiling Commission, the upper levels of big business remain mostly white and mostly male.[9] The Commission found that the **glass ceiling**—attitudes and actions that block the promotion of minorities and women into top management positions—is still very much in place. These barriers may exist because of individual prejudices and discrimination, or they may be rooted in the policies, procedures, and culture of a business. Other barriers, referred to as *glass walls*, make it difficult to move from one position to another at the same level. For example, minority employees sometimes find it difficult to transfer into those departments that eventually provide more chances to move into upper-level management.

---

journal entry

THINKING THROUGH DIVERSITY:
Have you or any member of your family ever encountered a glass ceiling or a glass wall?

---

3. Martin Luther King once called our time of worship the most segregated hour of the week. Despite the significant social changes during the past few decades, racial segregation remains in place at many religious services.

4. While the percentage of students of color is increasing significantly, racial diversification among teachers has not kept pace.

5. In recent years, there has been a resurgence of intergroup hostility and intolerance. This is not simply the work of a select few. When we think of intolerance, how many of us visualize a member of the Ku Klux Klan (KKK) or a skinhead? Unfortunately, intolerance can also come dressed in a three-piece suit, a military uniform, or more casual wear. College campuses throughout the country have recently witnessed an upsurge in hate crimes. Hate literature, graffiti on dormitory room doors, threatening e-mail and telephone calls, property damage, and physical violence can make it difficult for students to feel comfortable and concentrate on their studies.

People react differently to the social changes that result from the growing importance of diversity. Some adapt, others resist. In a way, it is a lot like the growing importance of computer technology. We may work to adapt and learn more because we know that if we do not become computer literate, our chances for success will be severely limited. The same holds true for diversity. Whether we realize it or not, diversity touches each of us on a daily basis. If we are not in a position to capitalize on diversity, we will be at a disadvantage socially and economically. In Chapter 2 we focus on the relationship between diversity and success.

▬▬▬ VIEWS OF DIVERSITY: ASSIMILATION AND PLURALISM

Throughout our nation's history, our diversity has been described as a *melting pot, tossed salad, rainbow, quilt,* and *kaleidoscope.* These images illustrate the fact that we are different. Our differences, and the way we view them, change constantly.

In the early twentieth century, a Jewish immigrant named Israel Zangwill offered this description of the United States in his book *The Melting Pot:* "There she lies, the great melting pot—listen! Can't you hear the roaring and the bubbling? There gapes her mouth—the harbour where a thousand mammoth feeders come from the ends of the world to pour in their human freight. Ah, what a stirring and a seething—Celt and Latin, Slav and Teuton, Greek and Syrian, Black and Yellow... Jew and Gentile."[11]

According to Zangwill, European immigrants would gradually lose their traditional ways of life and blend together. A new mixed culture would emerge from this process. This is commonly referred to as **assimilation**, the process in which people lose their cultural differences and blend into the wider society. International students as well as those born and raised in the United States sometimes sense their culture slipping away. They have many ways to deal with the pressure to assimilate. Some see it as inevitable and desirable. Others see it as something to avoid at all costs. Still others find themselves assimilating up to a point. As one of my students put it, "I do it up to a point, as long as it does not rob me of my identity."

It took 22 years for me to develop my own personality and goals despite the struggles I have and the struggles my race still has. By assimilating— that is like saying Dr. Martin Luther King died for nothing. That Malcolm X and all of the other people who gave their lives so that I would have a chance died for nothing. To me, assimilation is another word for slavery.

Work is a perfect example of how I assimilate my identity so that I feel comfortable. If changing the way I dress and act makes me feel more accepted on the job, then that's what I want to do.

My personal background provides me with a very strong belief that I am to be who I am. I think my Jewish background as well as my mother's influence help me deal with assimilation. I know who I am, as far as race, culture, and personality. And I know that I'm not changing for anyone. Therefore, when the idea of assimilation is presented in any way to me, I instinctively decline.

In America, everyone at some point and time will be forced to assimilate themselves with another culture or group. Being a young black male, assimilation is probably the most frequently used pattern of interaction in my life. In my neighborhood, especially with my circle of friends, it is a cardinal sin to assimilate with the white culture. We see ourselves as the shunned group. At every possible opportunity, we thumb our collective noses at white society. By learning the "rules of the game" a long time ago, I know that assimilating with the majority society is a must. When forced to assimilate, I just separate my two worlds. I'm always going to be black with black sentiments and I'll never compromise that for anything. However, I will play by the rules dictated, at least to an extent, to further myself and my people.

—Students' perspectives

Many now question whether the model of the melting pot fits our society. They argue that people want to be accepted for who they are. A growing number of people are unwilling to give up what makes them distinctive, even if it is only for a certain period of time each day. When they go to work or school, they do not want to leave their culture at home. They feel that like the ingredients in a salad or the colors of a rainbow, differences can coexist and complement each other (see Fig. 1.3).

Figure 1.3: "People call us a melting pot, but we never have been. What we really represent is a quilt of different colors, different textures, all held together by a common thread."—Kweisi Mfume, President of the NAACP. (Photo by Regina Bryan.)

▨ WHAT IS AN AMERICAN?

How would you define the term *American*? For some, the term applies solely to those living in the United States. Others maintain that those who inhabit any of the countries in North, Central, or South America are Americans. Still others feel that the term has a racial connotation. Toni Morrison, in her book *Playing in the Dark*, has observed "deep within the word 'American' is its association with race...American means white."[12] A student of color sums up her feelings this way: "Being an American is a phrase way down on my list of descriptive words. America has caused me to describe myself in a lot of ways—Black, woman, minority. The word *American* is not part of that list. I wish I could feel a part of this country. But everyday I am quickly reminded that I am not an American, but a nuisance."

Do you feel that you are an American? What does *American* mean to you? What does an American look like? In his book *A Different Mirror: A History of Multicultural America*, Ronald Takaki describes an experience he had while riding in a taxi. The driver, who looked to be in his 40s, asked him how long he had been in the United States. Takaki replied that he had been born in the United States. He further explained that his family came here from Japan more than 100 years ago. The driver's assumption was that he didn't really look "American."[13]

Why do we make this kind of assumption? According to Takaki, schools have to accept at least part of the blame. He argues that from kindergarten to college, teachers and textbooks have cultivated a narrow view of U.S. history. Typically, the experiences of African-Americans, Hispanics, Native Americans, and Asian-Americans have been ignored. In addition to schools, our upbringing can influence our thinking. A college student elaborates: "The way I was brought up was to think that everybody who was the same as me were 'Americans,' and the other people were of 'such and such descent'."[14]

Pluralism is a process through which cultural differences are acknowledged and preserved. By way of illustration, advocates of multicultural education argue that the study of U.S. history should be more pluralistic. History should reflect the distinctive cultural experiences of all people. According to this perspective, courses in history often ignore the experiences, perspectives, and contributions of women or people of color. Those who share this opinion argue that if history courses were truly inclusive, there would be no need for a Black History Month or a Women's History Month.

▬▬ DIMENSIONS OF DIVERSITY

Dimensions of diversity refer to specific traits viewed as distinguishing one person or group from another. Race, gender, and ethnicity are three examples. **Race** refers to a category of people who are *perceived* as physically distinctive on the basis of certain traits, such as skin color, hair texture, and facial features. Notice that what makes this group distinctive is our perception of their differences. The concept of race is discussed later in more detail.

Whereas race relates to physical differences, ethnicity focuses on cultural distinctiveness. **Ethnicity** is defined as the consciousness of a cultural heritage shared with other people. **Gender** has to do with the cultural differences that distinguish males from females. For instance, in any given culture, people raise males and females to act certain ways. Do not confuse the term *gender* with *sex*. Sex refers to biological differences, such as hormones and anatomy.

▨ SOCIAL CLASS DIFFERENCES IN THE UNITED STATES

Social class refers to one's status in society. In the United States, status is usually determined by a variety of social and economic criteria, including wealth, power, and prestige. Even though social class influences where we work, live, and go to school, its importance is addressed infrequently. Perhaps class distinctions are downplayed or ignored because we are uncomfortable, psychologically speaking, acknowledging the tremendous inequality that exists in this society. Moreover, the concept of social class is "fuzzy" and inconsistent. For example, how would we classify other students in our class? *Lower, middle,* and *upper class* mean different things to different people.

When we talk about the dimensions of diversity, social class, sexual orientation, age, religion, learning style, and family background are invariably ignored. Some people may perceive these and other dimensions to be more important than race or gender. When students are asked what makes them unique, their answers reflect a very inclusive view of diversity (see Diversity Box: Who Am I?)

▨ WHO AM I?

Students in a college success class were asked to write down five things that describe each of them. Then they wrote all of their descriptors on the board, as follows:

Jewish

African American   Protestant

American   student

baby boomer   mid-30s   family oriented

religious   flexible

member of intergenerational household

good mother

sincere   proud

female

young   poor   Christian

male

warmhearted

intelligent   young at heart

Indo-Guyanese   White

short   fat

WHO AM I?   outspoken

open-minded

artist

independent

single parent

strong-willed

hardworking   half Black/half Jewish woman

Roman Catholic

Irish American   child of two loving parents

product of interracial marriage   recovering alcoholic

caring   truthful

descendant of slaveholders   German

vegetarian   right-handed

southwesterner   family man

Polish

agnostic   mother of a special child

American of German and Irish descent

middle-aged menopausal

The meaning of the term *diversity* is expanding continually. Roosevelt Thomas, a leading expert on managing diversity in the workplace, makes this point in his book *Beyond Race and Gender*. He defines diversity in a way that includes everyone. According to Thomas, workforce diversity is not something that is simply defined by race or gender. Rather, it encompasses a variety of other dimensions, such as age, personal and corporate background, education, job function and position, geographic origin, lifestyle, sexual orientation, and personality.[15] To this list we can add ancestry, national origin, creed, religion, economic class, learning style, personality, family background, marital status, military background, and disability. The list goes on and on. In short, it includes whatever we think distinguishes us.

As you read about diversity and, in particular, various dimensions of diversity, keep these points in mind.

1. *Dimensions of diversity may be hidden or visible.* Diversity is not only skin deep. According to one theory, diversity is like a cultural iceberg. Only about 10 percent of it is visible. Most dimensions mentioned by students (see Diversity Box: Who Am I?) would be invisible in the classroom. For example, we would not know that a classmate was a descendant of slaveholders, a vegetarian, or a born-again Christian unless the person chose to share this with us.

2. *Dimensions of diversity are found within groups as well as within individuals.* People possess varied personalities and talents as well as different learning and communication styles. Similarly, everyone within a group is not the same. Differences within a group are often ignored when we distinguish between groups. Diversity within groups is addressed later in the chapter.

▨ MASTER STATUS

People are often identified and distinguished by their **master statuses**, positions that stand out in the eyes of society and hide one's individuality. Ask yourself what is the first thing that people see when they look at you? Is it your race, gender, disability, or some other master status?

In his autobiography, Malcolm X discusses his experiences as a student in Mason, Michigan, a town just outside Lansing. He was one of the top students in his class and excelled in English. He vividly remembers talking with Mr. Ostrowski, his English teacher, about his plans for a career. "'Malcolm, you ought to be thinking about a career,' said Mr. Ostrowski. 'Have you been giving it thought?' The truth is, I hadn't. I never have figured out why I told him, 'Well, yes, sir, I've been thinking I'd like to be a lawyer.' Lansing certainly had no Negro lawyers—or doctors either—in those days, to hold up an image I might have aspired to. All I really knew for certain was that a lawyer didn't wash dishes, as I was doing.

continued

Mr. Ostrowski looked surprised, I remember, and leaned back in his chair and clasped his hands behind his head. He kind of half-smiled and said, 'Malcolm, one of life's first needs is for us to be realistic. Don't misunderstand me, now. We all here like you, you know that. But you've got to be realistic about being a nigger. A lawyer—that's no realistic goal for a nigger. You need to think about something you *can* be. You're good with your hands—making things. Everybody admires your carpentry work. Why don't you plan on carpentry? People like you as a person—you'll get all kinds of work.'

The more I thought afterwards about what he said, the more uneasy it made me. It just kept treading around in my mind."[16]

It is clear from this excerpt that race was a master status during this period of Malcolm X's life. Although Mr. Ostrowski knew that Malcolm X was intelligent, he also understood the social norms that were in place at this time. From Mr. Ostrowski's point of view, it did not matter that Malcolm X was smart. He had to learn that aspiring to be a lawyer was at odds with the "place" reserved for him in the wider society.

3. *Dimensions of diversity are in a constant state of flux.* In different situations, we see ourselves and are seen by others differently. In some situations a student might want to be seen as a Muslim female. In another situation, she might simply want to be viewed as a student.

4. *Dimensions of diversity are not always clear-cut or easily defined.* Diversity means different things to different people. A good example is the term *race*. Even though we talk about race as if it can be biologically defined, there is no easy way to distinguish people based solely on their skin color, hair texture, shape or color of their eyes, or any other physical trait. Racial mixing has blurred the boundaries between races. Skin color, for example, is a common but unreliable indicator of race. There are Whites who are more dark-skinned than some Blacks. Many Hispanics have dark skin but do not consider themselves Black. Anthropologist Ashley Montagu addressed this issue in his book *Man's Most Dangerous Myth: The Fallacy of Race.* According to Montagu, the term *race* has no scientific basis and cannot be applied to real life.[17] There is almost total agreement among scientists today that race is arbitrarily and socially defined. Yet it is important because we make it important, and we model its importance for children (see Fig. 1.4).

In summary, diversity is multidimensional. Various dimensions may be hidden or visible. Moreover, they may or may not have anything to do with race or gender.

Figure 1.4: *(By permission from Copley News Service.)*

◼︎◼︎◼︎ DIVERSITY BETWEEN AND WITHIN GROUPS

The United States is home to one of the most culturally diverse populations in the world. Nevertheless, we often ignore or gloss over these differences. When we focus our attention on race, we think in terms of Blacks and Whites or sometimes Latinos and Whites. Our society, and even our communities, are described as biracial rather than multiracial. This can be particularly uncomfortable and offensive to those who are constantly stereotyped or left out of the picture. An Iranian student describes how she has struggled with this dilemma: "I am an Iranian woman, one who can't pass as white because I'm too dark, but certainly can't pass as black because I have Middle-Eastern features...When I date black men, I receive animosity from those who feel that black men belong with black women. When I date white men, I've been accused of selling out and trying to be white. Iranian men who expect me to fit within a certain mold find me strange. I also seem to have this peculiar power to make people at airports and train stations visibly uncomfortable." She describes her feelings when she was informed she would not be allowed to join the BLSA—the Black Law Students Association—at her college. "My first impulse had been to argue with the man sitting behind the table with the introductory flyers. He looked me in the eye and said, 'Look, if you're not black, then as far as I'm concerned, you're white.' She goes on to say: "What was I to do, start an 'ILSA' of which I would be the sole member?"[18]

We may paint diversity with such a broad brush that we fail to capture the differences that exist within groups as well as between them. Indeed, the differences within groups are often greater. For instance, we tend to get caught up with how men and women differ from each other. We forget or ignore the significant differences that can be found when we simply look at a group of men or a group of women. Women can be assertive or passive, dependent or independent, and supporters or opponents of feminism. Similar differences exist among men.

Differences exist among the largest ethnic groups in this country. These groups include African-Americans, Latinos, Asian-Americans, and Native Americans. For this reason, we cannot talk about the Latino family any more than we can talk about the white family. Discussing *the* Asian-American or *the* Latino experience in this country ignores the diversity that exists within groups and individuals from these populations. Asian-Americans include Chinese, Japanese, Filipinos, Vietnamese, Laotians, Cambodians, Hmong, Koreans, Native Hawaiians, Samoans, and others. Latinos are also distinguished by a wide range of skin colors, ethnic or cultural lifestyles, religions, and languages. Many object to the term *Latino* or *Hispanic* because it masks the uniqueness of the particular culture. *Mexican, Puerto Rican, Cuban*, or some other term identifying one's nationality may be preferred.

DIVERSITY MYTHS

Diversity is a concept that means many things to many people. It can trigger a wide range of positive and negative feelings. Unfortunately, what we learn about this subject is often incomplete and inaccurate. Some of the more common misconceptions that surround diversity follow.

Myth 1: Diversity = women + minorities. Diversity includes everyone. All of us, for example, bring differences to school. This includes white males.

Myth 2: Diversity is a new phenomenon. There has always been diversity, but now it is receiving more attention. Some changes are not as new as we might believe. As an example, statistics indicate that more women are entering the job market than ever before. This masks the fact that a large percentage of women of color have always worked.

Myth 3: Diversity = deficiency. This myth is based on the premise that diversity results in standards being lowered. Today, professionals increasingly view diversity as a resource rather than a deficit. Big businesses such as IBM, Xerox, and Digital Equipment approach diversity as good business. According to the international diversity manager at Digital Equipment Corporation, "It's in the best interest of each and every one of us to do the personal growth work that valuing differences is about. We will be more synergistic, we will share power, we will be more collaborative, and we will be more creative, and at that point, we'll make more money."[19]

An advertisement by Atlantic Richfield Company (ARCO) makes the same point. The top of the ad reads, "The value of diversity is priceless."

Underneath the ad is a picture of foreign currency and these words: "As a multinational corporation, ARCO is committed to filling the needs of our customers at home and around the world. Diversity in our staff and in our business relationships help enhance our effectiveness in the global marketplace. It's a win–win situation, because diversity increases opportunity for others and strengthens our own organization. Diversity makes sense. And pounds, francs, yen…"

Myth 4: Diversity = divisiveness. Many assume that our society is divided because of our differences. Does the problem lie with our differences or our inability to respect and learn from these differences? Being exposed to diversity can bring people together.

In *What Matters in College?* Alexander Astin discusses findings from his research on 217 colleges and universities.[20] He found that a student's diversity experiences in college can be a potent way of bridging the gap between various groups and easing tensions. These experiences might take the form of a workshop or a course on diversity. Equally important was the frequency with which students interacted socially with persons from different racial and ethnic groups.

Myth 5: Diversity is to be feared. By focusing exclusively on our differences and ignoring our similarities, we create fear. Fear is cultivated by our ignorance of differences and similarities. Fear is compounded by our inability to communicate with people who disagree with us about difficult issues. People often shy away from talking about diversity because it is so emotionally charged. As one student put it, "All it takes is one slip of the tongue." In a video entitled *The Color of Fear*, a group of men of varying racial and ethnic backgrounds attend a retreat and "open up" to each other about the issue of race. After a few days, it appears the racial divisions among the men are almost insurmountable. Their fear and mistrust almost make it impossible for them to communicate effectively. Toward the end of the retreat, they begin to connect with each other by confronting their fears, sharing intimate feelings, and really listening. They become more aware of some of the feelings they have in common.

The kind of dialogue that unfolds in this video is rare because it is genuinely open and honest. Consequently, it can be very painful at times. Toward the end of the video, one of the participants comments on the anger and hurt that surfaces during the group's discussions. "Sometimes," he says, "the cure for the pain is in the pain."[21]

Differences aren't necessarily a burden but a blessing.

—A student's perspective

WHAT IS DIVERSITY CONSCIOUSNESS?

The definition of consciousness in the dictionary is being fully aware or sensitive to something. Another way of defining it is the full activity of the mind or senses. This state of mind is necessary to develop **diversity consciousness**; understanding, awareness, and skills in the area of diversity.

journal entry

THINKING THROUGH DIVERSITY:
Should we always treat everybody the same and ignore differences? Are there any situations in which you should treat people differently?

Diversity consciousness is not simple and straightforward. It cannot be manufactured during a one-hour TV talk show or a day-long training session. Try to keep the following points in mind as you read about diversity consciousness.

Diversity consciousness is not

- *Simply common sense.* Common sense is not sufficient. We need to educate ourselves and each other. At the Boston Campus of the University of Massachusetts, the training of faculty includes dealing with diversity issues and instructing students from diverse backgrounds. Each year, employees at American Telephone and Telegraph (AT&T) are required to take 40 hours of continuing education courses in diversity and tolerance.

- *The result of good intentions.* I have heard people say, "If my heart is in the right place, that is enough." Trying extra hard to be fair and respectful of others or having the best of intentions are a good start, but only a start. It is possible to show insensitivity and ignorance even though you have the best of intentions. People who talk to adults with disabilities in a childlike manner may think that they are being kind. People who tell you to forget our differences and just "be human" may think they are offering helpful advice. Leonard Pitts, a columnist for the *Miami Herald*, writes, "I've lost count of the times well-meaning white people have advised me to quit being black and 'just be a person.'"[22]

- *The result of some simple formula or strategy.* This is a reflection of the "McDonaldization" of our society. Sociologists use this phrase to describe our preoccupation with doing things quickly and efficiently, much like McDonald's restaurants. However, diversity consciousness requires life-long soul searching, self-reflection, and learning.

- *Important for just some of us.* At your college, are events held during African-American History Month more apt to attract students and faculty of color than white students and faculty? Similarly, are Women's History Month events usually attended by more women than men? All of us need to be culturally literate and responsive to survive and succeed in the twenty-first century. According to Dr. Benjamin Carson, one of the world's most renowned surgeons, it is a mistake to think that it's not my problem or it doesn't affect me. "All of our ancestors came to this country in different boats. But we're all in the same boat now. And if part of the boat sinks, eventually the rest of it goes down too."[23]

○ *Simply ignoring differences and treating everybody the same.* It is necessary to distinguish between sameness and equal opportunity. Should an instructor, for example, always treat everybody the same? On one hand, she should have high expectations for all of her students regardless of who they are. That same instructor, however, will have to distinguish among students in determining how she can teach the material most effectively and how she can help individual students succeed.

○ *Some "feel good" activity.* Diversity consciousness is not a matter of merely feeling good about ourselves and others. It goes deeper. Superficial acceptance is replaced by a deeper and more critical understanding.

○ *A passing fad.* Diversity has always been with us, and responding to it effectively will become more and more important. A good example is our increasing life span. Census predictions point to a much grayer population by the year 2050 because we are living longer. America's "baby boomers" will begin to reach age 65 in the year 2010. By 2020, nearly one-fifth of the U.S. population will be 65 years of age or older.[24] People are not only living longer, but they are also healthier and retiring at a later age. Therefore, the older population will be a growing part of the diversity that surrounds us daily.

■ DIVERSITY EDUCATION

Diversity has always been a powerful, even a necessary, catalyst for intellectual progress.

—David H. Porter, President Emeritus, Skidmore College

Diversity education refers to all the strategies that enable us to develop diversity consciousness. Through diversity education, we develop awareness, understanding, and a variety of skills in the area of diversity. Throughout the book, these skills are referred to as **diversity skills**. Among these are flexible thinking, communication, teamwork, and leadership skills, as well as the ability to overcome personal and social barriers.

Diversity education takes many forms. It is something we can initiate and control, such as reading a book, attending a workshop, and exchanging ideas about diversity issues with thousands of people over the Internet. One form of diversity education, which has proliferated throughout the country in recent years, is study circles. Anyone can form a study circle.

⊞ STUDY CIRCLES ON DIVERSITY

The idea behind this kind of study circle is to involve communities in ongoing dialogues on diversity. Anyone or any group can initiate a study circle. In many communities, organizations such as churches, businesses, schools, and clubs sponsor study circles. Support from the Study Circles Resource Center (SCRC) is also available at no charge. SCRC provides free discussion materials and assistance.[25]

People who join study circles agree to meet regularly over an extended period of time. This long-term proactive approach to dialogue allows study circle participants to get to know one another and begin to share their innermost feelings. Everyone is given a "home" in the conversation. By participating in study circles, everyday people gain ownership of issues that relate to diversity. Typically, the discussion focuses initially on personal experiences and perspectives.

Participants then examine how personal and community issues interrelate and what action needs to be taken. Unlike many other forms of diversity education which do not go beyond dialogue, study circles combine talk with action.

The experiences of study circles throughout the country show promise. In some cases, hundreds and thousands of people participate in community-wide dialogues. Roughly 500 people and 30 organizations in Minneapolis/St. Paul are involved in study circles on the challenge of racial segregation in housing and education. A statewide program in Oklahoma helped initiate sweeping changes in the corrections system. In Miami, Florida, the "Many Voices, One Community" project is addressing a number of diversity issues, including immigration and education, race relations, language differences, and job opportunities.

Typically, long-term relationships form out of circles. I have a best friend that I met in a study circle. Often, there is a need for a second level of the same circle that further narrows the focus. If the first circle was good, the participants are reluctant to leave. There is a bonding that takes place that transcends culture and race. This makes us simply human beings who have gained a wiser understanding of one another and the need to know more.

—A student's perspective

Unlike many other forms of learning, true diversity education requires continual, fundamental change. Change of this nature, what best-selling author Stephen Covey terms *real change*, takes place "from the inside out." In *The Seven Habits of Highly Successful People*, Covey elaborates. Real change "doesn't come from hacking at the leaves of attitude and behavior with quick fix personality ethic techniques. It comes from striking at the root—the fabric of our thought, the fundamental essential paradigms which give definition to our character and create the lens through which we see the world."[26] In other words, fundamental changes involve growing as a person, both intellectually and emotionally. Although change of this nature is not easy, the rewards are worth it.

Much of the dialogue regarding diversity in recent years equates diversity with diversity education. They are not the same. Diversity simply refers to our individual and collective differences. Without education, diversity is simply untapped potential.

In summary, the cultural landscape in the United States is changing due to the influence of demographic, technological, and social changes. The term *diversity* has gained new meaning; it does not simply refer to racial, ethnic, and gender differences. Despite the attention diversity receives, our views and understanding of diversity are often influenced by myths about diversity and the role it plays in our lives. Diversity education enables us to move beyond these myths and develop our diversity consciousness.

In the next chapter, we focus on skills that enable us to capitalize on diversity. We examine how diversity skills make us more successful at school and on the job. Additionally, we explore the numerous ways in which organizations benefit from the diversity skills of their employees.

Exercises

IN-CLASS

Exercise 1: The Diversity within You

Each student will need the following materials for this exercise: 1 square foot of aluminum foil, 4 toothpicks, 2 paper clips, a foam cup, and a marker.

Directions for Instructor

1. Ask each student to create something from these materials that represents his or her diversity as an individual.
2. Once everybody has finished, ask each student to share his or her creation with other members of the class and explain what it represents.

Exercise 2: What Is an American?

Directions for Instructor

1. Ask students, "What does it mean to be an American?" Each student should write down a response that is no more than two sentences.
2. Ask students to form groups of two. Compare answers. How are their definitions of an American similar? How are they different?
3. Ask the entire class to share and analyze their responses. Who is included and excluded in their descriptions of an American?

OUT-OF-CLASS

Exercise 1: What Is Diversity?

1. Ask 10 students not in this class to complete this sentence:
   Diversity is _____.
   Record their responses.
2. Write a paragraph summarizing the responses of the 10 students. Do any of their responses reflect diversity myths? Explain.

Exercise 2: Thinking through My Cultural Diversity

Describe, in a reasonable amount of detail, your background in terms of the following dimensions of cultural diversity.
- Your early environment: the kind(s) of community(ies) in which you grew up (large city, suburb, small town, rural area)
- Your social class as you grew up, the jobs and levels of education of those who raised you, and the social class levels of your neighbors
- Your social heritage—specifically, your racial, ethnic (cultural), and religious background (you may not necessarily identify with all three)—and its importance to you
- The culture other than your own that has had the greatest impact on you, and why

Exercise 3: What's in a Name?

1. What is your full name? How do you feel about your name? Why?
2. Find out as much as you can about your name. For example, what is the history and significance of your name? What is the meaning of your name?

INTERNET ASSIGNMENT

1. Go to a search engine site such as www.Yahoo.com or www.hotbot.com. Do a search on "diversity education" (put the two words inside quotes so that the search is for that exact term).
2. Read the selection of links you receive and choose one that interests you. Go to that site and print either the home page or an article of interest.

3. Write a two-paragraph summary of what you learned from visiting this Web site and any links that you visited.

NOTES

[1]"Inclusion," *Book and Video Catalog* (Manhattan, KS: The MASTER Teacher, 1999), 5A.

[2]Vincent N. Parillo, *Diversity in America* (Thousand Oaks, CA: Pine Forge Press, 1996), 65.

[3]U.S. Bureau of the Census, *Historical Statistics of the United States, Part II*, Series Z 20-132 (Washington, DC: U.S. Government Printing Office, 1976)

[4]U.S. Bureau of the Census, *Statistical Abstract of the United States 1997*, 117th ed. (Washington, DC, U.S. Government Printing Office, 1997), 44.

[5]Barbara Fraser, "U.S. Colleges Step Up Recruiting in Latin America," *Chronicle of Higher Education*, XLIV(10), Oct. 31, 1997, A58–A59.

[6]Barry McLaughlin and Beverly McLeod, "Educating All Our Students: Improving Education for Children from Culturally and Linguistically Diverse Backgrounds." Online. World Wide Web. June 1966. Available: http://www.ncbe.gwu.edu/miscpubs/ncrcdsll/edall.htm.

[7]Marshall McLuhan, *The Mechanical Bride: Folklore of Industrial Man* (Boston: Beacon Press, 1967).

[8]William Frey, "The Diversity Myth," *American Demographics*, June 1998, 38–43.

[9]Federal Glass Ceiling Commission, *A Solid Investment: Making Full Use of the Nation's Human Capital* (Washington, DC: U.S. Department of Labor, 1995), 6.

[10]Southern Poverty Law Center, "E-mail on Trial," *Intelligence Report*, Winter 1988, 5.

[11]Israel Zangwill, *The Melting Pot* (New York: The Jewish Publication Society of America, 1909), 198–199.

[12]Toni Morrison, *Playing in the Dark* (Cambridge, Mass.: Harvard University Press, 1992), 47.

[13]Ronald Takaki. *A Different Mirror. A History of Multicultural America.* (Boston: Little, Brown, 1993).

[14]Ruth Frankenberg, *White Women, Race Matters: The Social Construction of Whiteness* (Minneapolis, MN: University of Minnesota Press, 1993), 198.

[15]Roosevelt Thomas. *Beyond Race and Gender: Unleashing the Power of Your Total Work Force by Managing Diversity* (New York: American Management Association, 1991).

[16]Malcolm X, *The Autobiography of Malcolm X* (New York: Ballantine Books, 1965), 36.

[17]Ashley Montagu. *Man's Most Dangerous Myth: The Fallacy of Race* (Cleveland, OH: World Publishing, 1964).

[18]Amanda Enayati, "Not Black, Not White," *The Washington Post*, July 13, 1997, C1.

[19]L. A. Kauffman, "The Diversity Game," *Voice*, Aug. 31, 1993, 31.

[20]Alexander Astin. *What Matters in College? Four Critical Years Revisited* (San Francisco: Jossey-Bass, 1993).

[21]*The Color of Fear* (video) (Oakland, CA: Stir Fry Productions, 1994).

[22]Leonard Pitts, Jr., "Watching Whites Struggle to Understand Their Whiteness," *The Sun*, Apr. 21, 1997, 9A.

[23]Benjamin Carson, "Carson Philosophy Is 'Think Big,'" *The Sun*, Aug. 24, 1997, 6H.

[24]Richard W. Judy and Carol D'Amico, *Workforce 2020: Executive Summary* (Indianapolis, IN: Hudson Institute, 1997), 3.

[25]For more information, contact Study Circles Resource Center, P.O. Box 203, 697 Pomfret Street, Pomfret, CT 06258; tel: 203-928-2616; fax: 203-928-3713.

[26]Stephen Covey, *The Seven Habits of Highly Effective People* (New York: Simon & Schuster, 1989).

2 DIVERSITY SKILLS AND SUCCESS

chapter objectives

Upon completion of this chapter, you will be able to:

○ Explain **sociocultural theory**.

○ List and discuss **diversity skills** that promote success at school.

○ List and discuss diversity skills that promote success at work.

○ List and discuss the ways in which organizations benefit from the diversity skills of its employees.

○ Explain why a lack of diversity skills is costly to individuals and organizations.

To be a black man in this society is hard, but not that hard that I shouldn't push to make my goals come true. Now I'm your average brother who plays basketball. Beside worrying about the white man trying to knock me down, there are people that I love doing the same thing (putting a brother down).

It all started when I found out I was going to a college in New Jersey to play ball. I got that chance to get an education while doing something I loved. Everyone was proud of their son, as well as their boy for taking the chance to better his self in today's cruel world. Besides the man using me to win him a championship in basketball, everyone I knew wanted me to get them out of the hood with me. Of course I'm going to help my boys that I grew up with. This was my ace boon koons, we did everything together since we could walk. If you think about it, they were the ones who got my game to where it needed to be to get me in school anywhere. So I owe them a lot, and I know this.

A small problem arised when I came home after the first year ended. Everything I said or did, I was acting White or I was a gay guy. Everything I would say was wrong, because they said that I was trying to be better than them. All of a sudden jealousy rose between my boys and I. The situation was getting on my last nerve because I could not understand why my peoples were dogging me out because I was in school. In class one day, we were talking about how if you are trying to make it in today's world, no matter what the race, there is always someone trying to bring you down. That helped me understand what I was going through but that is today's society. You got to live with it or kill yourself. I know that I got things to achieve for my two sons and I, so don't look for my funeral arrangements yet. For my boys, I rubbed off on a couple. They are in school trying to get their GED. For the others we still have love for one another.

—A student's perspective

◼◼ DEFINITIONS OF SUCCESS

We define *success* in a variety of ways. One meaning, according to the dictionary, is the attainment of wealth, honors, and position. Another is simply: to achieve what you want to achieve. In this book, success means to achieve your goals. Since our focus is on college and the workplace, those goals might be a good job, a degree, or simply doing your best. No single goal applies to everyone.

journal entry

How do students define success? Often, the emphasis is on achieving a personal goal: getting through another day or earning a certain grade. Other definitions tend to focus more on helping others: being a good role model or learning to work with others. Sometimes, students equate success with certain personal qualities such as character, self-awareness, or peace of mind. The following definitions reflect some of the markedly different ways in which students view success.

Success is fulfilling your goals. Success is when one works hard for something and achieves it.

Success means establishing goals for yourself, and then not allowing anything to stand in your way.

Success is reaching a goal that seemed out of view. It is something you feel when you graduate after many years of schooling.

Success is having the bills paid, food in the fridge, a place to live, a car to drive, and the opportunity to live just one more day.

Success is not only materialistic. It is having a spiritual belief that values every person as your brother.

Success is striving to be a better person by learning all that I can from numerous sources. Success for me is being able to learn something from a 2-year-old to the drug addict on the corner. It is being grounded enough to be able to communicate to people on their level and accept them for who they are.

Success is being aware of oneself. It is learning and growing from new experiences, being able to examine your strengths and weaknesses honestly, and having the courage to change if needed.

—Students' perspectives

When I ask my students whom they consider to be highly successful, many list big-name entertainers, sports stars, and well-known political and business leaders. Interestingly, many more students include the names of people whom they know on a personal basis, including parents, friends, teachers, and others. Once in a while they mention themselves. In many of these cases, success is not the result of a single accomplishment. It is a culmination of many events: some positive, some negative.

One person who is at the top of my success list is my mother. Before dying, she changed her life of prostitution and drugs after 20 and some odd years. My aunt is also on my list because she just bought a car, something she'd been waiting for forever, but never seemed to have the money because of more important factors like her children.

My father, and for one reason only. Because he is now a part of my life. When I really, really need him now, he is there. It wasn't always so simple.

My brother, who is now 21 years old. He struggled with his asthma, and the fact that our father was never really around. He stayed in a depressed state for a couple of years. He overcame his depression with a lot of love from my mother and me. At 22, he started working and moved into his own apartment. Now, he holds a manager's position at a local shoe store.

—Students' perspectives

Too often, we sell ourselves short. We fail to appreciate just how much we have to offer and all that we have accomplished. One of the things I do at the end of each semester is ask students to bring something to class that makes them feel special and successful. I tell them it should be something they feel comfortable sharing with their classmates. It is one of my favorite class sessions because it brings out a wonderful mix of success stories.

It is impossible to predict what students will choose to "show and tell." For instance, in one class, a student brought a picture of her family. Her pain was etched in her face as she recounted how she was abused as a child and how she has coped. A few brought in pictures of their children, each child described with such pride and love. One older student showed the high school diploma he earned in 1993. He explained that he was supposed to graduate in 1961 but dropped out of school during his senior year. "I was never satisfied until I got it," he said. A middle-aged male passed around a 50-cent coin that he had found as a little boy. As he described it, the coin had a picture of Booker T. Washington's face on one side and a slave cabin on the other. "My father," he explained, "preached to me that the only thing out there for black men is to be laborers. As long as I held on to that coin, I felt I could do more." With each student, a success is revealed and acknowledged. Even though their successes are markedly different, they unite through feelings of accomplishment and pride in themselves and each other.

I believe that my major barrier to success is myself. When I lose focus on what is really important to me in this life, success takes a back seat. Another barrier is when I listen to society's definition of success. I have to keep reminding myself that even though I am a part of society, I don't have to fit their mold. Success is contentment and it is something that is learned. It does not matter whether I have a lot or very little, because it will not change who I am. My success is achieved through a peaceful heart, a calm spirit, and a content state of being.

—A student's perspective

Success stories are all around us and within us. They come in a wonderfully diverse assortment of shapes, sizes, and colors. Some are more obvious than others. As one of my students suggests, they can be found by looking for beauty in the ugliest of circumstances. At times, only we can appreciate the grandiose nature of what we accomplish.

What constitutes success and the paths to success vary from person to person. Consequently, there are an infinite variety of success stories. Too often, we hear only the success stories that make the news and involve the "rich and famous." It is of utmost importance to remember that success is relative. It depends on where we start, how far we come, and the obstacles we encounter along the way.

I have learned that success is to be measured not so much by the position that one has reached in life as by the obstacles which he has overcome while trying to succeed.

—Booker T. Washington

◾ SOCIOCULTURAL THEORY AND SUCCESS

When you evaluate your successes, is there anyone beside yourself who has influenced you for better or worse? Although any attempt to make sense of your success must focus on you, you are only part of the picture. The bigger picture includes your social environment, both past and present. This explanation of success is closely tied to **sociocultural theory**, a perspective that focuses on the social and cultural context of one's thoughts and actions.

According to sociocultural theory, we do not live in a vacuum. Those around us, such as family, peers, and community members, significantly influence who we are. Attitudes, character, knowledge, and other individual attributes can be fully understood only when these and other social influences are taken into consideration.

By the same token, each of us has a choice in how we react to situations, people, and events. *Every* response to *every* situation is something we can choose and ultimately control. Although our life experiences may *influence* who we are, they do not *determine* who we are. In *Sermons from the Black*

Pulpit, Samuel Proctor says: "It does not matter where we were born, what kind of rearing we had, who our friends were, what kind of trouble we got into, how low we sank, or how far behind we fell. When we add it all up, we still have some options left, we still have some choices we can make."[1]

I'm 27. I live in a homeless shelter with other women. Living in that homeless shelter and coming to college is hard. When I'm at the shelter, I don't really get into what I'm doing that much because there is the envy and the jealousy among the other women and the counselors. I do a lot of downplaying. I keep it real low key. It can be very stressful. It's not that I feel I'm trying to be better than them. I feel there is enough for everybody. I always stress that you can do what I am doing if you really want it.

I have to build my self-esteem. That's a daily thing. I think what helps me is my will, my determination. I am strong willed. I've been down. I want to be a power of example to the best of my ability. I want to be able to say "Look at me. I did it. You can."

—A student's perspective

Too often, we arrive at simplistic explanations of success by failing to look at all individual and external influences and the interrelationships among them. The idea that "no one is going to hire me because of the way I look" ignores the importance of motivation and hard work. These and other individual traits can help us overcome such barriers if indeed they exist. Equally naive is the thinking that "I don't need anyone" and "I can make it on my own."

Maureen, a college student, offers a more inclusive and empowering perspective. She acknowledges the origin of her values: "My mother instilled good values in me just like her mother did for her. She always told me I could get anything I wanted out of life if I worked hard enough." Furthermore, Maureen is aware that her ethnic background shapes her goals and influences the way some people view her. In Maureen's case, this awareness becomes a motivator. "I feel as though some people view Latinos as lazy people who don't want to better themselves. They think all Latinos want a free ride, or welfare, which is not true because I go to college and I also work at night. It is this perception of Latinos that has motivated me to work hard at making life better for my daughter."

journal entry

THINKING THROUGH DIVERSITY:

One way of relating sociocultural theory to your life is to think of the bridges you have crossed to get where you are. People, both past and present, can be bridges in that their efforts make it possible for you to do the things you do. Oprah Winfrey once talked about the bridges in her life: Sojourner Truth, Harriet Tubman, Fannie Lou Hamer, and others. What people have been bridges for you?

By relating sociocultural theory to our own lives, we will be better able to understand the importance of diversity skills. For example, my son Jimmy has autism. Autism is a severely incapacitating, lifelong disability. People with autism have tremendous problems relating to others and life's daily occurrences. They frequently act in a way people find strange and unacceptable. These behaviors, which may be continual and almost impossible to control, seriously limit the autistic person's ability to be independent.

As Jimmy's father, I become more empowered in many different realms as I realize I need the help of my wife and family, friends, social agencies, support groups, teachers, and therapists. For a long time, I was tempted to try to isolate myself from the rest of society. However, to get through each day and find the support and services I need, I have to develop my teamwork and interpersonal skills. I am more sensitive to others who may encounter the looks, ignorance, and insensitive comments that continue to be part of my daily life. Because I chose not to remain isolated, I developed diversity skills I would not have otherwise. Being aware of sociocultural influences helps us make the connection between our own lives and the resources that surround us.

WHY DIVERSITY SKILLS ARE IMPORTANT

Diversity skills are those competencies that allow people to interact with others in a way that respects and values differences. Diversity skills such as communication, teamwork, and self-evaluation are key components of diversity consciousness. As defined earlier, diversity consciousness is more than just being knowledgeable about or aware of differences. It is the awareness, understanding, *and* skills that allow us to think through and value human differences. As our awareness and understanding expand, so do our diversity skills. Similarly, developing and refining our diversity skills increases our awareness and understanding (see Fig. 2.1).

We often ignore or trivialize the relationship between diversity skills and success. This is due, in part, to our limited perception of diversity. Traditionally, the idea of diversity has revolved around some of the more obvious differences among people, such as race, ethnicity, and gender. In this chapter and throughout the book, we adopt the more current, inclusive view of diversity. Dimensions of diversity also include learning styles, multiple intelligences, personalities, personal expectations, and a wide variety of other differences that often remain hidden. By broadening our conceptualization of diversity, we are better able to develop an array of skills that can motivate and empower us. These skills are referred to throughout this book as diversity skills. A comprehensive list of these skills can be found in Chapter 4, page 95.

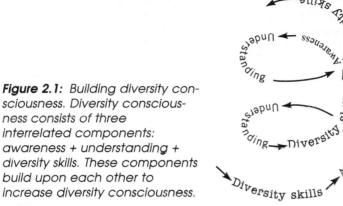

Figure 2.1: Building diversity consciousness. Diversity consciousness consists of three interrelated components: awareness + understanding + diversity skills. These components build upon each other to increase diversity consciousness.

Success at School

If we develop our diversity skills, we can be more successful in the classroom. Research, case studies, and student experiences underscore the importance of diversity skills. As you read about five of these skills, examine yourself. Which are strengths of yours? Which need a little or a lot more work? What might you do to improve certain skills?

1. *Flexible thinking.* This is the ability to understand and adapt to a variety of perspectives, depending on the situation. One good example of flexible thinking is being able to understand and respect **learning styles**, the way people learn. A good deal of research has identified numerous learning styles. For instance, some students find they learn best when they interact with others in small groups. Some prefer a highly focused lecture format. Whereas some are visual learners, others prefer listening. There are students who can learn from anybody, but others find learning nearly impossible if they cannot relate to their instructor. Research has shown that you can change and expand your learning style. Learning to do this will benefit you.

Involvement in Learning, a report by the Study Group on the Conditions of Excellence in American Higher Education, concludes that students can be more successful by taking control of their own education.[2] Being aware of your learning styles as well as becoming a more flexible learner can help you identify your strengths and avoid problematic situations. Begin by asking yourself: "How do I learn best?" There are numerous tests available to identify learning style preferences and strengths.

Once you have a better idea of how you learn, you are better able to monitor, adapt, and ultimately improve your learning. In a given class, you may determine that your learning style conflicts with your instructor's teaching style. Perhaps you learn best when *you* talk about something but your instructor is a straight lecturer. Knowing this, you might compensate by forming a study group and talking about the lecture after each class.

I have a physics instructor who speaks and pronounces words a lot differently than I do. These differences between her language and mine created a conflict at first because I kept telling myself I can't learn from this woman. But I began to pay closer attention and improve my listening skills. She also helped me learn I cannot depend on my instructors to teach me everything. I also have to use my textbooks and talk to others to get a full understanding of the subject at hand.

—A student's perspective

In recent years, researchers have also focused on different intellectual strengths or intelligences. These strengths may come into play during the learning process (see Diversity Box: Multiple Intelligences). A greater awareness of the variety of intelligences as well as learning styles can empower us and maximize our chances for success. Also, it can help us acknowledge and value the large variety of individual capabilities we will encounter in the classroom and elsewhere. However, it is important not to use our own differences in learning styles as an excuse.

When I am faced with a teacher whose strategies of teaching conflict with my learning style, I try to adapt instead of giving up. All teachers have different strengths and weaknesses. I think that in order to succeed in the classroom, you have to take the responsibility for adjusting to all kinds of teaching styles.

—A student's perspective

▨ MULTIPLE INTELLIGENCES

In 1983, Harvard University professor, Howard Gardner, identified a number of different intelligences.[3] Currently, Gardner theorizes that while each of us possesses at least eight intelligences, some are more fully developed than others. This theory may help explain why we

Diversity Consciousness: Opening Our Minds to People, Cultures, and Opportunities

can pick up some things very easily and other tasks come much harder. It also sheds light on why a particular subject might be difficult for you but not for some other students in your class.

Gardner identifies the following eight intelligences: linguistic, logical-mathematical, spatial, bodily-kinesthetic, interpersonal, intrapersonal, musical, and environmental. Throughout our school years, most of us are taught by teachers who use linguistic and logical-mathematical strategies. Our ability to understand them depends on our capacity to use language and understand logical reasoning and problem solving. Those of us with undeveloped skills in one or more of these areas may be at a disadvantage. In some other classes, however, we may encounter teachers who use alternative teaching methods that tap other types of intelligence.

Picture yourself in Professor B's math class. You are someone who has a long history of problems in math. However, your grades in this class are good for a change. You think it might have something to do with the way Professor B teaches. She seems to connect very well with students and employs a variety of teaching styles. One technique in particular seems almost funny at first but you find it helps. She creates raps out of different formulas and mathematical definitions. The class then does the rap together and some of the students "really get into it." The following is one example. It is a rap that helps you remember the steps to follow when graphing a line.

The Slope-Intercept Form Rap

$y = mx + b$

b's the y-intercept, so plot it first, ya' see?

m is the slope—rise over run

So go up or down and to the right and then you're done.

According to Professor B, raps such as this make learning easier because it taps a number of different intelligences, including musical, interpersonal, and bodily-kinesthetic. The rhythmic nature of rap, for example, appeals to those students who have a well-developed capacity to hear and remember musical patterns. Bodily-kinesthetic intelligence, the capacity to use hands, arms, and other body parts to take in knowledge, feeds into the rhythmic feel of rap. Furthermore, the fact that it is an interpersonal activity utilizes still another type of intelligence.

What can we learn from this experience? It is not enough to view this one class as a positive, unique experience and leave it at that. It might be helpful to seek out other teachers who teach this way. But realistically speaking, how many Professor B types are there? Maybe a better strategy is to realize how much this way of remembering helps you and use this technique in another class. In your next math class, you might try putting some of the new formulas to rhythm. Another idea is to get together with a group of other students from Professor B's class and try to create similar ways of remembering math or maybe another subject.

2. *Ability to appreciate and maintain pride in one's background and culture.* In her book *Affirming Diversity*, Sonja Nieto describes her research on a diverse group of "successful students." In this study, success meant that the students were still in school and planning to complete high school, or had recently graduated. They also have good grades, generally enjoy school, have plans for their future, and describe themselves as successful. Nieto concludes, "one of the most consistent, and least expected, outcomes to emerge from these case studies has been the resoluteness with which young people maintain pride and satisfaction in their culture and the strength they derive from it."[4] Furthermore, Nieto states that learning about one's culture, and how it informs and enriches us, is not easy. Chapter 4 elaborates on this important area of diversity consciousness.

I am an Orthodox Jew and it is very important for me to practice my religion. I cannot go out and act any old way. Two nights a week I go to Talmud classes and I am not allowed to go to school or study on the Sabbath or Jewish holidays. When I am at school, I say a blessing before and after I eat lunch. I also pray three times a day. When I am studying with someone during the time I observe afternoon prayer, I simply tell that person I have to stop and pray for a few minutes. I understand that the world does not revolve around the Jewish calendar. Therefore, I have learned to focus on my religion no matter who is around or what the situation is. This has made me a stronger Jew and a stronger student. I take pride in my difference—in my strong family and religious background.

My grandparents were both from France. My grandfather served in the French calvary and lost his leg in World War I. Henriette, my grandmother, came to this country alone. Even though she only knew a few words in English, she somehow managed to find a job and save enough money to buy a house. Her husband and children then joined her. Henriette and I were very close. She made me proud of my French heritage. She also made me proud to be an American citizen. When things get difficult, especially at school, it helps to remember Henriette. Doing this puts things in perspective, and gives me strength.

My relatives raised me to have self-esteem, to know of my history. We were taught that from the time we could read, when there weren't any black coloring books. My mother used to color the kids in the coloring books black. Jack and Jill were black. They might have been coal black but we understood where they were coming from.

Later on, I went to a racially mixed high school and I never felt inferior to anybody. And it got me into trouble because I do not allow that kind of stuff to filter into my mindset. I was always arguing with the teachers because I refused to answer questions a certain way. I would say "look at Ethiopia, look at the pyramids, look at this, look at that."

—Students' perspectives

THINKING THROUGH DIVERSITY:
How has your cultural background affected who you are?

3. *Ability to network and learn from everyone and anyone.* In his national study (1993) of undergraduates, Astin examines whether students' direct involvement in "diversity experiences" affects their academic progress. One of these experiences was the frequency with which students socialize with persons from diverse backgrounds. Astin found that interaction of this nature has a significant positive effect on practically all measures of students' academic development and satisfaction with college.[5] In other words, we increase our chances for success by expanding and diversifying our social network. In so doing, we learn more about who we are and our ability to relate to others. This, in turn, helps us develop our diversity consciousness. In chapter 4 we elaborate on this.

4. *Ability to deal effectively with barriers.* Much research examines the relationship between expectations and success. In many cases, our own expectations or the expectations of others act as barriers. According to the concept of the self-fulfilling prophecy, students conform to the expectations of teachers. However, we need to direct more attention at students' expectations of themselves. For example, there are teachers who say their course is hard and one-half of the class will drop by midsemester. While some students respond by mentally preparing themselves to drop the course, others react differently. They view expectations of this nature as a challenge and do everything in their power to complete this course "successfully." Barriers to success, and their relationship to diversity, are the focal point of chapter 3.

The fact that I know everyone expects me to fail causes me to work very hard. I am on a mission to prove to everyone that I am capable. Every time I experience racism I tell myself that my ancestors experienced worse. I want to be an example of what my people are capable of; so I strive to accomplish the impossible.

From the time I was little, my parents taught me to believe in myself and what I could do. With great pride, they took me to museums and replicas of pioneer villages to show me what my culture had produced. When school gets discouraging, I find myself thinking back on what I was taught. I believe I can get through anything if I work hard enough.

⟶⟶⟶

My cultural background has been an important factor in my success at school. Because of my major, I had to take biochemistry at the beginning of my sophomore year. The class I attended had only three African-American students. About three weeks into the course, we had our first test. All three of us failed. I remember feeling embarrassed and very intimidated. I felt like quitting, but I didn't want my classmates to think that all African Americans are dumb plus quitters. I vowed that I would be in the top percent of my class. When the next test was announced, my instructor informed the other two students and myself that we needed to study because there was an academic standard that must be upheld at this school. I felt she had purposely singled us out because other students had failed and yet they didn't get the same kind of warning. At this point, it became a matter of principle to do well on the test. Initially I was going to do well just for my own pride. But after the teacher's remark it became something more. It seemed to me that if I didn't do well on this test, she would forever think that I and all other African Americans were not capable of meeting the academic standards of the school. On that test, I made a 97, which was the second-highest grade in the class. I continued to study hard and made very good grades until I received my diploma.

⟶⟶⟶⟶⟶⟶⟶⟶⟶⟶⟶⟶ Students' perspectives

🪶 PUNJABI STUDENT EXPECTATIONS

The Punjabi families who reside in the California community of "Valleyside" are immigrants from India. They offer valuable insight into the relationship between expectations and success. Punjabi students are highly successful. Their families teach them that they are responsible for their own success. These students have high expectations of themselves. They know they must study hard and succeed in school for the honor of themselves, their family, and their community. If not, they put themselves at risk for being withdrawn from school and sent back to work in the fields.[6]

---

journal entry

THINKING THROUGH DIVERSITY:

If someone were to write your life history, what would we learn about the relationship between hard work and success?

5. *Ability to balance "fitting in" and "being yourself."* When students attend college, they may encounter a cultural setting that is unfamiliar and uncomfortable. As one example, due to their social class background, students might encounter an environment that makes it difficult to learn and succeed in school. Some students may feel they have to deny or cover up their social class in order to fit in with students from higher or lower socioeconomic backgrounds. Making this cultural adjustment on a daily basis can have profound implications. Like other diversity skills, the ability to make this kind of adjustment is connected with our diversity consciousness. More specifically, each of us can develop this ability as we learn to understand and value ourselves, individually and culturally.

Sometimes, certain ways of accommodating or fitting in are necessary. For example, some rules and expectations must be followed. Mastery of English or the language of instruction is critical. Some students resist talking standard English or even getting good grades because they equate it with "selling out." Willie Jolley, a motivational speaker who grew up in one of the poorer neighborhoods of Washington, DC, recounts how one of his friends took his books to and from school in a plastic bag because he did not want to appear too studious.

Findings from research[7] point to the potential benefits of transculturation. **Transculturation** is the process by which a person adjusts to another cultural environment without sacrificing his or her own cultural identity. In analyzing the factors that affect the academic achievement of Native American and white students attending college in South Dakota, Huffman discovers fundamental differences. High school grade-point average and parental encouragement to attend college relate significantly to the academic success of Whites. Among Native Americans, the retention of traditional cultural heritage is the most important predictor of success.

A middle-aged woman talks about making the necessary adjustments at college without assimilating or losing her cultural distinctiveness. "When we go to school we live a non-Indian way but we still keep our values.... I could put my values aside just long enough to learn what it is I want to learn but that doesn't mean I'm going to forget them. I think that is how strong they are with me."[8] Although this study focuses on Native Americans, transculturation can benefit all of us. You empower yourself when you learn you can adjust to any situation without sacrificing or compromising your beliefs.

My culture is in my soul all the time.

—A student's perspective

THINKING THROUGH DIVERSITY:
How do you know when to adjust and when to resist?

journal
entry

With our workforce demographics rapidly changing, managing diversity has become a critical managerial skill for those desiring to succeed in corporate America. In healthcare and in particular at the Johns Hopkins Hospital, we have long served patients from around the world. Now, our employees increasingly come from a variety of backgrounds and experiences. The extent to which our caregivers understand differences and have respect for each other as well as our patients will be the extent to which we will be successful in delivering excellent patient care.

—Ron Peterson, President, Johns Hopkins Hospital
(ranked by *U.S. News and World Report* as the nation's #1 hospital)

We believe that to survive and thrive in today's multicultural business environment, we must appreciate differences in education, backgrounds, experiences and perspectives. In doing so, we create a stronger team and a better workplace.

—Max Messmer, Chairman and CEO, Office Team
(the nation's leading staffing service, specializing in highly skilled office and administrative support professionals)

There is a mismatch today between the skills that college graduates bring to the workplace and what employers need (see Fig. 2.2). According to a recent study by the American Management Association, new hires were found seriously lacking in a number of skills that employers consider crucial.[9] Each of these skills relate to diversity. Specifically, new hires were deficient in "speaking one-on-one," "relating to others," and "working as a team player" (see Fig. 2.3). Comments from leaders in business and education throughout this chapter provide further insight into the importance of key skills related to diversity.

Diversity skills are clearly very much in demand. Employers value them. Thus, having these skills enhances your chances of landing a job and becoming a highly valued, successful employee. With this in mind, ask yourself the following question. Given your background, knowledge, and experience, how well can you meet employers' needs in the following areas?

1. *Interpersonal skills.* In subjects ranging from business management to health care to success in college, it is not uncommon to see entire chapters in

Figure 2.2: *(By permission from United Media.)*

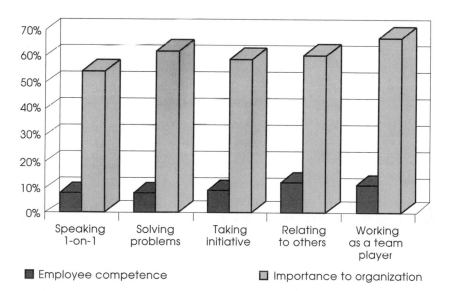

Figure 2.3: *Workforce skills among new hires. (Data from American Management Association, 1997.)*

textbooks devoted to the subject of interpersonal skills. Increasingly, educators and employers are realizing that strong people skills are just as important as technical expertise. A study by Dowd and Liedtka, commissioned by the faculty at the University of Virginia's Darden Graduate School of Business, examined what corporations are seeking in the MBAs they hire. Analysis of interview questions by corporate recruiters nationwide revealed that one of the most desired capabilities is interpersonal skills. These skills include the ability to adapt to the feelings and concerns of others, motivate people, and deal effectively with adversity and conflict.[10] In another case, the Secretary of Labor's Commission on

Figure 2.4: *In addition to being technically proficient, students need diversity skills. In the words of one dental hygiene instructor, "If one of my students leaves one small piece of plaque or calculus, that's not the most important thing. What is really important is whether that student connects with the patient. The patient should feel like she or he is the most important person in the world."*

Achieving Necessary Skills determined interpersonal skills to be one of four critical competencies in today's workforce. More specifically, the commission concludes that employees need to function effectively on teams, teach others, serve customers, lead and negotiate, and work well with people from culturally diverse backgrounds.[11] Interpersonal skills are discussed at length in the chapters on communication (Chapter 5) and teamwork (Chapter 6).

Employees need to relate effectively to the customer at the point of encounter (see Fig. 2.4). This requires interpersonal skills which some businesspeople refer to as *emotional intelligence* (see Diversity Box: Emotional Intelligence). Profits in any service-oriented industry depend to a large degree on employees who greet and service the public. A well-trained receptionist with excellent interpersonal skills can make a customer feel valued. Conversely, a salesperson or security guard who lacks these skills and is insensitive to diversity can hurt business.

The importance of treating people with respect and sensitivity was evident in a recent incident involving Eddie Bauer, a large upscale clothing store chain. Alonzo Jackson, a young black male, was detained by store personnel

Diversity Consciousness: Opening Our Minds to People, Cultures, and Opportunities

as he was leaving an Eddie Bauer outlet in the Washington, DC metropolitan area. Eddie Bauer employees had no legitimate reason to suspect that he was wearing a stolen shirt. Yet they forced Jackson to take his shirt off and only returned it when he came back the next day with a receipt. They did not apologize. Jackson later filed a lawsuit against the company. Eddie Bauer's lawyers countered by arguing that the individual employees themselves, not the company, should be held responsible. Eddie Bauer lost the case and alienated many customers.

⊠ *EMOTIONAL INTELLIGENCE*

In his best-selling book *Working with Emotional Intelligence*, Daniel Goleman analyzes those skills that distinguish average performers from superstars.[12] On the basis of data collected from more than 150 business firms, he concludes that "emotional intelligence" skills are the key. **Emotional Intelligence** is the ability to acknowledge, value, and manage feelings so that they are expressed appropriately and effectively, laying the groundwork for meaningful relationships and true teamwork. Goleman goes on to say that it is not enough to be technically proficient and possess a high IQ. Although "school smarts" might get you into the office, your ability to handle emotions and relate to people effectively allows you to excel on the job.

As an example, Goleman points to a 1997 study cited in the *Journal of the American Medical Association*. This study reports physicians who lacked empathy got sued more often. On the other hand, physicians who never had a malpractice suit possessed better interpersonal skills. They were empathetic and took time to communicate at length with their patients.[13]

2. *Flexible thinking skills and adaptability.* Perhaps you are a single parent who has struggled though difficult times. Maybe you have a military background that has given you the opportunity to live in numerous countries throughout the world. These kinds of experiences may help you think creatively and flexibly. Gene Polisseni, a vice president of marketing for a highly successful processing firm, is typical of many employers nowadays. He wants "people who are upbeat...who know life isn't always perfect and can go on when they hit a pothole."[14]

Flexible thinkers do not lock themselves into one mode of thought. Rather, they can adjust mentally to different situations. More and more companies need and want employees who are problem solvers, who can do more with less by examining both the familiar and unfamiliar from a variety of perspectives. This kind of thinking requires practice and a will to learn. In Chapter 4 we examine how flexible thinking enables us to understand and appreciate diversity.

In his book *A Kick in the Seat of the Pants*, Roger von Oech describes the flexibility of thought that characterizes creative thinkers. "Like race-car drivers who shift in and out of different gears depending on where they are on the course, creative people are able to shift in and out of different types of thinking depending on the needs of the situation at hand. Sometimes they're open and probing, at others they're playful and off-the-wall. At still other times, they're critical and fault-finding. And finally, they're doggedly persistent in striving to reach their goals."[15]

3. *Teamwork skills.* More and more organizations are turning to teams to solve problems and create better products and services. Consequently, people need to prepare themselves to join and contribute to teams. According to Andrea Dolph, coauthor of *How To Hit the Ground Running in Your New Job*, new graduates are sometimes insensitive to the needs of other team members in the workplace. She recalls when she started her career. "I was ambitious and often insensitive to some of the issues and priorities other people at work had to deal with."[16] When working on any team, it is important to remember "you're working with people from a variety of age groups and with different events in their lives—people with elder care issues or children for example. Have respect for the differences among people in your workplace."[17] In Chapter 6 we focus entirely on the subject of teamwork.

4. *Cultural awareness and understanding.* Awareness and understanding make it possible for you not only to recognize cultural differences and similarities, but also to grasp their meaning and significance. This learned skill is absolutely essential, at home or abroad, given a customer base that is becoming increasingly multinational and multicultural. As the buying power of minorities in the United States increases, businesses are directing more of their attention to minority marketing. Numerous advertising agencies now specialize in Asian-, African-, and Hispanic-American marketing. As the marketplace expands, a lack of cultural awareness and understanding is even more of a liability. It is clearly difficult to design and develop merchandise for markets you do not understand.

Kentucky Fried Chicken found this out the hard way. Their advertising slogan "finger-lickin good" became "Eat your fingers off" when translated into Chinese.

5. *Self-evaluation.* Stephen Covey, best-selling author and business consultant, says a common complaint of business leaders is that they cannot find workers who will take on the responsibility for making good things happen.[18] To do this requires continuous self-evaluation. By being open to feedback from others and monitoring yourself, you are more apt to realize why diversity skills are so important and what skills you may need to develop. Rather than simply relying on someone else to make this happen, you take the initiative. Self-evaluation, or what I term in later chapters "checking up on yourself," is a key area in the development of diversity consciousness.

In subsequent chapters, flexible thinking, cultural awareness and understanding, teamwork, communication, self-evaluation, and other basic diversity skills are discussed in more detail. Improving skills such as these allows us to develop our diversity consciousness. The benefits are numerous. We grow more aware of the value of human differences and the limitations imposed by close-mindedness. At the same time, we do not preoccupy ourselves with differences. This means that we can acknowledge, respect, *and* see beyond differences. In so doing, we relate to others more effectively and capitalize on human potential—our own as well as that of others.

◼◼◼ DIVERSITY SKILLS AND INDIVIDUAL/ORGANIZATIONAL BENEFITS

Understanding, celebrating and embracing differences provide a rich environment and taps into the best of everybody.

—Frank Blethen, CEO of the Seattle Times Company
(winner of the 1997 Ida B. Wells Award for his leadership in hiring,
training, and advancing minorities in media careers)

If businesses are going to succeed, regardless of their goals, they need to understand the business case for diversity. It will honestly determine their success.

—Carl Jefferson, Diversity Manager, Interstate Hotels Corporation
(the largest hotel management firm in the United States)

In our rapidly changing business, high-technology companies need people who come from diverse backgrounds and who can contribute different talents and perspectives to problem solving. Diversity is key to problem solving and problem solving is key to technology. To be the best, we must utilize the talents of all segments of the population. I believe diversity and valuing individuals has helped Texas Instruments grow into a stronger and more competitive company.

—Tegwin Dyer Pulley, Vice President, Texas Instruments (the world's leading designer and supplier of digital signal processing solutions)

journal entry

THINKING THROUGH DIVERSITY:
Select one school you attend(ed). If you were to grade this school on its ability to capitalize on diversity, what grade would you give, and why?

The Individual

Diversity skills provide people with more opportunities. If people have more opportunities, their chances for success will be greater. If you are looking for a job, these opportunities are particularly obvious. Take a look in the employment section of any major newspaper in the United States. What follows are some actual, typical ads for a variety of positions.

- "Great communicators wanted. Talk is cheap. Communicating is what really counts. After all, this is the Information Age. And if you don't have it, you won't be around very long." (communication specialist)
- "Demonstrated ability to bring about constructive change using participatory processes and strong human relations skills." (college administrator)
- "We require excellent communication and customer service skills. Fluency in French or Spanish strongly desired." (sales and service representative)
- "Excellent interpersonal and communication skills. Communication experience on a global level a plus." (marketing/promotional writer)
- "Candidates must have strong computer programming and analytical skills, leadership potential, and the interpersonal skills needed to work effectively in a demanding team environment." (technical associate–information)

- "We are looking for a team-oriented professional to provide leadership, direction, and technical expertise to support the current reporting infrastructure across our global enterprise-wide organization." (program analyst)
- "The position requires an individual who is a quick learner of new technologies with proven qualities of leadership, effective teamwork, and communication... Our people are diverse, and we capitalize on that diversity as we help each other grow and develop our talents in our areas of expertise." (Web application development and support)
- "Outstanding client relationship skills. Outstanding communication (written and verbal) skills. Strong self-starter, self-motivated, and willing to take on responsibility as an absolute team player." (computer assurance services)
- "We develop innovative programs and treatment modalities to meet the complex needs of an increasingly diverse population...need someone to help foster effective interaction with facility staff, patients, consumers, their families, and locally based providers to deliver a progressive continuum of mental health services." (mental health facility director)

Another indication of the importance of diversity skills is the emergence of diversity training into a highly competitive and profitable industry. Schools, government agencies, and major companies such as Levi-Strauss, IBM, Dow, Digital, and Avon spend millions each year on training of this nature. Often, diversity training in the workplace is mandatory. In some cases, the evaluation of an employee's contributions in the area of workforce diversity is one of the performance criteria that determines his or her salary and bonuses. There are also a rapidly growing number of training videos, seminars, books, and journals on managing and valuing diversity. "Diversity managers" are now commonplace in Fortune 500 companies.

▓ INTERACTIVE DRAMA AT XEROX CORPORATION

At Xerox Corporation, managers are evaluated on their ability to deal with diversity issues. Managers attend special interactive theater productions around the country as part of their training. These dramas represent a joint effort by the Theater Department at Cornell University and Xerox. Actors portray a variety of scenarios in which managers interact with employees who may look, think, and act differently. Then managers evaluate the choices made and offer suggestions. The productions' aim is to make managers more aware of discrimination and give them the tools to deal with it.

Diversity is a plus rather than a minus. But the plus doesn't come easily. The plus comes from appreciation and hard work.

—James Tschechtelin, President, Baltimore City Community College

We are in an industry that historically has not been inclusive. To move forward we need to learn how to communicate effectively with people who are different. Diversity efforts are critical components of reaching our business objectives.

—Richard Gaskins, Vice-President, Diversity Resource Center, American Express Financial Advisors (one of the largest financial planning and money management companies in the United States)

Diversity has tremendous power. The work we do involves dealing with a few pieces of information. We make a decision based on that. With a diverse group of people, we can be more objective. In a diverse group, I get a more balanced view of a problem than if I was looking at the data myself.

—Jose Arreola, Vice President of Research and Development, Cypress Semiconductor (a $600 million international supplier of high-performance semiconductors for the computer, networking, and telecommunications industries)

Why is it important for you to understand why organizations seek employees and others with diversity skills? In the course of your lifetime, you will deal with many **organizations**, groupings of people organized to achieve one or a number of goals. Many organizations are employers, including businesses, government agencies, educational institutions, and charitable agencies. Examining how and why organizations operate the way they do will allow you to assess what skills are in demand. Also, you will be better able to understand how diversity skills affect the organization and its members. Why, for example, do people at all levels and in all positions need these skills? How do diversity skills affect productivity? Why do surveys consistently show that CEOs of large and growing companies believe diversity is essential to their ongoing success? Whatever your position and function, you need to develop a perspective that is organizational as well as individual.

At the organizational level, the advantages afforded by a workforce with diversity skills are numerous.

1. *More innovation and adaptability.* Diversity skills generate a variety of innovative responses to challenges. In dealing with technological advances, international developments, and other social and economic changes, there is less reliance on tradition and more of a focus on creative problem solving. In the business world, the result is typically better products and better services, new customer/client populations, and the expansion of existing markets. For example, U.S. companies alter their marketing strategies as they grow more aware of the buying power of all types of minorities. American Telephone and Telegraph (AT&T) mailed brochures depicting three couples in affectionate poses: two women, two men, and a man and a woman. The slogan reads "Let Your True Voice Be Heard." Other companies, such as Saab, are now running their usual ads in gay publications.

2. *Better communication.* It is not enough to have employees with diverse talents and backgrounds. In sports, this is why the most talented team may not always win. A team with less talent but better communication is able to maximize its collective talent. In other words, team members work with and feed off each other.

The same thing holds true in the workplace. Without effective communication, teamwork suffers and talent is wasted. An example of this is **groupthink**, conformity to the expectations of a group, which in turn limits understanding of an issue. For example, an employee might think of a radically different approach to a group problem. However, she is hesitant to share it because of the vibes she has gotten from other group members in the past. Her ideas are often dismissed as far-fetched and idealistic. Rather than take a chance, she ends up going along with the group because she doesn't want to "rock the boat." This scenario, which is very common in work teams, produces mediocre solutions to difficult problems.

3. *Recruitment and retention of the best employees.* Those organizations with the best reputation for attracting and maintaining an inclusive and highly competent workforce will be at an advantage in terms of recruiting and keeping the best talent. The consequences of limiting the talent pool are obvious when we examine intercollegiate athletics. Formerly all-white southern colleges and universities did not recruit Blacks and other students of color. Consequently, they denied themselves some of the best athletic talent available at that time.

4. *Less likelihood of incurring the costs of discrimination.* Discrimination is very expensive. It creates conflict, siphons off people's talents and energies, and leads to the underutilization of human potential. A fact finding report by the Glass Ceiling Commission states that "barriers persist," slowing down the advancement of women and minorities and depriving companies of the talent and diversity they need to compete globally.[19]

5. *Greater productivity.* If you feel valued, you are going to be more productive. This is the rationale behind "managing diversity." **Managing diversity** does *not* imply control or manipulation; rather, it means creating an environment that enables everyone to contribute their full potential.

A person who possesses diversity skills is a more valued employee. These skills can help the members of any organization work together to improve the quality of their product or service. This, in turn, will increase profits. Therefore, the importance of diversity skills is not some "feel good" issue. It relates directly to the "bottom line"—productivity and profit.

> *Valuing and creating a work environment that is diverse is a priority at Xerox. If it's a priority, then it needs to be tracked and rewarded. If objectives are not met, then there needs to be a consequence.*
>
> —Pat Elizondo, Vice President and General Manager, Xerox Corporation (Xerox is the 1995 winner of the first award given by the Federal Glass Ceiling Commission for commitment to diversity

THE COSTS OF INADEQUATE DIVERSITY SKILLS

> *People with business backgrounds need to have strong interaction skills and EI (emotional intelligence). There's such a big learning curve when new employees walk through the door. Often, they are not ready to produce.*
>
> —Carl Jefferson, Diversity Manager, Interstate Hotels Corporation

Mr. Riley is one of a number of recruiters attending a job fair at a local college. He describes himself as multiracial. Years ago, he lost his arm while serving in the army and he now wears a prosthesis. He represents a growing company that develops and manufactures high-technology products for industrial and medical uses. His company, with plants around the globe, takes pride in the fact its employees have no titles or so-called bosses. Employees communicate as equals and work in small, multidisciplined teams. From his point of view, good hires are a necessity. Although a student's academic background is important, it is also necessary that he or she have the right attitude and the necessary people skills. With this in mind, is Mr. Riley going to take a chance on any of the following interviewees?

1. Tim has excellent credentials, including a 3.50 GPA. During much of the interview, he seems uncomfortable and distracted. It is almost as if Tim fixates more on Mr. Riley's physical differences than anything he says.

2. Frieda has good grades and excellent references. However, her communication skills are suspect. At numerous points during the interview, her body language appears to contradict what she is saying.

3. Terry seems very sure of himself. His résumé is lengthy and impressive. He has had virtually no experience working or living in a multiethnic environment. Another concern is a remark he made before the interview began. Both Mr. Riley and Terry were talking about their plans for the upcoming weekend.

Terry jokingly referred to a Kwanzaa celebration being held at the college. Mr. Riley felt the comment was clearly inappropriate.

When people lack necessary diversity skills, the implications are significant. As a student, you may find it difficult to learn from instructors and other students who do not share your background, personality, values, or learning style. Lacking the skills to be a "team player" may make it difficult for you to work with others in study groups. Beyond resulting in alienation and emotional stress, poor communication skills can make it difficult for you to find the help you need in and out of class. For example, some students do not know how to interpret and respond to both verbal and nonverbal cues. When they interact with someone who may not share their perspective, they find it difficult to listen actively and think flexibly. As a result, they may alienate others and not even know it.

Organizationally speaking, people with poor diversity skills will strain interpersonal relationships, threaten team spirit, and waste time. Costly lawsuits are more likely to occur. Ultimately, the reputation of an organization may be undermined.

With each of the following real-life examples, the individual and organizational costs are significant.

1. Tom interviews for a college teaching position. He meets a team of six people, only one of whom is female. Tom is highly qualified for the position and answers all the questions flawlessly. However, when it is time to rank the candidates, the lone female on the search committee observes that Tom addressed the male interviewers' questions more fully. In addition, she is the only person with whom he did not establish eye contact. The committee decides that he is not worth the risk and does not offer him the job.

2. At Yankee Stadium a few years ago, a relief pitcher for the Baltimore Orioles, Armando Benitez, triggered a brawl by hitting a New York Yankee player with a fastball. Many thought it was intentional, although Benitez denied it. A day later, the Orioles general manager tried to explain Benitez's actions. "You have to understand Armando comes from a different culture, a different background." He added, Latinos "can be quite emotional and become frustrated" in situations. Although these comments were made with the best of intentions, they alienated baseball fans, players, and the public. Besides stereotyping Latinos, the comments seemed to excuse Benitez's behavior.[20]

3. American Telephone and Telegraph (AT&T), widely acknowledged as a corporate leader in managing diversity, experienced a public relations nightmare as a result of a cartoon published in its employee magazine. It showed customers on various continents making a telephone call. Four customers in different parts of the world were represented as people: a white man in North America, a white woman in South America, and a white man and woman in Eastern and Western Europe. The caller in Africa was a gorilla. After a flood of complaints from angry customers, employees, civil rights groups, and politicians, AT&T management apologized for the "racist" illustration.

4. In 1994, Denny's restaurants paid $45 million to settle class-action suits. African-American customers charged that they were treated differently by the chain's waiters and managers.

5. In 1996, a suit filed against Texaco alleged racial and religious discrimination. A secret recording of Texaco executives making disparaging remarks about African Americans and Jews added to the evidence. Texaco paid out $176 million in damages. As part of the settlement, the company agreed to spend millions on programs designed to "wipe out" discrimination.

6. Mitsubishi Motors recently agreed to pay $34 million in a sexual-harassment settlement. The settlement will be shared by 350 women who worked at the Mitsubishi auto plant in Illinois. The suit stemmed from complaints about male co-workers and supervisors kissing and fondling women, calling them "whores" and "bitches," posting pornographic drawings of the female workers, demanding sexual favors, and retaliating against women who refused. Furthermore, it was alleged that company managers did little to stop the mistreatment. Twenty Mitsubishi employees have been fired as a result of the case.

The relationship between diversity skills and success has been examined throughout this chapter. Numerous research findings, personal anecdotes, student perspectives, and comments from business leaders attest to the critical importance of diversity skills. Through education and constant practice, each of us has the power to improve our diversity skills and enhance our chances for success. By developing these skills, you will become a better student and a more valued employee. Conversely, ignoring these skills will be very costly.

Subsequent chapters focus on these and other diversity skills, and their relationship to diversity consciousness. A number of questions are addressed. For example, how do we develop and refine diversity skills? How do these skills enable us to overcome barriers to success? Finally, why will these diversity skills become even more important in the future?

Exercises

IN-CLASS

Exercise 1: The Meanings of Success

Directions for Instructor
1. Seat students in pairs.
2. Have each student read each of the following questions, writing down their individual responses.

○ How do you define success?

○ How have your life experiences shaped your attitudes regarding what constitutes success?

○ What three names would be at the top of your list of successful people? For each person, explain why you include her or him.

3. Have students share their responses with their partners.

4. As a class, ask all students to examine their lists of successful people. Are there any traits or talents that seem to distinguish most or all of the people on their lists? If so, what are they? Record these traits on the board.

Exercise 2: A Picture of Success

Directions for Instructor

1. Give each student a large sheet of paper and make available pencils, felt-tip markers, and crayons.

2. Ask them to think of experiences in school that have contributed to their success.

3. Instruct students to draw one of these experiences on the sheet of paper. They should not use words in their drawing. If possible, display the drawings where everyone can see them.

4. Ask each student to describe what her or his drawing represents and how it relates to success.

OUT-OF-CLASS

Exercise 1: Social Class and Success

1. Has your social class background shaped your definition of success in any way? Explain.

2. What advantages and disadvantages have you experienced due to your social class background?

3. Imagine that you wake up tomorrow and discover that you have inherited $100 million from an unknown benefactor. How would this change your definition of success? Would your educational and career goals change? Explain.

Exercise 2: Learning and Teaching Styles

Below are some sample student evaluations of two different instructors.

Instructor A:

Taneka: "I feel I learn a lot in this class, and I think I will get a good final grade. I really like the way the instructor uses examples from everyday life and lets us work in groups so much. It makes it easier to understand and more interesting. I usually do not participate much in discussions. But this class is different. I think the instructor has a lot to do with this. She is very friendly and informal."

Luis: "I have a hard time understanding why I have to take this course. I find the course to be pretty boring. I am always listening to students. I am taking this class to find out what the instructor knows about the subject. After all, that is what we're going to be tested on."

Michael: "This class is always interesting and I like the instructor, but I don't think I'll get a decent grade. I have a hard time figuring out what I need to study. Sometimes, we spend too much time discussing the readings. I would rather just focus on what I need to know for the tests."

Instructor B:

Schuzan: "I really didn't think I was going to like this course. I heard a lot about this instructor, how hard he is. But his lectures are really good. I can tell how much work he puts into them. I do not see how anyone can do poorly in this class. The instructor writes practically everything on the board. Also, the handouts make it easy to take notes and study for the test."

Alice: "If anything, he needs to move a little faster. He is always stopping and writing everything on the board. Also, we never get to talk about the subject. We are always listening. I have the feeling he is more interested in the subject than in his students. That makes it hard for me to pay attention."

Esther: "I can tell this instructor really, really cares about his field. It shows in his lectures and it really helps me learn. I just wish we had more opportunities to work in small groups and talk about what we are studying."

Answer the following questions.

1. Do you identify with any of the students above or with any of their comments? If so, which one(s)? What do you think this says about your learning style?

2. Which instructor would you prefer? Which specific characteristics of this instructor appeal to you? How well does his or her teaching style fit your learning style?

3. Which instructor's style does not appeal to you? If you found yourself in this instructor's class, what could you do to increase your chances for success?

Exercise 3: Instructor Interview

Interview. Schedule an appointment with one of your instructors. Explain that you would like to conduct an interview with this person for a class assignment. Prior to the interview, make a list of possible questions. Include questions that cover the following points, but do not hesitate to explore other topics as well.

- What is the instructor's name and position?
- What is the instructor's professional and educational background?
- What does he or she share in common with other instructors?
- In what ways does this instructor feel different?
- How has the instructor's individual and cultural background influenced his or her teaching?
- How does this instructor define success?
- How has the instructor's individual and cultural background influenced his or her definition of success?

Follow-up questions are a good way of getting more information or of clarifying certain points brought up during the course of the interview.

Summary and Analysis. List each of the questions you asked. After each question, summarize the interviewee's response. Briefly analyze the interview. How do you think it went? What did you learn?

 ## INTERNET ASSIGNMENT

Search the World Wide Web for a site that is about some dimension of your diversity. It could refer to your cultural heritage, race, religion, learning style, sexual orientation, position at work, age, or some other dimension. This Web site should be of a positive nature, promoting the value of what you have chosen without demeaning others. After reading the Web site and going to any appropriate links, do the following.

1. Print the information you found to be particularly inspiring or insightful. Include the URL address.

2. Write a paragraph on each of the following questions: What did you learn about your diversity? Why did you find this information inspiring or insightful?

ANSWER to Diversity Box: "Thinking Outside the Box" (see page 44)

Directions: Draw four straight lines, without lifting your pencil, that touch all the dots.

This problem illustrates the idea that sometimes the only way you can solve a problem is to go beyond your usual way of thinking. Most people when trying to solve this problem will not extend their lines past the dots—staying "in the box." The only way to solve the problem is to "think outside the box."

NOTES

[1]Samuel D. Proctor and William D. Watley, *Sermons from the Black Pulpit* (Valley Forge, PA: Judson Press, 1984), 38.

[2]National Institute of Education, "Involvement in Learning: Realizing the Potential of American Higher Education," *Report of the Study Group on the Conditions of Excellence in American Higher Education* (Washington, DC: U.S. Department of Education, 1984), 17.

[3]Howard Gardner, *Frames of Mind: The Theory of Multiple Intelligences* (New York: Basic Books, 1983).

[4]Sonia Nieto, *Affirming Diversity: The Sociopolitical Context of Multicultural Education* (White Plains, NY: Longman, 1996), 283.

[5]Alexander Astin, "Diversity and Multiculturalism on the Campus: How Are Students Affected?" *Change*, Mar./Apr. 1993, 44–49.

[6]M. A. Gibson, "Parental Support for Schooling," paper presented at the annual meeting of the American Anthropological Association, Dec. 1986.

[7]Terry Huffman, "The Transculturation of Native American College Students," in *American Mosaic: Selected Readings on America's Multicultural Heritage*, Young I. Song and Eugene C. Kim (eds.) (Englewood Cliffs, NJ: Prentice Hall, 1993), 211–219; Sonia Nieto, *Affirming Diversity: The Sociopolitical Context of Multicultural Education* (White Plains, NY: Longman, 1996).

[8]Terry Huffman, "The Transculturation of Native American College Students," in *American Mosaic: Selected Readings on America's Multicultural Heritage*, Young I. Song and Eugene C. Kim (eds.) (Englewood Cliffs, NJ: Prentice Hall, 1993), 211–219.

[9]American Management Association, "What Do Organizations Really Want?" *AMA Catalog of Seminars*, Oct. 1997.

[10]Karen Dowd and Jeanne Liedtka, "What Corporations Seek in MBA Hires: A Survey," *The Magazine of the Graduate Management Admission Council* (Winter, 1994), 38.

[11]Anne-Lee Verville, "What Business Needs from Higher Education," *Educational Record*, 76(4), Fall 1995, 46–50.

[12]Daniel Goleman, *Working with Emotional Intelligence* (New York: Bantam Books, 1998).

[13]Wendy Levinson, Debra Roter, John Mullooly, Valerie Dull, and Richard Frankel, "Physician–Patient Communication: The Relationship with Malpractice Claims Among Primary Care Physicians and Surgeons," *Journal of the American Medical Association* (February 19, 1997) 553.

[14]Christina LeBeau, "Attitude Adjustment," *Rochester Democrat and Chronicle*, Oct. 19, 1997, 1e+.

[15]Roger von Oech, *A Kick in the Seat of the Pants* (New York: Harper & Row, 1986), 5–21.

[16]Lynda P. Clemens and Andrea T. Dolph, *How to Hit the Ground Running in Your New Job* (Lincolnwood, IL: VGM Career Horizons, 1995).

[17]Sheryl Silver, "New Grads: Make the Most of Your First Job, *The Washington Post High Tech Horizons*, Aug. 3, 1997, M19.

[18]Stephen Covey, "How To Succeed in Today's Workplace," *USA Weekend*, Aug. 29–31, 1997, 4–5.

[19]Scripps Howard News Service, "White Men Still at Top of the Business Heap, Study Finds," *Carroll County Times*, Mar. 16, 1995, A7.

[20]Ann O'Hanlon, "Lost in the Translation," *The Washington Post*, May 24, 1998, D1+.

3 PERSONAL AND SOCIAL BARRIERS TO SUCCESS

Upon completion of this chapter, you will be able to:

○ Differentiate between **personal** and **social barriers**.

○ List, explain, and give examples of the six barriers to success.

○ Explain and give examples of each of the four combinations of **prejudice** and **discrimination**.

○ Discuss the strategies for acknowledging and overcoming diversity barriers.

I believe that in the United States there are barriers. People get tired of bumping their heads against those invisible walls. And I speak from experience. Years ago, I went to a predominantly white college. I got in trouble for things that were overlooked for Anglo students. But that didn't stop me from trying to get an education.

I became a supervisor at a predominantly white hospital. I was told, "Don't hire too many Mexicans because we don't want this place to become a barrio." And I didn't let that stop me from being fair in my hiring. When I worked at another hospital, there was discrimination but it was swept under the carpet. They would say, "We didn't do that," or "We didn't say it that way." Or they would go back and rewrite their policies when someone would file a grievance.

I feel that for those of us who pretend this kind of thing does not happen, it's like sticking your head in a hole. But I don't feel like any of us should allow the barriers to stop us from moving ahead. Nobody can hold you back. It's your own thinking that holds you back. I don't feel like I'm looking for discrimination all the time. I just feel like I am a realist.

—A student's perspective

How do we explain why some people are more successful than others? Is it simply a matter of individual talent and motivation? Cornel West, author of nine books and a professor at Harvard University, is highly critical of conventional explanations of success. In his writings, West zeros in on the issue of race and its implications for climbing up the social ladder. However, his analysis could apply to gender, class, and any number of other dimensions of diversity.

At first, West takes issue with the idea that people can solve problems such as poverty and inequality simply by changing individual values and behaviors. He rightly points out that many poor African-Americans remain poor despite their strong work ethic. Second, he criticizes the notion that more government and economic programs can eliminate racial inequality. West argues that the problem is not strictly a matter of economics. In short, he views approaches to racial inequality that focus entirely on the individual *or* the larger society as simplistic and incomplete. West argues that we will be successful only if we stop pointing our fingers at a single source of the problem.[1]

We can take West's analysis and apply it to our discussion of diversity, success, and the barriers to success. Barriers to success may stem from the individual or may be found in the larger society. **Personal barriers** refer to those individual factors that get in the way of our success. Our focus is on factors that relate to diversity. These barriers include one's lack of self-awareness, cultural ignorance, and underdeveloped diversity consciousness. Personal barriers would also include a person's biases and discriminatory behaviors. **Social barriers** focus more on society. They refer to those factors that are external to the person and impede her or his success. Among these barriers are the perceptions, thoughts, and actions of others. Ethnocentrism, stereotypes, prejudice, and discrimination are barriers that can be personal or social, depending on the situation. Also, it is important to remember, as West mentioned earlier, that interrelationships exist between personal and social barriers. For example, encountering prejudice and discrimination in the larger society may reinforce our personal biases. Similarly, our biases can adversely affect our friends, classmates, and co-workers.

I am from a small island in the West Indies. I have an accent where I do not speak clearly. People do not understand me, or laugh. As for my instructors, they look at me as spaced out. They think I do not know what is going on because I do not talk a lot in class. Sometimes if I think I have a good answer, I will second-guess myself. When the instructor asks me something, the first thing I'll do is get hot and sweaty and scared. I'll feel like my answers are not as good as anybody else's.

—A student's perspective

In this chapter we examine personal and social barriers that impede our success: perceptions, ethnocentrism, stereotypes, prejudice, prejudice plus power, and discrimination. We focus on those barriers that are obvious as well as those that are not easily recognizable. Additionally, we examine a number of strategies for overcoming such barriers.

THINKING THROUGH DIVERSITY:
journal entry | **If someone were to write your life history, what would we learn about personal and social barriers?**

■■■■ SIX BARRIERS TO SUCCESS

Barrier 1: Limited Perceptions

The scene: You just return to campus after the spring break. As you approach the library, you see a number of statues. Upon closer examination, you notice that each of these statues represents a student. Two appear to be

African-American students. One of the African-American students is twirling a basketball and the other is balancing a book on her head. The single Asian-American student is carrying a violin. Each of the white students is shown holding a number of books. What are you feeling as you study each of the statues? Individually and collectively, what do these statues say to you? Are you offended? Do you plan on sharing your thoughts and feelings with anyone else? Why? Will you be able to put your feelings aside and concentrate on your studies for the rest of the day?

This scene took place at the University of North Carolina (UNC). Each year the graduating class gives the university a gift. Not long ago, one class hired a well-known sculptor to create a number of statues depicting the diversity of UNC's student population. The artist sculpted the figures described earlier. Once they were placed in a prominent place on campus, they immediately caused an uproar among students. Many complained that the statues reinforced stereotypical images. The African-Americans, they argued, were portrayed as being less studious and less intelligent than the Whites and Asian-American. In their eyes, it reinforced the stereotype that African-Americans are athletes first and students second. Other students felt that people were making a big fuss over nothing. In response to the growing tension among students, the statues were relocated to another spot on campus that was much less visible.

The scenario just described provides insight into the potential barriers that limited perceptions of diversity can create. Did the sculptor consider the different messages these statues might convey? Did the sculptor have any understanding of the backgrounds and perspectives of the students, faculty, and staff at UNC? What about the people who hired this sculptor and oversaw the project? Most important, what did the students learn from this?

For a moment, put yourself in the place of certain students who might walk past these statues. What if you were a student who was constantly asked "Do you play sports?" because of your height or skin color? Suppose that you often encounter instructors and other students who make a habit of assuming that you got into college because of your athletic talent rather than your intelligence. Or imagine that people assume you are gifted and extremely intelligent simply because of your cultural background or your looks. Taking on the role of each of these students, or at least trying to, can help us understand the multiple worlds in which we live. It can also make us more aware of the barriers we may create by perceptions, thoughts, and actions.

Perceptions refer to the way in which we receive and interpret information from any of our senses. Thus perceptions can be understood as a link between a person and his or her surroundings. However, what we perceive does not necessarily reflect reality. Furthermore, two people can look at the same image or witness the same event and see something completely different (see Fig. 3.1). When we interact with others or even take a look at ourselves, our perceptions come into play. They can affect the way we feel, think, and act. Hence, it is important to understand those factors that can influence our perceptions.

We do not interact with others with an entirely blank mind. Rather, our perceptions are rooted in past experiences. Throughout our lives, we are

Figure 3.1: *What do you see? Two faces looking at each other? A vase? Because of the shapes and coloring in the picture, you might see either. This image, which appears in the book* Can You Believe Your Eyes? *by J. Richard Block and Harold Yuker (New York: Brunner/Mazel, 1992), was first published around 1915.*

exposed to a variety of human images via our interaction with the media, school, peers, friends, family, community members, and others. The images we experience and how we interpret these images color our perceptions.

A well-known psychological experiment illustrates how our perspective may distort what we see. In this experiment, a person was shown a picture of a white man holding a knife, who is standing next to a black man. The person was asked to describe the picture to another person, who then relayed what he or she was told to the next person. This process went on until everybody in the group had a turn. The last person, asked to describe what the first person saw, explained that there were two men standing next to each other, one Black and one White, and the black man was holding a knife. The experiment shows how our racial biases can radically alter what we see.

✄ PERCEPTIONS OF PEOPLE WITH DISABILITIES

The relationship between perceptions and environment is illustrated dramatically in a study of high school seniors in Berkeley, California. The study compares students' attitudes toward people with and without disabilities. Students were shown videotapes of a man who was variously identified as disabled or able-bodied. Each student then rated the man on intelligence, work, competence, morality, and sociability. In comparison to the negative ratings found in similar studies conducted elsewhere, the overall rating of the person with a disability was much more positive.

In explaining their results, the researchers point to the uniqueness of Berkeley. As the home of one branch of the University of California, Berkeley has many students with disabilities. Mainstreaming and other educational innovations are opening up opportunities for persons with disabilities and increasing their visibility. As a result, "the nondisabled population is exposed to persons with disabilities who cope and live within the community" and "get to know them and their abilities beyond the disability."[2]

Psychologists conduct extensive research on perceptions. Research indicates that we can only experience and digest a certain portion of our vast social world. Because of this, we have a tendency to take shortcuts to understanding others. We often perceive what we want to perceive. This is called **selective perception**. In other words, we focus on those things that support our assumptions and beliefs. We ignore information that refutes our thinking. In this way we can store and process information in neat, simple categories.

Research by Bodenhausen illustrates the potential dangers of selective perception. Bodenhausen asked students to take on the role of jurors in a fictitious court case. Some students were told that the defendant's name was Carlos Ramirez and his home was Albuquerque, New Mexico. Others were informed that the defendant's name was Robert Johnson and he was from Dayton, Ohio. Moreover, students learned of these names either before or after the evidence was presented. The study's findings revealed that students who were told that the defendant was Carlos Ramirez *before* the evidence was presented were the most likely to find him guilty. Initially, these students formed an image of the defendant based on his name. This image had a direct bearing on their perception and interpretation of the evidence.[3]

Limited perceptions work against us for a number of reasons:

○ We tend to be unaware of the blinders or obstructions that distort our perceptions in some way. This makes it difficult to acknowledge, much less remove, these obstructions. The end result is that our senses do not operate at peak efficiency.

○ We absorb only a small fraction of the world around us. In other words, we experience only a slice or, in some cases, a sliver of life. More often than not, we experience things from one perspective rather than from a variety of perspectives.

○ We tend to tune into those things with which we agree. Although this might make it easier to make sense of the world around us, the end result is that we miss out on a lot. In an increasingly diverse world, we fail to experience and appreciate much that the world has to offer. Moreover, there is a tendency to view more and more people as homogeneous masses with whom we have little in common.

○ Our perception of others reflects on ourselves. According to an African proverb, "when you judge others, you do not define them…you define yourself."

If I am to have a successful medical career, I can't afford to walk around with blinders on or refuse to treat someone because that person is "different" from me.

—A student's perspective

Barrier 2: Ethnocentrism

Culture envelopes us so completely that sometimes it is difficult to realize that our perspective is one of many. **Ethnocentrism** refers to the assumption that our way of thinking and acting is naturally superior to any other. As a result, we use ourselves or our culture as the yardstick by which we measure what is right or desirable. Therefore, we may devalue or ignore differences. This kind of thinking produces "tunnel vision." Rudyard Kipling, in his poem "We and They," describes how ethnocentrism locks us into an "us" and "them" mindset. "Father, Mother and Me, Sister and Auntie say All the people like Us are We, And everyone else is They."[4]

▨ TAKING A CRITICAL LOOK AT MAPS

Consider the way you look at maps. Students are generally not taught to question maps. After all, the world can only be drawn one correct way. Right? Imagine a sphere like a hollowed-out pumpkin or an orange peel. What happens if you try to make it flat? It would not be possible without damaging or wrinkling it in some way. Now think of what happens when we take the earth's curved surface and try to make it lie down on a map. There has to be some distortion. This is why mapmakers utilize projection. Over 200 techniques have been used to project the earth onto a flat map. All are distorted to some degree.

A commonly used map in American schools is the Mercator Projection Map. This map was created by Gerardus Mercator in 1569 in Germany. At this time, European colonial powers dominated much of the world. Although the Mercator

Projection had navigational benefits, it also reflected the Europeans' sense of importance and power at that time. It made European countries look bigger than the rest of the world. Other areas, such as China, Mexico, and Africa, appeared much smaller than they really were.

During the past few decades, Arthur Robinson is one of a number of cartographers who has created a projection that corrects this bias. Cartographers consider his map, the Robinson Projection Map, to be a major improvement. It displays the relative sizes of continents and countries much more accurately. For example, the true relative size of Africa is shown on the Robinson Projection Map; unlike the traditional Mercator Projection, the Robinson Projection shows Africa to be considerably larger than Greenland (see Fig. 3.2, next page).

It is important to realize that no one person, group, or society has a monopoly on ethnocentrism. We are all ethnocentric to some degree. For example, we might view our customs as the right way and, in some instances, the only way. When we encounter someone from another culture, we might think to ourselves: Why can't she think the way I think? Talk the way I talk? Act the

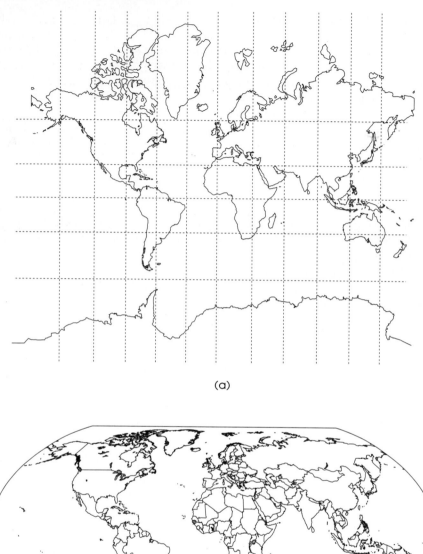

(a)

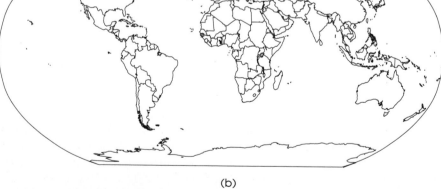

(b)

Figure 3.2: *(a) Mercator and (b) Robinson projection maps of the world. Compare the size of the continents on the traditional Mercator Projection and the Robinson Projection.*

way I act? That kind of thinking can build group solidarity and pride. It becomes a liability when we get so caught up in our own thinking that we cannot see the value of other ways of life. As an example, the ethnocentrism shown by some corporations has been very costly (see Diversity Box: The Human and Financial Costs of Corporate Ethnocentrism).

▓ THE HUMAN AND FINANCIAL COSTS OF CORPORATE ETHNOCENTRISM

In the 1960s and 1970s, the world-wide infant formula industry was dominated by Nestlé of Switzerland and several U.S. companies. These firms saw the large populations in less developed nations as a growing, untapped market for their product. Nestlé planned its marketing strategy and targeted new mothers and professionals in these countries. Mass media and billboard ads showed happy mothers with their beautiful, bottle-fed babies. Free samples were given to health personnel and new mothers in hospitals. Face-to-face sales efforts pushed the nutritional value of formula.

The reaction from abroad was not what Nestlé or any of the other firms expected. Critics charged that selling formula put babies at risk. When sub-stituted for breast feeding, babies were denied the nourishment of their mothers' milk. Many of these women were illiterate and therefore could not read the directions. In many areas, there was no refrigeration to keep the formula from spoiling.

The controversy culminated in a worldwide boycott of Nestlé from 1977 to 1984. The boycott was called off when Nestlé agreed to alter its marketing practices and comply with the marketing code established by the World Health Organization (WHO). When activists discovered that Nestlé was continuing to supply free or low-cost formula to hospitals, the boycott was reinstated. In 1991, Nestlé agreed to discontinue this practice. The company lost between $3 and $5 million as a result of the boycott.

Ethnocentrism can be very subtle and difficult to recognize. In the examples that follow, ask yourself what assumptions are being made? What are the implications for success?

1. Gloria is a manager of a large department store. She feels very proud of her success on the job and takes pride in the fact she is the only employee with a college degree. Gloria attaches a lot of importance to academic degrees and credentials. When she meets with store employees, she tends to be close-minded even though she pretends to listen. She finds it particularly difficult to give much credence to the views of lower-salaried employees without a college education. Many of these employees sense this and keep their ideas to themselves.

2. Karlton is completing a lengthy research study in which he examines the short- and long-term effects of daily doses of aspirin. In compiling his data, he relies exclusively on research that studies only men. He operates under the assumption that what he finds true of men also applies to women. Now, a prominent fellow researcher is criticizing this assumption as ethnocentric and questioning the validity of his research.

3. Bob is a 54-year-old, single, white male. As a veteran lawyer, he is proud of his accomplishments working for a large law firm in Chicago. He attributes his success to the tremendous amount of time and energy he invests in his job. Recently, he attended a diversity training workshop. Along with other participants, he was asked to make a list of the firm's unwritten rules. The lists were then shared. One rule mentioned by a number of minority lawyers was "If you're not a white male, you won't succeed." Although Bob did not say anything at the time, he thinks any mention of race or gender is a "cop-out." According to Bob, "These people have to be willing to sacrifice like I did."

Ethnocentrism is universal. It affects us all. The challenge of ethnocentrism is realizing not *if* but *when* it influences our thinking and judgment. Similarly, it is necessary to recognize the *costs* of putting ourselves and our culture at the center of everything. We become narrow-minded and lose sight of opportunities in realms outside our own. We impair our ability to relate to others. Most important, we fail to learn and benefit from the collective wisdom and experiences of all people.

Barrier 3: Stereotypes

As you were growing up, what stories or comments did you hear about people who were viewed as different for one reason or another? They might have been members of another race, social class, or religion. From whom did you hear these things? Did you believe them at the time? What about now? Often, what we hear and accept as true takes the form of a **stereotype**, an unverified overgeneralization that we associate with a group of people. Our social environment provides us with a set of images. Many of these images are stereotypes. When we stereotype, we lump people in a category and assume they are all alike.

Each of us is exposed to stereotypes starting at an early age. Wilma Mankiller, former chief of the Cherokee Nation, recalls her first encounter with stereotypes. Her schoolmates would sing a song, "Mankiller, Mankiller, how many men did you kill today?" or they would make war-whoop noises. Stereotypical images, whether associated with Native Americans or any other group, are learned through family, peers, school, religion, the media, and other social influences. Over the course of many years, these stereotypes are reinforced and internalized in the same way that they were initially learned. As a result, stereotypical thinking tends to be very rigid and difficult to change.

I was raised in a single-parent household headed up by my mother, as were most of my friends. As a result, I grew up believing that African-American men were irresponsible, selfish, and afraid of commitment. They cared nothing about their children or the women who bore these children. As I've grown older and explored other communities and cultures, I've learned to question what I see around me. I've learned that the absentee African-American father is not the norm.

—A student's perspective

There is no shortage of stereotypes in today's world. Stereotypes revolve around every dimension of diversity, such as job position and function, race, ethnicity, religion, social class, language, learning style, and sexual orientation. In many instances, stereotypes relate to physical appearance, such as skin color, age, or gender. Another dimension, one that is more subtle and rarely mentioned, is physical attractiveness. Psychological research shows that many people in our society equate character with looks. According to the *attractiveness stereotype*, we view people who are attractive as "more sensitive, kind, interesting, strong, poised, modest, sociable, outgoing, and exciting, sexually warm, and responsive." Furthermore, we tend to assume that they will "hold better jobs, have more successful marriages, and happier and more fulfilling lives."[5]

Like other stereotypes, the attractiveness stereotype can affect the way we think and act. This was borne out in recent research by Wesley Kayson and Andrea DeSantis of Iona College. These researchers recruited 160 college students, faculty, and office workers. Each participant was asked to serve as a juror in an imaginary burglary case. After reviewing a fact sheet describing the crime, the participants studied the photographs of men and women described as defendants. The attractiveness of each defendant had already been rated by 10

BEAUTIFUL AND DISABLED

People with disabilities in our society constantly encounter stereotypical images of beauty that do not look like them. Some accept society's norms of attractiveness and enjoy trying to live up to them. Others, such as Ellen Stohl and James Box, do not. Stohl, who has a spinal cord injury, posed for *Playboy* in 1987. This was *her* way of saying that a woman with a disability can be beautiful and sexy. Box, a paraplegic and founder of a high-tech wheelchair company, uses advertising to challenge the public's perceptions of people who use wheelchairs. One ad shows a sexy blond woman lying on her back, tipped over in her wheelchair. According to Box, ads such as these show that people in wheelchairs do have sexual lives. Even though some people are uncomfortable with his ads, he says that is fine. His point is to show real people in real situations.

psychology students on a scale of 1 to 7. The participants were then asked to recommend a jail sentence. On average, good-looking defendants received much shorter sentences than those rated as less attractive.[6]

Before we can change our thinking, we need to acknowledge our stereo-typical assumptions. However, this is not easy. Coming to grips with a stereo-type we have held for a long time can make us feel uncomfortable and vulnerable. Additionally, we tend to be more aware of other people's stereo-types than our own. As one of my students said, some stereotypes are "difficult to see because they are buried deep within our souls."

If students feel a certain level of trust and comfort, the classroom can be a place where students take a more critical and rational look at their thinking about diversity. In my classroom, I use an activity that focuses on the subject of racial stereotyping. Students sit in a tight circle. I ask them to recount a story or comment they have heard about members of another racial or ethnic group. One by one, each student gets a chance to share his or her story. What they share is typically negative and stereotypical.

I heard that French people were rude, sex starved, and unclean. When I finally got the opportunity to travel to France, I learned that the French were just like Americans in many ways.

In elementary school, I was taught that Africans lived in huts, in villages. They were starving and poor. Even though my mother is from Zambia, I still had trouble picturing Africans having the same things Americans have, such as homes, communities, and streets.

I used to believe that all white people were rich and their problems could be solved within 30 minutes.

I grew up thinking that Asians—Vietnamese, Chinese, and Japanese— were all the same. For a long time, I believed that all Asians were smart.

People would say that all Jews were penny pinchers. I grew up believing that all Jews were cheap and very cautious with money.

Growing up, I viewed the English as very uptight, unathletic human beings. I pictured them as always wearing suits and trench coats. I pictured the women always dressed as if they were going to a ball and most wearing fine jewelry all the time. I figured all of the English always drank tea and ate only freshly cooked, expensive dinners.

When I was growing up, I heard that you can't trust white people. They'll act like they're your friends and they'll laugh and joke with you. But when it comes down to a confrontation, they'll turn on you.

As a child, I heard that people from Haiti and the Islands in general always lived with like 30 people to a bedroom. So many lived in an apartment they had to sleep in shifts.

—Students' perspectives

Interestingly, there are also many stereotypes that revolve around two sensitive subjects we rarely discuss in public: sex and hygiene. For example, many students have been "taught" that other races are unclean and sexually deviant.

Once every student has had a chance to participate, I ask them to examine critically what was shared. Do they think that any of these stories are based on fact? Why? How do we share and perpetuate these stories? What assumptions are found in each story? Can we make this assumption about all members of a racial or ethnic group? Inevitably, the students teach each other. For example, the comment, "All Whites can't be trusted" is picked apart. What does this mean? How do we know for sure? Does this apply to all Whites or just some? Can people of the *same* race necessarily trust each other? For some students, it is the first time they openly discuss issues such as this in a racially and ethnically diverse group. The value of critical thinking becomes more apparent as students weigh whether the evidence supports certain assumptions. They also begin to share how their thinking is changing as a result of personal experiences.

It is not enough to recognize and critically evaluate stereotypical thinking. We also need to understand that this kind of thinking can limit our opportunities. When we stereotype, we see people as labels rather than individuals. We base our actions on images that are distorted, incomplete, and usually negative. This limits our ability to interact effectively and learn from others.

When others stereotype us, we may feel vulnerable and our self-esteem may suffer. Claude Steele refers to this as **stereotype vulnerability**, the danger of not performing up to our ability because of our anxieties and fears about perpetuating a stereotype.[7] For instance, Paul is an older employee who hesitates to ask for help when he has computer questions at work. He has to deal with a supervisor and others who assume that he cannot keep up with younger co-workers when it comes to computer know-how. Because of this stereotypical assumption, he keeps to himself and does not ask questions because he does not want to appear computer illiterate. Consequently, his skills never improve.

Steele, a social psychologist at Stanford University, has conducted experimental studies which reveal that vulnerability to stereotypes is a significant factor in academic achievement. According to Steele, certain groups of students find themselves constantly wrestling with stereotypes. As an example, women deal with the image of being mathematical klutzes and African-Americans contend with assumptions about their lack of academic ability. Steele maintains that fear of conforming to stereotypical expectations creates a pressure-packed situation for these students. As a result, students who are otherwise competent often do not perform up to their ability.

Carol, a visually impaired African-American student, is a friend of mine. Recently, she confided in me that she was having problems in school. When I asked her if she had met with her teachers to discuss her poor grades and some of the difficulties she is having, she said no. Surprised by her response, I asked why. After a moment of hesitation, Carol said, "I didn't want them to think I was dumb." Still I did not understand. Carol is intelligent, outgoing, and a hard worker. She then elaborated. "My teachers think I'm dumb because I'm blind. They think I'm dumb because I'm black. And they think I'm dumb because I'm a female. I just don't want to give them another reason to think I can't do the work."

Steele's research focuses attention on cultural expectations that undermine achievement, but it is equally important to examine the reactions of many different students. For some, stereotypes can motivate them to work that much harder. Some students manage to turn the negatives they encounter at school into a positive.

I believe my cultural background has definitely affected my success in school. My parents, who are not very familiar with this country and did not feel very safe, push me in the only way they know to secure a decent future for me, and that is through studying and working hard. My gender and skin color also make a difference. In some instances, I feel that being a female makes it more of a challenge for me, and that I have to prove myself. In other instances, the color of my skin makes me instantly stupid. In still other instances, I am expected to be a genius. These dramatically contrasting experiences teach me more than anything to do the best I can. In instances when less is expected of me, I actually work harder to prove the teacher wrong. It is almost a personal challenge that I am determined to win.

᚛᚛᚛᚛ ᚛᚛᚛᚛ ᚛᚛᚛᚛

I sat down in my statistics class, looked around, and saw that the students appeared to be about 10 percent African-American, and 90 percent Asian and European mixed. As the African-American students entered the class, they would look around to see who was in the class. This did not appear to be unusual to me. Once the instructor entered the class, the majority of African-American students grabbed their book bags and exited the room. I found it hard to believe that they were all in the wrong class. Later on that day, I ran into one of the African-American students and asked him why he left. He informed me that he noticed that the majority of the class was Asian and the probability of him getting a good grade was

*slim because Asians "mess up a curve." As one of the few remaining
African-American students, this made me even more determined to stay in
the class and be successful.*

—Student's perspectives

Stereotyping is a way of putting people in our own mental boxes. The problem with these boxes is we do not individualize them; rather, we use a "one size fits all" mentality. Therefore, something important gets left out. Imagine trying to solve a mathematical problem without being given all the necessary information. Maybe your information is inaccurate as well as incomplete. Stereotyping is no different. When we put others into a "box," we lose or distort potentially valuable information and diminish our ability to relate effectively to others. Plus, in those cases in which we are targets of stereotyping, we may feel vulnerable and less confident in our abilities.

Barrier 4: Prejudice

I think my instructors feel that because I am older, I should perform at a higher level. Some don't seem to understand that some of the material is just as new to me as to my younger classmates. I notice some irritation and disappointment from some of my instructors when I do not perform up to their expectations.

There are people who assume certain things about me because I am white. Even though they don't know me, they act like they're angry at me. They assume that I think I'm superior. They assume my parents did not have to struggle to make ends meet. They assume that being white is a ticket to success.

—Students' perspectives

Prejudice is an irrational and inflexible opinion, formed on the basis of limited and insufficient knowledge. Stereotypes, which were discussed earlier, often give rise to prejudice. Exposure to exaggerated and rigid images of a particular group might lead us to prejudge anyone we identify with that group. A good example is what happened immediately after the 1995 Oklahoma City bombing. Because of prior news events and media coverage that had connected Muslims to terrorist acts, many Muslims in the United States became prime suspects even though there was no evidence to support this. Several mosques were vandalized and a number of Muslims received bomb threats. Even Arabic and Islamic schoolchildren were viewed suspiciously and mocked by some.

journal entry

When you met the instructor in this class for the first time, had you already formed certain impressions of him or her? If so, were your opinions based on what you had already heard from other students? Did your instructor's race, gender, or age influence your first impressions?

More often than not, talk about prejudice focuses on "them" rather than "us." Many of us can readily sense prejudice in others, but seeing it in ourselves is a challenge. When someone mentions the word *prejudice*, what comes to mind? Is prejudice something ordinary or extraordinary? Do prejudiced people look and act like you?

It is important to understand that we learn prejudice just like any subject at school. The lyrics of a song from the Broadway musical *South Pacific* tell us that the learning process starts very early in life. "You've got to be taught before it's too late, before you are 6 or 7 or 8, to hate all the people your relatives hate." Research indicates that children as young as 4 or 5 years of age begin to show signs of racial prejudice. At a young age, we are more apt to simply believe what we hear. By the time we are adults, prejudging people for whatever reason can become almost an unconscious habit. Additionally, prejudice affords us a quick and easy way of categorizing all the new and different people we meet each day. It takes much more time and effort to withhold judgment until we really know someone.

THINKING THROUGH DIVERSITY:

journal entry

Are you aware of your own prejudices? What do you do when you recognize prejudice in yourself? Specifically, how do you respond?

If we view prejudice as something that each of us learns, it is easier to examine ourselves. We begin to realize that uncovering prejudice in ourselves does not make us bad people. Rather, it simply shows us that we have some work to do. Ask yourself the following questions:

- ❍ Do you feel uncomfortable around certain people? Does your body language provide you with any cues? For example, are you comfortable talking to someone whose sexual orientation is different than yours? Are you comfortable sitting next to such a person?

As a gay man, I don't live my life looking for sex. My relationships are based on friendship, not sex. As a student, I remember being confronted by a student who lived in the same living unit as I did. He said "I don't care if you live here as long as you don't come on to me." His assumption was that if you were gay, you wanted to have sex with any man. Who that man was did not matter.

—A student's perspective

○ Do you have a tendency to judge other people because of the way they look, dress, and speak? Even the cars we drive can give rise to certain assumptions. Lorenzo, a young male student who describes himself as White, Black, and American Indian, drives a nice car to school. He constantly runs into people who assume that he stole the car or bought it with drug money. Getting stopped by police is a daily occurrence. "It messes my whole day up," says Lorenzo. It has gotten so bad he carries his pay stub beneath his license to prove that he can afford the car.

○ Are there times when you form an opinion about a person because he or she belongs to a particular group? Rafael Olmeda, a reporter for the *New York Daily News*, resents it when people assume they know something important about him because of his name. He remembers being a senior at the Bronx High School of Science. One day, Olmeda received a packet of unsolicited Harvard admission materials. Included was a Minority Student Information Request Card and information about the experiences of Hispanic students at Harvard. Even though he is proud of his Puerto Rican heritage, he resents being categorized this way. What did the people at Harvard really know about him?[8]

If we are honest with ourselves, we can begin to be more critical of our mental pictures of others. Only then can we begin to acknowledge that prejudice does exist. If somebody does complain about prejudice, it is important not to discount it. As one of my students says, sometimes the greatest gift you can give to other people is just to listen to them.

A while ago, I had developed a strong hatred for all white people. This hatred was caused by the deaths of some young black boys while under the custody of the police. The situation became so bad that my grades started slipping in school. I thought about just forgetting about school and I even thought about converting to the Nation of Islam. I was hearing all kinds of things about what happened and the police investigation. The story was in the news almost every night. Then, at school one day, I got a chance to express my feelings about the incident in one of my classes, as did every other student. Getting a chance to express what I was feeling really released some of the pressure that had been building up inside me. I realized that what I had been doing by assuming that all white people are bad was wrong, and I could not judge a whole nation of white people based on what a few dirty cops had done.

—A student's perspective

Some people minimize the importance of prejudice in the workplace. Since an employer cannot know what you are thinking, they argue, prejudice becomes an issue only when we act on it. Consequently, you can be held accountable only for your actions, not for your thoughts. The problem with this argument is that we cannot analyze behavior and perceptions as distinct entities.

Picture yourself driving to work. Your commute takes you by two men who appear to be Latino standing on a street corner. You pull up next to them as you stop at a red light. You wonder why they are not working. Trying to be as inconspicuous as possible, you check to make sure that your door is locked and continue on to work. At the office, you ready yourself for a series of job interviews you will be conducting throughout the day. When the last interviewee walks into your office, you notice that he is one of the two men you passed on the way to work. What are the chances that you will be able to judge this person fairly?

We cannot neatly compartmentalize prejudicial thinking. It is messy and can influence our behavior at the most inopportune times. Just ask people who are fired from their jobs because a racial slur they use at home finds its way into their conversation at work. We cannot turn prejudice on and off like light from a lamp. Whether or not we are conscious of it, our thinking can and does affect how we behave.

THINKING THROUGH DIVERSITY:
journal entry

Why is it that we can see prejudices all around us but not in us?

Prejudices, no matter how much we think we can cover them up, work against us. This is true of prejudices that we hold or those we encounter. Consider the implications when prejudice:

- *Prevents us from making accurate judgments about people.* According to various studies and court rulings, sometimes police stop a disproportionate share of minority drivers simply because of their racial or ethnic background. Many are searched as well. This practice is called *racial profiling*. Police, as well as the public, have recently focused more attention on the role of racial bias in police–citizen interaction and possible safeguards to ensure the equal treatment of all motorists.

- *Becomes a source of distraction. Race*, a book by Studs Terkel, captures the feelings of ordinary Americans about the sensitive subject of race. One person interviewed by Terkel shares what it is like to deal with racial prejudice in the United States. He compares it to wearing a shoe that does not quite fit. "It squeezes, it pinches, it cuts off circulation and sometimes it drives people to varying forms of distraction."[9] The man being interviewed goes on to say that it is not your race which has this effect. Rather, it is the assumptions that people make about you because of your race.

- *Results in resentment and fear.* Consider **xenophobia**, people's unreasonable fear of foreigners. People who are xenophobic often resent the academic and economic success of certain groups of immigrants. Furthermore, they devalue cultural differences, and no one benefits. A series of *Doonesbury* cartoons makes this same point. In the cartoon, neighbors complain to the parents of an Asian-American student. The parents are told that teaching their daughter to value discipline and hard work gives her an unfair advantage.

○ *Means the difference between life and death.* A Georgetown University Medical Center study reveals prejudices can and do affect the diagnoses and treatments doctors give their patients. Dr. Kevin Schulman of Georgetown University created videos with actors as patients. Black and white actors, wearing plain white hospital gowns, read identical scripts describing heart pain. Dr. Schulman then showed the videos to more than 700 doctors. These doctors were much more likely to recommend appropriate treatment for the white "patients." Dr. Schulman attributes this differential treatment to the subconscious biases of many doctors.[10]

○ *Results in psychological "wear and tear."* Howard Ehrlich, research director at The Prejudice Institute, reviewed research on the effects of prejudice on students at a number of college campuses. Based on his research, Ehrlich estimates that one in four minority students is "victimized for reasons of prejudice."[11] Many of these students report that prejudice interferes with their ability to study. For them, stress and discomfort may be an everyday occurrence.

▨ BLUE EYES AND BROWN EYES

In 1968, Jane Elliott was a third-grade teacher in a small, rural town in Iowa. She conducted an experiment in her classroom so that her students could learn a valuable lesson about the effects of prejudice. She divided them into two groups based on the color of their eyes. Over the period of a week, Elliott treated the children differently based on the color of their eyes. Elliott and the blue-eyed students initially treated the brown-eyed students as if they were inferior. The "brown eyes" were told to wear collars around their necks so they could be identified easily. It was not long before their schoolwork suffered and they felt angry and frustrated.

Furthermore, blue-eyed students who had always been their friends turned on them.

Midway through the experiment, Elliott convinced her students that she had made a mistake—in fact, the brown eyes were superior. Each brown-eyed student was instructed to take off his or her collar and put it on a classmate with blue eyes. Almost immediately, the brown-eyed children started feeling better about themselves and the quality of their schoolwork improved dramatically. A group lesson that had given them trouble when they were assumed to be inferior was now completed with ease. Now that they were viewed as superior,

continued

they refused to associate with the inferior "blue eyes." At the end of the experiment, even Elliott was amazed by the students' transformation. When asked what they learned from the experiment, one student mentioned how the collar made it difficult for her to think and pay attention. Another student said the collar made him feel like a "dog on a leash."[12]

Your prejudices, or the prejudices you encounter, can make it that much more difficult for you to achieve your goals. Prejudice can be a source of distraction and stress. It can produce resentment and fear. When people are prejudged, misunderstandings and ill feelings get in the way. For example, your academic success may be threatened when prejudice comes between you and a teacher or another student. Ultimately, no one wins in a situation such as this.

Barrier 5: Prejudice Plus Power

When people in power show prejudice, the consequences can be that much more severe. **Power** refers to the ability to influence and control others. Therefore, people with power are in a position to affect many more people by virtue of their prejudices. Imagine that you are looking for a highly competitive job and no one in upper-level management considers you a serious candidate because of your gender or class or ethnic background. Prejudice of this nature is more potent because it is backed up by economic power. This is particularly true if you encounter this kind of thinking everywhere you go.

The various "isms" are at work when we talk about prejudice plus power. **Isms** refer to the thinking by those in power that certain types of people are inherently inferior; therefore, unequal treatment is justifiable. A variety of isms exist, each focusing on a different dimension of diversity (ageism, sexism, classism,...). Of all the isms, probably none is more volatile or difficult to understand than racism.

⎰
journal
entry

THINKING THROUGH DIVERSITY:

What is the first image that comes to mind when you hear the word *racism*?

Definitions of **racism** vary. In some cases, it is defined as discrimination based on the belief that one race is superior to another. According to this definition, anyone can be a racist. However, some disagree. Racism, they argue, requires more than just acting out racial prejudice. It requires power. This means that those in power are the only ones who can be racist. The question then becomes who has the power. For some, only whites can be racist because they have the economic, political, and social power in the wider society. Still there are those who maintain that power shifts from place to place. For instance, in a specific locale, Latinos or African-Americans may be in a dominant position in terms of their economic or political status.

No matter how we define racism, we need to understand the importance of power and its implications. David Shipler examines the effects of racism in his book *A Country of Strangers*.[13] A former reporter for *The New York Times*, Shipler describes a workshop in which white participants are paired up with minorities. The facilitator asks participants to stand if they have to leave their culture at the door when they go to work. He then asks participants if they believe they have been stopped by police because of their color. Finally, did any of the participants consider not having children because of racism? After each of these questions, a number of minority participants stand up—but none of the Whites.

When I ask these same questions in a number of my racially mixed college classes, the pattern of responses is the same. It is important to note that *acknowledging* racism is not the same as *using* racism as an excuse for not getting ahead. When we discuss social inequality, minority students in my classes are generally highly critical of those who blame their lack of success on white racism or "the system." The views of some of my white students, especially those who are poor, are noteworthy as well. On numerous occasions, they cite instances where being white and poor works against them or someone they know. People assume that they do not need help because they are white. They feel denied rather than privileged. Clearly, it is difficult to talk about racism without addressing isms that connect with class and other dimensions of diversity.

In the larger society, we rarely talk about the issue of racism in public or in racially mixed company because it can be such an inflammatory and divisive issue. However, there have been times when discussions of racism have become more open and inclusive. One example in recent history is the trial of O. J. Simpson and the dialogue it triggered on college campuses.

▦ RACE AND THE O. J. SIMPSON TRIAL

In the mid-1990s, an African-American man, O. J. Simpson, was charged with killing his ex-wife and someone thought to be her lover. Both of the murder victims were White. Simpson was a well-known actor and sports commentator who had gained fame as a star football player in college and the pros. For many, the trial and society's reaction to the trial provided a window into race relations in the United States.

The lengthy and widely publicized trial elicited a wide range of reactions from students on college campuses throughout the country. Some Latino and Asian-American students complained about the media's portrayal of race-related issues in strictly white and black terms. When the jury found O. J. Simpson innocent, the response from many students was decisive and immediate. Media pictures of students showed African-Americans and

continued

Whites reacting quite differently. The image of African-Americans shouting and smiling was in striking contrast to the absolute silence and disbelief of Whites. The following comments provide a glimpse into students' feelings regarding the trial and the verdict:

- In my opinion, O.J. is guilty. I know my English is not good enough and maybe I did not understand something in his trial. But in fact two people died. He was beating and kicking his ex-wife. And what is the solution of jury? O.J.—absolutely free man, he is not guilty. My heart was broken....I thought there was no justice only in my former country, now I think—no justice here.

- O.J. was able to beat the system. He was able to do something that most African-Americans don't get to do—that is, prove himself innocent beyond a reasonable doubt.

- You call that justice?

- O.J. came across as articulate and calm. He was handsome and well dressed. This is so different than most of the black male images we see on TV.

- I don't like how the media talked about "playing the race card." Putting it this way trivializes race as an issue.

The different reactions to the verdict prompted some to exclaim that Whites and Blacks must be "living on different planets." Polls indicated that roughly two-thirds of the Whites in the United States thought O.J. was guilty. About the same proportion of African-Americans contended he was innocent. Keeping in mind that one-third of African-Americans and Whites surveyed did not follow this pattern, how can we explain this difference? Research by Bob Blauner, author of *Black Lives, White Lives*, shows that African-Americans are more apt to focus on **institutional racism**, racism that is found in the rules, policies, and procedures that govern the day-to-day operations of institutions.[14] Among these institutions are education, government, and the economy.

To many African-Americans, a racist law enforcement system was on trial. In other words, this trial was not simply about a few individuals. Rather, it dealt with everyday law enforcement practices that some felt single out African-Americans and treat them unequally. On the other hand, Blauner found that Whites tend to view racism differently. For them, racism is more of an individual than an institutional issue. It is seen as clear-cut, overt bigotry stemming from a single person's belief in racial superiority. When viewed this way, racism was seen as largely irrelevant to O.J.'s guilt or innocence.

When prejudice is coupled with power, diversity becomes a negative rather than a positive for everyone. Mistrust and divisiveness interfere with communication. Teamwork suffers. It becomes a matter of my group versus your group. People may start doubting themselves and acting unnaturally around each other. What is certain is that human potential will be wasted.

Barrier 6: Discrimination

Unlike prejudice, *discrimination* refers to behavior. More specifically, **discrimination** is defined as the unequal treatment of people on the basis of their group membership. Treatment varies because of race, age, gender, social class, or any number of other dimensions of diversity. As an example, a study by the Massachusetts Commission Against Discrimination reveals the pervasiveness of age discrimination.[15] The commission sent teams of "testers" to look for employment. With each pair, the older and younger tester were matched in terms of personality and qualifications. They were taught to interview in a similar fashion. After a series of 24 job interviews in Atlanta, certain patterns emerged. The younger testers were generally complimented, encouraged, and accommodated. On the other hand, the older testers were patronized and subtly discouraged. The response, "I'm sorry, but you're overqualified" was a common mask for age discrimination.

Results from this study are consistent with other research findings. Age stereotypes can and do influence who employers hire, promote, train, and evaluate positively. All too many managers mistakenly believe that older workers get sick more often, are less productive, have more accidents, and are more difficult to manage. Consequently, they deny many talented people the chance to compete on an equal footing.

▨ RELATION BETWEEN PREJUDICE AND DISCRIMINATION

While some people seem to see prejudice and discrimination everywhere, others are certain that prejudice and discrimination no longer exist. As difficult as it is, try to evaluate each situation with an open mind. Although prejudice and discrimination often go hand in hand, they do not have to. Four combinations may occur in a variety of situations (see Table 3.1, next page).

1. *The prejudiced discriminator.* This is someone who holds personal prejudices and discriminates. Example: A manager's prejudices related to age influence her decisions in a variety of personnel actions. The manager evaluates a younger worker more favorably than she does an older person who performs just as well.

2. *The prejudiced nondiscriminator.* In this case, a person's prejudiced attitudes do not lead to discriminatory behavior. Example: An employee feels prejudice toward his supervisor because of her gender but does not show it for fear of the consequences.

3. *The unprejudiced discriminator.* Someone who is not prejudiced discriminates nonetheless. There are times when a person may discriminate unknowingly by following certain commonly accepted policies or practices. In addition, someone may belong to a group and discriminate to conform to group expectations. Example:

continued

Even though a person is open-minded about the subject of homosexuality, he caves in to group pressure at school and discriminates against certain people who "act gay."

4. *The unprejudiced nondiscriminator.* This person is not prejudiced and does not discriminate. An employer conducting a job interview notices that an interviewee with a noticeable accent shies away from direct eye contact. As in every other interview, the employer puts the candidate at ease and focuses solely on the person's ability to do the job.

It is important to remember that each of these combinations applies to situations, not to individuals. We may or may not show any of the foregoing combinations, depending on the situation.

Table 3.1 PREJUDICE AND DISCRIMINATION

COMBINATIONS OF PREJUDICE AND DISCRIMINATION	IS THIS PERSON PREJUDICED? (ATTITUDE)	DOES THIS PERSON DISCRIMINATE? (BEHAVIOR)
Prejudiced discriminator	Yes	Yes
Prejudiced nondiscriminator	Yes	No
Unprejudiced discriminator	No	Yes
Unprejudiced nondiscriminator	No	No

Source: Adapted from Robert Merton, "Discrimination and the American Creed," in *Sociological Ambivalence and Other Essays,* Free Press, New York, 1976.

As long as I can remember, my grandfather was always telling jokes about Jews, though he used a more offensive term. Yet he worked in public education, was highly respected, even by many of the Jewish students that had been in his care. In fact, his boss was Jewish! He apparently worked quite well with the man, yet the continuous barrage of ethnic slights revealed the true nature of his heart.

—A student's perspective

Discrimination assumes many forms. There are times when it is obvious and clear-cut. At other times, we are not so sure that behavior is in fact discriminatory. Although a person might be at fault, there are situations in which we need to look beyond that. Here are some of the major forms of discrimination:

1. *Blatant versus subtle discrimination.* Discriminatory acts, some more obvious than others, are an everyday occurrence in public places. In towns and cities throughout the Southwest, certain people are stopped on a regular basis and required to prove their citizenship for no other reason than because of their skin color, accent, or surname.

On the other hand, some encounter more subtle discrimination, such as certain looks or what one Hispanic woman terms that "spoken or unspoken word." "Because I'm dark and have dark eyes and hair... If I entered a department store, one of two things was likely to happen. Either I was ignored, or I was followed closely by the salesperson. The garments I took into the changing room were carefully counted. My check at the grocery store took more scrutiny than an Anglo's. My children were complimented on how 'clean' they were instead of how cute."[16]

Joe Feagin, of the University of Florida, recently interviewed 210 upper-middle-class African-American professionals living in 16 cities. Those interviewed reported less "door-slamming exclusion" but more subtle discrimination, such as exclusion from informal networks that increase chances for promotion.[17]

THINKING THROUGH DIVERSITY:

journal entry

What subtle forms of discrimination have you encountered? How have you dealt with them?

⊠ *How Much Discrimination Exists?*

People often disagree about the extent of discrimination at the present. For instance, is it common or rare? How we answer this question has a lot to do with our race according to recent public opinion polls.

Results from a Gallup Poll show that Blacks and Whites tend to see things differently when asked the question, "Are Blacks treated less fairly than Whites?"[18]

ARE BLACKS TREATED LESS FAIRLY THAN WHITES...	WHITES SAYING "YES"	BLACKS SAYING "YES"
In the workplace?	14%	45%
In stores/malls?	19%	46%
In restaurants?	16%	42%
In interactions with police?	30%	60%

---

2. *Individual versus institutional discrimination.* Individuals are not the only ones who discriminate. Sometimes, institutional policies and procedures put certain people at a disadvantage. For example, a waiter at a restaurant may consciously or unconsciously give better service to some customers because of their looks, race, or gender. This is individual discrimination. When unequal treatment becomes a company policy, it is institutional.

Discrimination of this nature allegedly existed at Denny's not too long ago. In a class-action suit against the international restaurant chain, a former Denny's manager stated that he was instructed by his district manager "to implement policies designed to limit or discourage black patronage." According to the manager, a term used at district meetings was *blackout*, meaning that there were too many black customers in a restaurant at one time. He recalled: "We were taught to avoid blackouts by requiring black customers to pay for their meals in advance or simply to close the restaurant for a few hours when we started getting too many black customers."[19]

3. *Intragroup versus intergroup discrimination. Intragroup discrimination* occurs *within* groups, whereas *intergroup discrimination* takes place *between* groups. We often assume that discrimination occurs only *between* groups such as Latinos and Whites. However, intergroup discrimination is common and may be just as painful. One African-American student recounts how she got teased because of her skin complexion. In her case, most of the people who treated her differently were not Whites; they were people of her own race and even members of her family. "I was seen as a white girl and an albino. People gave me names like 'goldie locks' and 'light bright.' They called me 'light bright' because they said I was 'light, bright, and damned near White.' It was very humiliating as a kid because I got teased constantly about my complexion. My sister was the worst of them all because when she got mad with me she would tell me that I was adopted or that I was the milkman's baby."

▩ PUTTING A PRICE TAG ON DISCRIMINATION

Andrew Hacker's widely acclaimed book *Two Nations*, analyzes inequality between black and white Americans.[20] Hacker, a college professor, discusses an experiment he conducted with his white students to illustrate the costs of being treated unequally. He creates a scenario in which students are visited by an official who tells them a "mistake" has been made. The race of these students was identified incorrectly. Newfound evidence shows that they should have been identified as Black at birth. The official emphasizes that the mistake must be corrected immediately. From now on, the students will live their lives as Blacks. However, the organization represented by the official is willing to pay them for the inconvenience of changing their race. When Hacker asked his white students how much money they would request, most of them asked for approximately $1 million a year for the rest of their lives. Hacker analyzed this amount as the price these students attach to prejudice and discrimination.

For a moment, consider what Hacker might discover if he varied this experiment. In my classes, I modify Hacker's experiment to take into account that race, however important, is only one dimension of diversity and one possible reason for inequality. Moreover, I give students a choice. I simply ask students how much money they would want to change any of the following: race (which race you would like to become), gender (male/female), sexual orientation (heterosexual/homosexual), or age (add 10 years to your age). Interestingly, the vast majority of them would not change any of their statuses for any amount of money. They express satisfaction with their current status, even if it makes them the object of discrimination. Of those who do elect to change their status, most choose to add 10 years to their age. The price tag for doing this is typically in the millions. Interestingly, one category that is rarely changed is sexual orientation. When I ask students why, many respond by talking about the constant ridicule they feel they would have to endure if they became gay or lesbian.

Discrimination is a losing proposition for everyone. When discrimination occurs, factors other than merit become important. The financial and human costs are undeniable. Beside costly lawsuits, valuable human resources are lost. Discrimination feeds anger, tension, and fear. As one of my students says, it can "eventually get to you." When this happens, we sabotage teamwork and close lines of communication. Consider the amount of time and energy that is spent discriminating or coping with discrimination and its aftereffects. What would happen if we could somehow refocus this time and energy in a more positive direction?

■ ACKNOWLEDGING AND OVERCOMING DIVERSITY BARRIERS

Take a Mexican-American man in his early 20s and put him in a situation where he forces himself to go out into an all-white or predominantly white community. He's going to get some negative feedback, whether it's just looks, whispering. It can be anything...there's all types of negative feedback. It doesn't have to be verbal or physical. When things like that happen, that in turn makes that person not even want to try to interact or push himself into that kind of situation. It's like a foreseeable risk.

A person's race should not make a difference. I am a white male and I have lost out on scholarships and other opportunities because I was the wrong race.

—Students' perspectives

How do you deal with prejudicial beliefs, discriminatory behaviors, and other social barriers that you encounter in your environment? It is important to realize there is no single strategy that is right for everyone or appropriate for all situations. What may work for one person at one time may be ineffectual for someone else. One CEO says that he counters prejudice by doing his job beyond expectations. His habit of doing more than he is asked to do wins people over. A student of mine resorts to writing whenever she feels the sting of prejudice. For her, writing provides an emotional release. "Writing down what happens and how it feels puts some distance between me and the incident. I can look at it later with less emotion." Still another effective strategy was employed by Zora Neale Hurston. When people discriminated against her, Hurston did not get angry. Instead, she saw discrimination as a way in which others lost out. In effect, they denied themselves the pleasure of her company.[21]

Regardless of what strategy or strategies work for you, keep mindful of the following:

1. *Recognize that barriers sometimes exist.* That does not mean that you have to let them get in your way. In Ellis Cose's book *The Rage of a Privileged Class*, one highly successful African-American observes that business executives' attitudes and behaviors may be judged differently because of racial prejudice. "Recognize the fact, don't necessarily accept it, deal with it as the reality."[22] He goes on to say that, like every other obstacle, it can be overcome.

Prejudice...I can get over it, around it, above it. Sometimes I'm just too busy to even deal with it.

When you feel comfortable in your own skin, you simply find a way to get around the obstacles that roll down the road.

—Students' perspectives

---

2. *Develop and maintain pride in yourself.* Eleanor Roosevelt once said: "No one can make you feel inferior without your consent." Stephanie, a former student of mine, has had to deal with what she describes as "life's little cruelties and discomforts" because of her obesity. She recalls standing in a college biology class for two hours at a time, week after week, because she could not find suitable seating. No one, including the instructor, seemed concerned. Additionally, she remembers the instructor maintaining almost constant eye contact with her one day as he lectured about the dangers of being overweight. As she left the college campus that day, she had no plans to return and continue her college education. But she drew strength from her obese mother, who taught her that she is unique and deserves to be heard. Stephanie gradually

Diversity Consciousness: Opening Our Minds to People, Cultures, and Opportunities

Figure 3.3: *Jorge, a student, shared his Mexican heritage with his college community by assembling an altar in memory of a Mexican hero, Emiliano Zapata.*

changed her thinking. "I learned that I have a place in this world that is beyond the shadows. I learned I don't have to accept whatever is given to me. I have a right to be out there and make a living for my children."

3. *Develop and maintain pride in your culture.* When combating intolerance, cultural pride can be a source of strength. Jorge, a student from Mexico who attends a small, rural college in Maryland, emphasizes how important it is for him to be grounded in his culture. People who lack this grounding, according to Jorge, tend to be more confused and vulnerable. In Fig. 3.3, he is shown with folk art he brought with him from Mexico.

4. *If you encounter discrimination, whether it is directed at you or others, speak out if at all possible.* Sometimes it helps to record exactly what happens in writing. Using the *I feel formula* to convey how you feel about an incident can be particularly effective. Explain to others how *you* feel and why *you* consider it inappropriate (see Diversity Box: Conflict and Communication, pages 182–183). If you or others are personally offended by something that takes place in a group setting, consider the pros and cons of dealing with it immediately. If it involves only one or two members of a larger group, you might be better off waiting and talking to these people in private. On the other hand, speaking right away may result in a valuable learning experience for the entire group.

In determining how to respond to discrimination, consider whether your safety is an issue. If it is, use your common sense and do what is in your best interest. You may elect to ignore it for now or deal with it indirectly and remain anonymous. If you think that a law has been broken, report the incident to someone in authority—preferably a person or group you know and trust. Depending on the situation, this might be an instructor or manager whom you know and respect. It may be necessary to consult a lawyer or the local human rights commission. If you record what happens, this can be useful if you pursue the matter further at a later date.

5. *When people judge you immediately because of your distinctive looks or behavior, try to be as patient and understanding as possible.* Try not to act on emotion alone. Ask yourself what you hope to accomplish by reacting a certain way. Do you want to change behavior, raise awareness, or simply "blow off steam"? It helps to remember that the perceptions of others may have nothing to do with you as a person. More likely, they result from ignorance, mistrust, and even fear. Viewing other people's prejudices in this manner helps us deal with the walls of misunderstanding and mistrust that we encounter. Keep in mind those times when *you* jump to conclusions about others.

As a graduate student, I attended a small, rural, private college. I had just moved from a large city. I was very open about being gay. I felt like "I'm gay and damn you're going to like it." One night, I remember visiting one of my friends in his dormitory. On the way up to his room, I saw the quarterback of the football team. We knew each other and had talked before. Up to that point, I had always looked at him as a "dumb jock" and he saw me as a "stupid faggot." This time it was different. We related as humans, not as categories. I came to realize that if I tried to push my "category" on someone else, we would end up relating as categories.

—A student's perspective

---

6. *Fine tune your anger.* Many people who constantly face petty and not so petty slights find it necessary to pick their battles. Some pick their responses: shouting, whispering, or conversing. It may depend on the situation or how one feels that day. Karen Bates and Karen Hudson recently coauthored an etiquette book for African-Americans entitled *Basic Black: Home Training for Modern Times.*[23] Part of the book offers advice to those who suspect they are being treated a certain way because of the way they look. Bates and Hudson give the example of poor service at a restaurant. Perhaps the waiter is rude to you and polite to others. What if the maitre d' ignores you and your guests or your request for seating in a certain area of the restaurant? The authors suggest asking the person in charge if the waiter is having a bad day. If you suspect that your race is the reason for your treatment, ask the manager: "Can I assume that your restaurant does not want customers who look like me?" Low-key responses to subtle but hurtful slights can get results.

7. *Resist the urge to scapegoat.* When we **scapegoat**, we blame others for our own problems. In essence, scapegoating allows us to look outward, not inward. For example, some majority group members blame affirmative action for the ills of society. They argue that affirmative action has given minorities an unfair advantage and puts Whites at a disadvantage. When a close relative or friend is not promoted or hired, an underqualified minority is assumed to be the reason. Maybe this relative or friend was simply not the strongest candidate for the job. Similarly, some minority-group members see the white man as the root of all evil. One student of color comments: "A lot of the blame is toward the white man. When do we stop blaming and just accept that it happened and go on? They say the white man has oppressed us and is still oppressing us. I think in the long run we're oppressing ourselves because of our attitude. We have a lot of opportunities we are not taking advantage of."

8. *Try to keep the focus on the offensive behavior rather than the person.* This can be done by maintaining one's composure, using the "I feel formula," or possibly turning a question around. Instead of trying to answer an insensitive question by justifying or defending your behavior, turn the question around. By doing this, you keep the focus on what is said. For instance, a student who is gay might respond to the following questions this way:

Question: When did you know you were gay?
Answer: Well, when did you know you were straight?
Question: When did you come out of the closet?
Answer: Good question. When did you come out of the closet?
Question: Why do you like someone of the same sex?
Answer: Why do you like someone of the opposite sex?

9. *Seek out others for support.* Harvard psychiatrist Alvin Poussaint emphasizes the importance of sharing one's experiences and emotions with others.[24] Often, people assume that what they are going through is unique to them and may be their fault. By building relationships with others who have had similar experiences, you can release emotional pressure, make new friends, raise your consciousness, and work for change. Support groups take many forms. You can join or create one at school, work, or in any social setting. If your hectic schedule makes this impossible, consider using your personal computer to network online with people who experience similar problems. Forums, conferences, and chatrooms can function as a type of support group.

10. *Work with others to find new and effective ways to address intolerance and discrimination.* Consider joining a community or college-based organization working to promote the value of diversity. For example, at one college, a coalition of students with and without disabilities formed S.O.D.A. (Students Organized for Disability Awareness). At another college, a conflict resolution team offers assistance to students who request it. Team members include racial and ethnic minorities who speak a variety of languages, students with physical and learning disabilities, as well as students who are gay, lesbian, and bisexual. After a period of intense training, they work in small, diverse groups to help disputants settle their differences.

11. *Treat people as individuals.* Try to avoid what one of my students refers to as the "barracuda syndrome." She uses this phrase to describe people who feel as if they are constantly under attack and cannot trust anyone. As a result, they become so stressed and defensive that their performance suffers. Cecil, an African-American male college student with a background in theology, explains that he learns to look for the good in people instead of always focusing on the negative. In the past, he focused more on the young female who clutched her purse tightly as she walked by him. He would forget he saw a young male dressed like a "yo boy" help an elderly lady across the street.

12. *Combat the prejudices, stereotypes, and ignorance that exist within each of us.* When we look for barriers to diversity and ultimately our success, all too often we look outward rather than inward. In the next chapter the focus shifts to each of us. More specifically, what is the impact of our social isolation? What can we do differently to develop our knowledge and awareness of ourselves and others?

Each of us has the power to choose our reactions and overcome barriers that get in our way. One of the things I admire most about my students is their resiliency. When we talked about this in class one day, one student recalled how she has spent most of her life crying because of something somebody said. "There comes a time," she said, "when you simply have to stop crying and move on." In the course of the discussion, someone else talked about her "survival kit." When I asked her to describe its contents in writing, she listed:

- ○ A smile
- ○ A courteous attitude
- ○ An open mind
- ○ Questions
- ○ Answers
- ○ Help

THINKING THROUGH DIVERSITY:
If we open up your survival kit, what will we find?

Journal entry

Throughout this chapter we have examined a number of personal and social barriers that may interfere with our ability to be successful. These include limited perceptions, ethnocentrism, stereotypes, prejudice, prejudice plus power, and discrimination. Additionally, we have explored a variety of strategies that can help us acknowledge and overcome these diversity barriers.

In the next chapter we take an in-depth look at the process by which we develop our awareness, understanding, and skills in the area of diversity. We also explore a number of strategies that can help us open our minds and learn more about diversity.

Exercises

IN-CLASS

Exercise 1: Feeling Different

Directions for Instructor

1. Ask each student to think of a real-life situation in which he or she felt different: for example, being the only person in a group with a particular skill, look, or lifestyle. This should be a situation you feel comfortable sharing with another student.
2. Instruct students to answer the following questions briefly in writing.
   a. How did you feel in this situation?
   b. How did you react?
   c. If this situation occurs again, how would you like other people to react?
3. Divide students into small groups, preferably three students in each. Instruct them to take turns describing the situation in which they felt different and their responses to parts a, b, and c of question 2.

Exercise 2: People with Disabilities: Barriers at Your School

Directions for Instructor

1. Divide the class into groups of four. Each group should appoint a recorder, a leader, a mediator, and a reporter. Provide the recorders in each group with a flipchart and a felt-tip marker. The tasks are as follows:
   ○ *Recorder:* takes notes
   ○ *Leader:* keeps the group on task and encourages everyone to participate

○ *Reporter:* speaks for the group, uses recorder's notes

○ *Mediator:* makes sure that everyone understands and listens

2. *Brainstorming Activity.* The idea behind brainstorming is to generate as many ideas as possible. There are no "right" or "wrong" ideas for this exercise. The recorder should write down *all* the group members' responses to the following questions.

   a. What barriers do people with disabilities encounter at your school? (These barriers might take many different forms. The attitudes of students, faculty, and staff are possible barriers. Services and facilities that are or are not provided for students with disabilities represent another.)

   b. Which barriers are based on the thinking and behavior of individuals?

   c. Which barriers are more closely related to the school as a whole?

   d. Which barriers could be removed within the next year? What needs to be done to remove each barrier?

3. *Consensus Building Activity.* This activity requires that all members of each group reach a general agreement on:

   ○ *One* barrier that could be removed within the next year

   ○ What needs to be done to remove it

   Be as specific as possible. The recorder should take notes and later type this information on a single page. A copy of this goes to the instructor.

4. Instruct each group to share this information with an administrator who might be in a position to consider the feasibility of your recommendations. If possible, the group should arrange a meeting to discuss their concerns.

OUT-OF-CLASS

Exercise 1: Images of the Elderly

Journal. Keep a journal for a week. Every time you see an older person in a commercial, record it on a chart with the headings shown below:
<u>What Is Being Sold</u>   <u>Role of Elderly in Commercial</u>   <u>Possible Stereotypes</u>
Analysis. Given the entries in your journal, do you notice any patterns in the images you observed? For example, are the images of the elderly primarily positive or negative? What kinds of roles are associated with old age?

Exercise 2: Reflections on Being an Insider and an Outsider

Being an insider:

1. Describe a situation in which you feel like an insider. In other words, when do you feel people accept and respect you? Why do you feel this way?

2. What privileges do you have as an insider? Did you do anything to deserve these privileges? Explain.

Being an outsider:

1. Describe another situation in which you feel like an outsider. In other words, when do you feel a lack of acceptance or respect from others? Why do you feel this way?

2. What disadvantages do you have as an outsider? Did you do anything to deserve these disadvantages?

Being an insider and an outsider in different situations teaches us something. What do you learn about yourself and others by being an insider? What do you learn by being an outsider?

Exercise 3: Memory Maps

1. Draw a map of the world from memory alone.

2. Compare your map to a map of the world found in an atlas or other reputable source. What are the major differences? For instance, which hand-drawn continents are closest to their actual size and shape? Which are the least accurately drawn?

3. What does your map reveal about you and the way you view the world? What biases or gaps in knowledge does it show? Do you know best your own area of the world? Which area was the most difficult for you to visualize? Why?

Exercise 4: Hate Incidents

On college campuses, an increasing number of students are victims of hate incidents. These incidents affect students directly and indirectly. Indeed, the entire college community can feel the repercussions of a single act of intolerance. Pick *one* of the following real-life examples. Describe how you could respond effectively as a student. What would you do? Why? At whom would your response be directed? Why?

○ In the entranceway to a dormitory, a student writes on the dry erase board a message that describes Blacks as welfare recipients and STD spreaders.

○ A columnist on a student newspaper refers to Whites as "irredeemable racists" and calls for Blacks to "execute" Whites who pose a threat.

○ A college fraternity holds a "Mexican Border Party." To gain entrance, students have to crawl under a barbed wire barrier.

○ Leaflets depicting the Holocaust as a hoax are handed out in front of a building housing a Jewish student organization.

○ A group of students take it upon themselves to sell T-shirts with anti-homosexual slogans. One of the T-shirts advocates violence against gays and lesbians. Another has the words "Homophobic and Proud of It" printed on the front.

INTERNET ASSIGNMENT

Web sites of hate groups have proliferated in recent years. According to a recent report by the Southern Poverty Law Center, there were 163 active sites spewing racial hatred as of January 1998.[24] Additionally, there are a growing number of hate sites that focus on other dimensions of diversity.

1. Locate a hate group on the World Wide Web. Print the home page and include the URL address.

2. Analyze the site by responding to the following questions. What are the goals of this hate group? How does this group try to rationalize and "market" hate? What prejudices, stereotypes, and "isms" are revealed in this Web site? Be as specific as possible and give examples.

NOTES

[1]Cornel West, *Race Matters* (New York: Random House, 1993).

[2]Howard Schwartz, "Further Thoughts on a 'Sociology of Acceptance' for Disabled People," *Social Policy*, Fall 1988, 36–39.

[3]Galen V. Bodenhausen, "Stereotypic Biases in Social Decision Making and Memory: Testing Process Models of Stereotype Use," *Journal of Personality and Social Psychology*, 55, 1988, 726–737.

[4]Angus Wilson, *The Strange Ride of Rudyard Kipling: His Life and Works* (New York: Viking Press, 1978), 290.

[5]E. Berscheid and E. Walster, "Beauty and the Beast," *Psychology Today*, Mar. 1972, 46, 74.

[6]Andrea DeSantis and Wesley Kayson, "Defendants' Characteristics of Attractiveness, Race, and Sex and Sentencing Decisions," *Psychological Reports*, 81, 1997, 679–683.

[7]Claude Steele, "Twenty-First Century Program and Stereotype Vulnerability," unpublished study and program, Stanford University, Stanford, CA, 1995.

[8]Jim Slepper, "Liberal Racism," *The New Democrat*, July/Aug. 1997, 8.

[9]Studs Terkel, *Race: How Blacks and Whites Feel about the American Obsession* (New York: New Press, 1992), 124.

[10]George Strait, "Health Care's Racial Divide" [online]. Available: http://more.abcnews.go.com/sections/living/DailyNews/racial_healthcare990224.html (March 7, 1999).

[11]Howard J. Ehrlich, *Campus Ethnoviolence: A Research Review*, Institute Report 5 (Baltimore: National Institute Against Prejudice and Violence, 1992), 8.

[12]ABC News, *The Eye of the Storm* (video) (Mount Kisco, NY: Guidance Associates, 1981).

[13]David Shipler, *A Country of Strangers* (New York: Alfred A. Knopf, 1997).

[14]Bob Blauner, *Black Lives, White Lives* (Berkeley, CA: University of California Press, 1989).

[15]Massachusetts Commission Against Discrimination, as reported on ABC News Primetime Live, "Age and Attitudes," June 9, 1994.

[16]Gabriela Kuntz, "My Spanish Standoff," *Newsweek*, May 4, 1998, 22.

[17]Karen Winkler, "While Concern over Race Relations Has Lessened among Whites, Sociologists Say Racism Is Taking New Forms, Not Disappearing," *Chronicle of Higher Education*, Sept. 11, 1991, A10–A11.

[18]"Inclusion, Not Rejection, Will Spur Racial Harmony," *USA Today*, June 16, 1997, 18A.

[19]Stephen Labaton, "Denny's Gets a Bill for the Side Orders of Bigotry," *The New York Times*, May 29, 1994, E4.

[20]Andrew Hacker, *Two Nations* (New York: Ballantine Books, 1995).

[21]Zora Neale Hurston, as quoted in Dorothy W. Riley, ed., *My Soul Looks Back, 'Less I Forget: A Collection of Quotations by People of Color* (New York: Harper Collins, 1995), 318.

[22]Ellis Cose, *The Rage of a Privileged Class* (New York: Harper Collins, 1993), 168.

[23]Karen G. Bates and Karen E. Hudson, *Basic Black: Home Training for Modern Times* (New York: Doubleday, 1996).

[24]Ellis Cose, *The Rage of a Privileged Class* (New York: Harper Collins, 1993).

4 DEVELOPING DIVERSITY CONSCIOUSNESS

chapter objectives

Upon completion of this chapter, you will be able to:

○ Explain the importance of **diversity consciousness**.

○ List and explain the six areas of development.

○ Discuss at least three strategies for personal growth.

○ Explain why the development of diversity consciousness is a continuing process.

> *Not to know is bad.*
>
> *Not to want to know is worse.*
>
> *Not to hope unthinkable.*
>
> *Not to care unforgivable.*
>
> *—Nigerian proverb*

DIVERSITY CONSCIOUSNESS

In this chapter we look at how each of us can develop our diversity consciousness. We examine the roots and impact of our cultural isolation, as well as how we can become more aware of ourselves and others. This ongoing process is not sequential; it does not occur in steps that follow one another neatly. Rather, many things feed into this process as we continually open ourselves up to other perspectives.

Regardless of your educational or career goals, diversity consciousness is important for a number of reasons:

1. *It enhances your diversity skills.* These skills, discussed throughout the book, include:

- ○ Teamwork
- ○ Ability to balance "fitting in" and "being yourself"
- ○ Flexible thinking and adaptability
- ○ Ability to network and learn from everyone and anyone
- ○ Ability to recognize and respect diverse intellectual strengths and learning styles
- ○ Ability to appreciate and maintain pride in your background and culture
- ○ Ability to deal effectively with barriers to success
- ○ Interpersonal relations and communication
- ○ Self-evaluation
- ○ Pluralistic leadership
- ○ Conflict management
- ○ Critical thinking

These skills will open up your mind to opportunities in all realms of life.

2. *It expands your horizons and empowers you.* Knowledge is power. Learning about yourself and others helps you to cope with all kinds of situations. Knowledge can give you confidence and instill pride in yourself and your culture. Unlike material possessions, it cannot be taken away from you. Vu Duc Vuong, a Vietnamese immigrant, makes this point when he talks about the economic hardships endured by refugees. They "often lose everything they have; everything can be taken away from a refugee: money, house, car, gold, souvenirs, job, status, friends, relatives, spouses, and even their own lives. You have heard these stories, and some of you may have even witnessed them firsthand. But among all the losses, there is one thing that will always be yours, that is your learning. No person, no circumstance, no law, and no catastrophe can take away what is inside your head. So, you owe it to yourself to learn as much as you can the rest of your life. That is one possession that is completely within your control, that is completely yours."[1]

Knowledge is better than riches.

—Cameroonian proverb

---

3. *It allows you to expand and enhance your social network.* By making contacts and developing relationships with people from a wide variety of backgrounds, you expand your social network. Thus you open up social, educational, and business opportunities. As you grow to value diversity, you will meet new and different kinds of people and expand your circle of friends. At school, diversity consciousness allows you to relate more effectively to a wide variety of instructors with diverse teaching styles. It enables you to learn more from other students. Additionally, the skills you develop as you become more conscious of diversity increase your value at work. Your assets will include your flexibility, creativity, and ability to communicate and work with all kinds of people. These are the same qualities that will make you a more effective leader or manager.

Opportunity isn't necessarily going to come along looking, talking, dressing, and acting like you. The more different kinds of people you can get along with, the more opportunities you will have.

—An instructor's perspective

■ ISOLATION

Are you the typical college student? In comparison to most other students, what makes you similar or different? The following quiz tests your assumptions about college students in the United States today.

True or false?

1. Most college students are between 18 and 21 years of age.
2. Of all college students, fewer than 25 percent are part-time.
3. Roughly half of those who begin college drop out.
4. Most college students are paying, on average, around $10,000 a year for tuition and other fees.
5. People classified as "minority" or "foreign" make up approximately 15 percent of all college students.
6. The proportion of women completing college is greater than that of men.

Note: Answers to each of these questions are provided on the next page.

When we think of what is typical, we tend to start with ourselves and our own little worlds: our families, neighborhoods, schools, and communities. This kind of thinking often gives rise to ethnocentrism, a concept we discussed in the last chapter. Ethnocentrism leads us to judge others or the larger world by our own limited experiences.

Sometimes, our narrow perspective expands a bit through exposure to the media. Indeed, for most people in the United States, various media are their primary source of information about the larger world. This can be dangerous since many people do not critically evaluate what they see or hear on television, in the newspapers, or elsewhere. According to research, the media often provide information that is stereotypical, superficial, and incomplete.

For example, the research group Women, Men, and Media periodically reviews the gender of newsmakers found on the front page of large and small newspapers. In a recent survey of news coverage, this group found that women rarely make the front page of newspapers. When they do, it is often because of a tragedy such as death or due to their relationship to a male newsmaker.[2] Another survey by the National Council of La Raza found that television and film often depict Hispanics as low status and criminals.[3] Many stories on poverty that appear in the media reveal a bias as well. According to a recent Yale University study by Martin Gilens,[4] stories about the poor in national news magazines picture African-Americans 62 percent of the time. This is likely to create the impression that most poor people are African-Americans. However, U.S. Census data paint a different picture of poverty. While roughly 25 percent of Americans who fall below the poverty line are African-American, 75 percent are not.[5]

If we cannot rely on the media, what about our personal lives? Why can't we simply fall back on what we know as a result of our past and present experiences? Your perception of college students might provide some answers to this question. Think back to the quiz on college students that appears above. How do your answers compare with data provided by the U.S. Department of Education and the College Board?

Figure 4.1: *Lifelong learning is becoming a reality for all Americans, regardless of age. (Courtesy of Senior Net.)*

1. Most college students are between 18 and 21 years of age—*false*. More than half of all college students are 22 years of age or older, and more than one-fourth are 30 or older.[6] Many older students are returning to college to learn new skills (see Fig. 4.1). Others have raised their families and are finally able to think about their own education. Although most of your classmates may be 18 to 22 year olds, this is not the norm, especially for community colleges.

2. Of all college students, fewer than 25 percent are part-time—*false*. Approximately 40 percent of college students attend part-time.[7] Many of these students are employed and some are parents. They do not have the time or the resources to attend full-time. Many older students are getting a feeling for college before they become full-time. Many of these students tend to be less visible on campus because they attend school at night or on weekends.

3. Roughly half of those who begin college drop out—*true*.[8] This figure may seem high to some of you. However, retention is a serious problem in higher education. Students drop out for any number of reasons and often times, it has nothing to do with their ability to do the work.

4. Most college students are paying, on average, around $10,000 a year for tuition and other fees—*false*. We often read articles or watch news stories about tuition and fees rising above $20,000. However, this is true of relatively few schools. Most students attend public two- and four-year colleges where the average cost of tuition and fees ranges from about $1500 to $3100 a year.[9]

5. People classified as "minority" or "foreign" make up approximately 15 percent of all college students—*false*. Minority and foreign students account for almost twice this percentage.[10] In recent years, most of the growth in college enrollment has been among students classified as African-American, Asian-American, Native American, and Hispanic American.

6. The proportion of women completing college is greater than that of men—*true*. This statement is supported by the Census Bureau's analysis of education statistics. Before 1985, men topped women consistently. Between 1985 and 1995, the completion rate for men and women was so close that the difference was considered statistically insignificant. In 1996, the proportion of women completing college topped that of men and the lead is widening.[11] This trend indicates that more and more women want careers and recognize the economic value of a college education.

Our perceptions of college students are a reflection of our experiences. Sometimes those experiences are what we might term "typical," but often they are not. When we show ethnocentrism and assume that our way of living or doing things is not only typical but also the only way, we can easily offend others and limit our own personal growth.

Isolation: Before College

Social isolation starts at a young age. It is apparent throughout **socialization**, the lifelong process of social interaction that enables us to learn about ourselves and others. We are inclined to make friends with other people who are like us. In many cases, we attend schools and live in neighborhoods that are racially and ethnically segregated. Social isolation prior to college is one of the major reasons why college life can be such an adjustment. After living in relatively segregated communities, students tend to become much more aware of their cultural identity when they enter college. One student commented: "Like now, I feel white. I feel different. I feel really different compared to other people."[12]

Students may find it difficult to adjust to college life when the cultural backgrounds of their fellow students are unlike those of people in their home communities. Faced with this situation, students typically become more focused on their own culture or minority status. As one student remarked, "I'm used to being the minority, but I wasn't used to living it day by day by day, morning, noon, and night."[13]

Prior to college, exposure to other groups and ways of life takes place largely through the media and popular culture. Students tend to experience exposure to some groups more than others. Larger groups, such as Latinos and African-Americans, tend to be more visible than smaller groups, such as Asian-Americans and Native Americans. Even when images in the media are accurate, they may lack balance. By way of illustration, a movie such as *The Joy Luck Club* provides us with certain negative images of Asian-American males. These images might accurately reflect *some* Asian-American men. However, these images are not adequately balanced by other, more positive portrayals.

Many students bring to school negative preconceptions about differences. Often, students form these views as a result of isolated experiences with members of another group. Some of these experiences are associated with considerable emotion and even pain. For instance, one student confided in me she had been raped by a Jamaican male. As a result, she makes a habit of staying away from any man who appears to be Jamaican.

Isolation: At College

College typically exposes students to a wider variety of human differences. However, this exposure does not necessarily lead to greater acceptance and interaction across group boundaries, due to a number of factors.

1. *Research shows that throwing diverse students together in the same setting is no guarantee that they will interact or get to know each other.* Whites, African-Americans, Latinos, and other minority students often are unlikely to develop personal relationships outside their group. Students in general may find it easier to socialize with others who they perceive as being more like them. Also, negative prior experiences or personal biases may make some students hesitant to develop any kind of meaningful relationship with someone who does not share their background or even their physical appearance.

This kind of self-segregation, in which people "keep with their own kind," is relatively common on college campuses. It occurs in residence halls, athletic teams, social clubs, and support groups. Contrary to popular belief, research findings indicate that self-segregation is more common among white students than among students of color. This is one of the major conclusions found in *The Impact of Diversity on Students*, a research report published by the Association of American Colleges and Universities.[14]

THINKING THROUGH DIVERSITY:
journal entry
Take a look at your close circle of friends. How diverse is this group?

2. *The campus climate is "chilly" for some students.* **Campus climate** refers to the level of comfort that students experience in the classroom and on campus. Students may feel uncomfortable for any number of reasons, including gender. In *The Classroom Climate: A Chilly One for Women?*, a female student recalls: "I was discussing my work in a public setting when a professor cut me off and asked me if I had freckles all over my body."[15] A chilly climate can make it more difficult for students to focus on their schoolwork, communicate with others, and develop relationships with faculty and students. Unfortunately, research findings show that students feel there are very few opportunities to express their concerns about campus climate.[16]

3. *Opportunities to learn about diversity, and students' inclination to take advantage of these opportunities, vary greatly.* When it comes to providing students with opportunities to become more knowledgeable about diversity, some colleges do a lot and others do relatively little. At certain colleges, all students are required to take at least one course dealing with cultural diversity. An increasing number of college instructors are infusing diversity in their courses. Student and faculty programs, workshops, and activities dealing with diversity issues are commonplace.

Nevertheless, learning about diversity is not always a college-wide priority. Sometimes, it is only an issue if a particular student or faculty member makes it an issue. At some schools, diversity is seen as relevant only for a small group of students majoring in the social sciences or related areas. Consequently, many students discover that during their years in college, learning about diversity is up to them. If you take responsibility for learning more about others regardless of the college you attend, your diversity consciousness will grow. If you don't, it won't.

THINKING THROUGH DIVERSITY:

journal entry

Look at what is being taught in your college classes. Do the readings, lectures, and discussions reflect the contributions of many cultures?

✦ CULTURAL IMMERSION PROGRAM

The University of Indiana and the University of Nebraska have recently begun what they term a *cultural immersion program* for education majors. As part of their educational program, students are required to teach and live in a predominantly bilingual/bicultural setting. The program addresses the growing need for elementary and secondary school teachers with multicultural skills and training.

■ SIX AREAS OF DEVELOPMENT

Diversity consciousness is not an ideal level of awareness and understanding that we reach, after which we remain static. Rather, it is dynamic. Developing our diversity consciousness means committing ourselves to constant learning

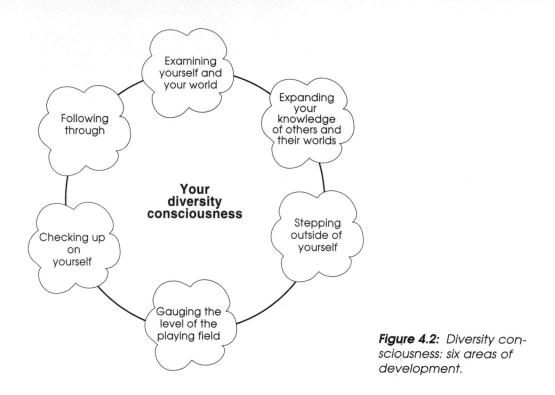

Figure 4.2: *Diversity consciousness: six areas of development.*

and change. In this sense, it is a lot like developing computer know-how. There is always something new to learn and practice.

The development of diversity consciousness can be broken down into six areas (see Fig. 4.2): (1) examining yourself and your world, (2) expanding your knowledge of others and their worlds, (3) stepping outside of yourself, (4) gauging the level of the playing field, (5) checking up on yourself, and (6) following through. In the following sections we describe each of these areas.

Examining Yourself and Your World

It is a huge mistake to assume that we already have full knowledge of our own history and culture. Zora Neale Hurston, a well-known writer and anthropologist, stated: "I couldn't see it [culture] for wearing it. It was only when I was off in college, away from my native surroundings, that I could see myself like somebody else and stand off and look at my garment. I had to have the spyglass of Anthropology to look through at that."[17] Like many of us, Hurston was unaware of her culture because she was so immersed in it. When she went to college, she found herself in a different cultural and academic setting. By experiencing and learning about cultural diversity in this new environment, she was able to "stand back" and take a more critical look at her culture.

Before we begin to make sense of other cultures and cultural differences, we need to become aware of who we are. We do this by focusing on ourselves and the enormous diversity that exists within each of us. Each person is different and each is unique.

Our uniqueness is a reflection of both nature and nurture, which work together. **Nature** refers to our biological makeup. This includes our inborn or genetic traits. "Who we are," therefore, has something to do with nature. However, we cannot examine nature apart from nurture. **Nurture** includes those aspects of the environment that mold and shape us. Essentially, nurture simply describes how schools, families, peer groups, and other parts of our culture influence us. Each of us is reared in a distinctive environment. Even children from the same family are treated differently by their parents, watch different television shows, read different books, and have different friends.

You can reveal your own diversity by asking a number of questions about your background. What makes you unique? Is it your work ethic, talents, personality, sense of humor, or maybe all these things? Your upbringing, schooling, family background, and cultural roots further distinguish you from other people. Your answers to the following questions will provide greater insight into your diversity.

1. What is your name? What is the meaning or significance of your name?
2. Where were you born?
3. What is your family background? Who raised you? As you grew up, who did you consider "family?" Where did you live? Who were your closest friends?
4. What schools did you attend? In general, did you feel like you belonged, or did you feel like an outsider at school? Were the values you learned at school similar to the ones you learned at home? Did you feel the need to "leave your culture at home" in order to be accepted at school?
5. How has your identity been influenced by your race, gender, religion, ethnic background, sexual orientation, and/or social class?
6. What about your personality makes you unique? How are you different from other members of your family?
7. What motivates you? What are your interests and hobbies? What are your goals in life? How do you want to be remembered?
8. What kinds of learning experiences are meaningful for you? What kinds are not?

Every person has a name, and also his own story about his name. My name is Yuan Cai. I don't know what you think about that, but to me it just feels upside-down because I used to be called "Cai Yuan" or "Yuan

*Yuan." That's why when I speak English I just tell you my name is "Yuan."
"Yuan" is the end character of my name, so I feel I have told you all. You
know, giving best names to children is so important in China. They look
up in dictionary and search for the most beautiful sounds, perfect meanings, special and elegantly simple characters, and require the characters
to have some relationships between family members. So you can imagine
how hard a job it was for my parents to give me my name.*

—A student's perspective

Examining our own diversity entails learning about our culture. This is a
bigger job for some than others. How much do you know about your ancestors? Although most of us have an immigrant past, few of us know much about
it. Whereas some students are very conscious of their cultural backgrounds, others are hardly aware of it at all. Still others wrestle with the history of their culture and how it reflects on them.

Sometimes, learning about your history can be difficult. In the book
Tearing the Silence, Ursula Hegi talks about "what it means to be linked to two
cultures."[18] Hegi, a German-American, devotes much of her book to the personal histories of Germans who were born during or after World War II and
later migrated to the United States. When they arrived, they expected to find an
open and tolerant society. Instead, they encountered many who scorned and
mocked them because they were assumed to be Nazis.

Many of the German-Americans interviewed by Hegi wanted to leave their
past behind. As one person put it: "I have a very difficult time dealing with the
Holocaust. I think there is a collective burden in our generation because it is
just so tremendous, so horrible. On the other side, I must say that we have this
'Gnade der spaten Geburt'—the grace of late birth. It's an easy way out....But
it came to my mind that there is a shadow of a collective guilt. At the same time,
I feel it is not my personal guilt, and there's nothing I can do."[19]

Your own cultural identity may be more or less visible to you for a number of reasons. For example, some students are more apt to be reminded of
their cultural background on a daily basis. Language, music, food, holidays, and
customs all serve to reinforce our sense of cultural belonging. Being treated as
an outsider serves as a reminder as well. Because of their background, some
students continually find themselves in situations in which they must decide
whether to try to "fit in." Frequently, they may have to weigh the pros and cons
of being "true" to their cultural roots, assimilating, or some combination of the
two. On the other hand, other students do not have to make these choices.
Their culture is the norm at school, home, and work.

There are also times when some students feel their culture is slipping
away. "I was so anxious to assimilate, to blend in, that I started to forget who
I was.... I just felt it wasn't cool to be a poor Latina girl from Harlem. It was
better to mosh than merengue and to be able to go to a country home on
the weekends. I almost forgot who I was and where I came from, and it's

important not to do that. Remember, you come from beautifully vibrant cultures filled with rich music and traditions. Share that. Enlighten others with your history.... Try new things but don't forget the old.... Remember who you are."[20]

In the course of becoming aware of our cultural roots, it is important to remember that our environment has a lot to do with who we are. An African proverb states: "A person is a person through other people." We cannot escape the influence of culture; we are not the totally independent thinkers and learners we may think we are.

Up to this point we have focused on who we are and how we are interconnected with others. Frequently, it is difficult to make that connection for a number of reasons, including the following:

1. *The emphasis on individualism in U.S. society makes it difficult to see social influences.* In most cases, people in the United States are raised to believe that they think and act on their own. Consider the sayings, "Be all that you can be" and "You are your own worst enemy." Now contrast those with the African proverb, "It takes an entire village to raise a child." Asian cultures also tend to be more oriented toward "we" than "me." As an example, Japanese have a saying, "the nail that stands up gets pounded down." This notion that personal goals are not as important as the goals of the group is at odds with the saying in this country that "the squeaky wheel gets the grease."

▨ BASEBALL IN JAPAN AND IN THE UNITED STATES

Think for a moment about how we view baseball in the United States. How might people in other countries, such as Japan, view it differently? Some differences are captured in an article that appeared in *Sports Illustrated*.[21] While U.S. professional ballplayers are encouraged to "do their own thing," *kojinshugi* (the Japanese term for individualism) is frowned upon in Japan. In the United States, it is commonplace for a player to hold out for more money and sell his services to the highest bidder. This is highly unacceptable in Japan because it shows that a player is more concerned about himself than about his team. In the United States, each player gets himself into shape, whereas in Japan, everyone follows the same training regimen, even the superstars.

2. *Our cultural environment is so close to us that sometimes we do not see it.* Often, we do not even think about certain beliefs that are deeply embedded in each of us. Consequently, it is hard to step back and take a long hard look at our environment or imagine that anyone could think any other way. In *Patterns of Problem Solving*, Moshe Rubinstein provides us with insight into how people from different cultures might view the following hypothetical situation.[22] Imagine that you are in a boat with your mom, spouse, and child. If you could save yourself and only *one* of these three people, who would you save, and why? Most students in my classes answer child. They argue their children have their whole future ahead of them. Some students mention that their children are "part of them." Very few choose mom or spouse. Rubenstein relates how a man from an Arab culture chose "mother." Given this man's cultural background, he could not imagine choosing anyone else. His reasoning was that you can always have another child or spouse. However, you can only have one mother.

3. *Some people rarely experience what it is like to be viewed as an outsider.* Because of this, they have a difficult time seeing beyond their own world. On the other hand, if you are constantly being judged because of your race, class, or religion, you are apt to be more aware of its social significance. For example, consider an American history instructor who constantly calls on the only Mormon student in class to get "her people's" point of view. This experience may make this student feel like an outsider because she is constantly being singled out. In addition, the student may realize that other students in class are not called upon to represent their religions.

journal entry

THINKING THROUGH DIVERSITY:
How can learning about others help us learn more about ourselves?

Expanding Your Knowledge of Others and Their Worlds

Learning about others is instrumental in laying the foundation for diversity consciousness. Furthermore, it enables us to learn more about ourselves. Anthropologists, for example, do not just study cultures that differ from their own. They also work to understand and interpret their own culture, often using what they learn about other cultures to do so. Visiting another country, similarly, can make you more aware of your cultural biases and provide you with a basis for comparison. After visiting another country, you may have a whole new outlook on parts of your culture that you take for granted, such as housing, recreation, education, or friendship.

I come from Zaire and one thing that I miss here most is the friendship of my neighbors and friends. In my country, and in Africa in general, people are hospitable. Friendship is the most important thing in life. In my country, you can't perish from hunger or illness, because members of your family must assist you and help you to improve your life. It's an obligation. Even the neighbors give you their assistance. For instance, when you are sick and you can't go to a hospital because you don't have enough money or you don't have a car, the one in your neighborhood who has a car must transport you to the hospital without hesitation. He has to do it with all his heart. You can even stop a car passing your way, to get help.

In America, however, I think this is not the same. People live in mistrust of each other. You can't count on your neighbors because either they don't know you or don't want to be involved. You are condemned to live without any moral support from anyone in the neighborhood. You can be ill and can die alone in your apartment and no one is likely to notice it. Here I think friendship takes place only when there is an interest. Last week I finished my milk and went to ask a neighbor for a half cup of milk. She gave it to me, but a few days later, she asked for some sugar from me and gave it back to me in the evening. I was very surprised because this is not done among neighbors.

Maybe I am wrong in my opinion, but the facts show that friendships in America are very different from friendships in my country.

—A student's perspective

Malcolm X, in his autobiography, talks about his visit to Saudi Arabia as well as a number of countries in Africa as being one of the turning points in his life.[23] His experiences in that part of the world gave him an entirely different view of race relations in the United States. Moving to another country can provide students with new insight into their ethnic background. A college student from Colombia talks about her interaction with other Latin Americans in the United States. "I have met a lot of Latin Americans. Although we have the same cultural background, we are different. We have different accents in our language and use different words to mean the same things. I have learned about exotic foods from other Latin American countries that I have never seen before. It's incredible that I have learned about Latin American culture in a non–Latin American country. When you are in a foreign country, you have the opportunity to recognize your own roots because you see things from a different point of view."

Differences

Typically, students learn about cultural differences by sampling and studying a few noteworthy events and people. A good example of this is the "group of the month" approach adopted by many schools. With this approach, students are exposed to various elements of African-American culture during Black History Month. Similarly, there are months reserved for women, Latinos, Native Americans, people with disabilities, and other groups.

This kind of approach may be attractive because it is simple and easy to implement. Unfortunately, it promotes a superficial and distorted view of differences. The historical experiences of African-Americans or women, for example, cannot be separated and studied in any kind of meaningful way in a single month. At best, this approach gives us a "taste" of a few noteworthy people or events. At worst, it excludes some students who wonder why their groups are never a "group of the month." Such an approach can also lead to even more stereotypical assumptions.

Although sampling different ways of life may have some value, it is not without dangers. After riding in a wheelchair for 15 minutes or attending a one-hour lecture on disability awareness, some people may begin to feel that they now know what it is like to have a disability. They may generalize what they learn or experience to all people with disabilities. In addition, they may forget the lesson learned shortly thereafter, unless it is reaffirmed time and again.

What then is the best way to learn about differences? A number of specific strategies will be discussed later in the chapter. It is impossible to know every aspect of every culture. However, we need to approach cultural differences with a number of things in mind:

1. *Do not simply sample differences from a distance.* This promotes an "us" versus "them" attitude. In the mid-1970s, I remember a student in one of my classes correcting me on something I had said about Black Muslims. The student, Lola X, was a Black Muslim. She then invited me and my wife to her local temple. We accepted. When we arrived, we were frisked for our own safety. At that time there were concerns about the threat of violence. We were then taken into the temple. My wife was seated with the women on one side and I took my seat with the men. We discovered that we were the only two Whites in a congregation of more than 300 people of color. The sermon was powerful and positive. Everybody, it seemed, tried to make us feel welcome. After the service, a number of people came up to us, introduced themselves, and invited us back. As I look back at that experience, I realize how being there helped me learn and appreciate Lola and her religion. Based on what I had read and heard, I fully expected to be surrounded by people who were angry and hateful toward Whites. What I saw and felt were strong, loving people who went out of their way to make my wife and me feel at home.

2. *Seek to understand how the histories, perspectives, and contributions of different cultures are interconnected.* In 1927, the American historian Carter Woodson made this point with regard to "Negro history." Woodson argued that the focus should be on the Negro *in* history rather than on Negro history.[24]

3. *Try to decrease the social distance between you and those groups or individuals about whom you know little if anything.* **Social distance** is a concept that was coined by a scientist named Emory Bogardus.[25] It refers to the degree to which we are willing to interact and develop relationships with certain racial and ethnic groups. Bogardus created a scale to measure whether we would accept certain people as neighbors, classmates, co-workers, or even spouses. He found that we tend to separate ourselves from others who we think are not like us. This is particularly true of our inner social circles. Take a look at your close friends. How closely do they resemble the racial, ethnic, and social class mix of the students in your school? Would you be comfortable bringing someone of a different religion or sexual orientation home for a few days to spend some time with your family? Our tendency to gravitate toward people who are like us promotes **cultural encapsulation**, meaning a lack of contact with other cultures.

In your life, what groups or cultures are most socially distant?

4. *Focus on ordinary people and occurrences.* Learning about a few remarkable people and events from another culture is not sufficient. Often, stories like these tell us very little about a culture. You can learn a lot more from people who do not make the headlines or the history books, such as a friend, a fellow student, or the employee who works in the cafeteria. Think about the "student perspectives" that appear throughout this book. What have you learned from them?

Similarities

Too often, we preoccupy ourselves so much with individual and cultural differences that we ignore our similarities. Some similarities are harder to see because they lie beneath the surface. In a poem entitled, "Underneath We're All the Same," a student addresses the fact that we all share certain feelings.

> *He prayed—it wasn't my religion.*
> *He ate—it wasn't what I ate.*
> *He spoke—it wasn't my language.*
> *He dressed—it wasn't what I wore.*
> *He took my hand—it wasn't the color of mine.*
> *But when he laughed—it was how I laughed,*
> *and when he cried—it was how I cried.*

> —Amy Maddox, as quoted in *Teaching Tolerance* Magazine[26]

Picture yourself in one of your classes. With whom do you have the most in common? Perhaps it is someone who looks like you or shares your cultural background. It might be the Hispanic student who sits next to you: Even though your race is different, you both grew up in a middle-class, urban neighborhood and are very close to your families. Then again, it might be the white woman who sits in front of you. Unlike you, she is married and has five children. Yet she is the one person in class who shares your passion for computers. Both of you hope to find jobs as computer programmers. Our differences often hide our similarities. Until we really get to know a person, we often fail to realize just how much we share in common.

As students encountering each other for the first time, we tend to notice differences. During the course of a semester, similarities among races, cultures, and other groups can become more apparent. The following comments were written by students who were part of a semester-long study group on racial and ethnic diversity.

I look at things differently because with me being a single parent, I do struggle and I realize that it's not just a "black thing." Everybody struggles.

I learned that Whites hurt just like I do, they cry just like I do. I never knew that some Whites have the same fears about race that I have.

I remember the day we listed the qualities that make us who we are. I realize most of us are alike in a lot of ways, and different in fewer ways. It was very reassuring to see other students agree with me on the same qualities.

—Students' perspectives

Stepping Outside of Yourself

One way to step outside of yourself is to put yourself in somebody else's place. For instance, when you study for a test, you might try to put yourself in the place of your instructor. You might say to yourself: "What questions would I ask on the test if I were the instructor?" This can give you valuable insight into what your instructor is thinking and what to study.

The ability to "put yourself in somebody else's moccasins" increases your awareness, understanding, and diversity skills—your diversity consciousness. By stepping outside of yourself and your culture, you can gain a deeper appreciation of other people's experiences. As a result, your ability to think flexibly and to communicate effectively improve.

Stepping outside of yourself is important for other reasons as well. It increases your awareness of your own frame of reference and how this shapes what you see. By adopting another perspective, you become more aware of your own. You also begin to realize that your perspective is just one of many.

journal entry

THINKING THROUGH DIVERSITY:
Imagine that you are being forced to change your gender (select male/female) or your race/ethnicity (select a "new" racial/ethnic group) or your sexual orientation (select homosexual/heterosexual). Which would you change, and why?

Joshua Solomon, a white student at the University of Maryland, remembers the day he read the book *Black Like Me* by John Howard Griffin.[27] He spent the entire day reading it and thinking about little else. Back in 1959, Griffin, a journalist, took a drug to change his skin from white to brown. He then traveled throughout the South and recorded his experiences. (A white woman by the name of Grace Halsell did something similar in the 1970s. Over the course of three years, she wrote three books about life as a Hispanic, Native American, and African-American woman.)

Solomon decided that he too would change the color of his skin and venture into the South. He did some research and talked to a physician at Yale University. He found the drug that Griffin had taken. Once he started taking it daily and spending time at a tanning salon, the effects became very noticeable.

Solomon decided to visit Atlanta, Georgia first. Almost immediately, he found himself trying to be polite when people stared at him or looked away. Even though he had never had any difficulty making friends, this was no longer true. People acted differently toward him. A hostess at a half-filled restaurant made it clear to him that there would be a long wait. A police officer stopped him and gave him a warning even though he had done nothing wrong. And a lady who sat next to him while he was eating warned him not to venture into an all-white area north of Atlanta. She made it clear that "you people" ruin white neighborhoods.

Solomon cut short his "experiment" after a couple of days because he had grown increasingly angry and depressed. He had always thought that many black people used racism as a crutch or an excuse. Because of this experience, he developed new insight into how pervasive and debilitating racism can be.

For some, learning to step outside of your own world can be a matter of survival. W. E. B. Dubois addresses this issue in his book *The Souls of Black Folk*.[28] According to Dubois, **double consciousness** refers to a person's awareness of his or her own perspective and the perspective of others. It is like looking at the same thing in different ways. Double consciousness makes it possible to shift your perspective back and forth continuously.

Why is shifting one's perspective so important? Imagine driving through the Deep South years ago. For many, driving through Mississippi or Texas on a long trip was like driving anywhere else. They drove as far as they wanted and then stopped for gas, food, or rest. They stopped when it was convenient. Others may recall their trips through this part of the country differently. They had to be constantly aware of where they were at all times. Some remember filling their car with gas and then driving for miles without stopping for gas, food, or lodging. Given the racial climate in the area, they may have even feared for their lives. They found themselves in two worlds divided by race. As they drove, they had to understand the perspective of people who lived in the surrounding areas. If they did not, their safety might be at risk.

Gauging the Level of the Playing Field

For some of us, college is the first time we really wrestle with inequality. This is particularly true of students who have lived around people of similar means all of their life. George Pillsbury, heir to the Pillsbury Flour Company family fortune, recalls that he never saw people living in poverty during his youth. He grew up on a private estate, attended an elite boarding school, and spent his leisure time at a country club. When he started attending classes at Yale University in New Haven, Connecticut, he was exposed to a radically different social world. "It was the first time I'd ever lived in the city—a real city with housing projects with poor people. I began to see poverty where I never had before....I saw the inequities and felt them personally for the first time. I felt a lot of guilt at first, but then it became an emotional and intellectual process toward dedicating myself to positive social change."[29] As Pillsbury discovered, learning about diversity means coming to grips with social inequality.

THINKING THROUGH DIVERSITY:

Are you *solely* responsible for opening and closing the doors of opportunity in your life?

Social inequality refers to the unequal distribution of resources, such as wealth, power, and prestige. In *Where Do We Go From Here*, Martin Luther King addresses the fact that people have different amounts of power.[30] He says, "There is nothing essentially wrong with power. The problem is America's power is unequally distributed."

As a result of social inequality, we belong to different social classes. A **social class** is a category of people who share similar amounts of wealth, power, and prestige. As mentioned earlier, social class is one dimension of diversity. Social class in the United States is not simply a matter of economics. Education, lifestyle, interests, and values relate to one's class position as well.

Diversity and social inequality are closely related. A sense of worth is often attached to differences. For example, in the United States we attach a lot of significance to age. We distinguish between old and young people, and unlike many other countries, we value youth. Billions of dollars are spent each year by people trying to avoid being perceived as old. A relationship exists between social inequality and people's perceptions. One example of social inequality is **ageism**, discrimination on the basis of age. Other examples of social inequality revolve around other dimensions of diversity, including gender, race, ethnicity, class, religion, and sexual orientation. In each case of social inequality, we categorize certain people as different and treat them unequally.

Thinking through inequality is difficult. Living in this society constantly exposes us to advantages and disadvantages connected with social inequality. However, in our own lives, we somehow fail to see many of our *advantages.* Think back to the example of George Pillsbury. He was surrounded by economic advantages throughout his childhood, yet he was not really aware of them because of his social isolation.

Why do we remain oblivious to many of our advantages or privileges? Why are we more aware of our disadvantages than our privileges? Why do we assume that we deserve these privileges and that others do not? **Unearned privileges** are those benefits in life that we have through no effort of our own. Perhaps we were born into a wealthy family or maybe we have certain benefits in school because of our religious background, gender, or race.

Unlike my wife, I was challenged by my teachers to pursue science or math as a possible career. I did not think twice about this advantage until my wife shared with me that she was always led to believe that math was for males. As a result, she opted not to pursue her interest in math even though she exhibited a tremendous amount of potential in this field. After graduating from college and teaching music for a number of years, she went back to school to pursue her lifelong dream of being a mathematician. She is now teaching this subject to high school students.

Privileges are invisible for a number of reasons. When we have something, we tend to take it for granted. For example, we might not truly appreciate freedom until we lose it. Those with privileges naturally want to hold on to them as long as possible. One way of preserving privileges is to discount or ignore them. The education we receive in schools typically focuses on how certain groups are disadvantaged, not advantaged. Discussing individual privileges is seen as too personal and threatening. We also live in a society that values individual achievement, competition, and equality. Because of this, we do not like to acknowledge our privileges, especially those that we do not earn. If we are privileged in some way, we assume that we deserve it. If others are not, we assume that they are not as good or worthy or qualified.

Thinking through privileges and disadvantages requires more than just learning about these things in an abstract way. Rather, we need to recognize them in our own life and in the lives of others. In each of our lives, we have an assortment of privileges as well as disadvantages. The power, number, and consequences of these privileges or disadvantages vary from person to person. Ask yourself: How are you privileged? What privileges do you enjoy? Did you earn them? Writing them down might help you bring them into sharper focus. One of the exercises at the end of this chapter will ask you to do this.

In *White Privilege and Male Privilege,* Peggy McIntosh talks about some of the privileges of being White. She examines an "invisible, weightless knapsack of special provisions, assurances, tools, maps, guides...." McIntosh cites some of the privileges operating in her own life, such as "I am never asked to speak for all the people of my racial group." Another one of the 47 unearned privileges mentioned by McIntosh is: "I can be pretty sure that if I ask to talk to 'the person in charge,' I will be facing a person of my race." In addition, she states "I can easily buy posters, post-cards, picture books, greeting cards, dolls, toys, and children's magazines featuring people of my race."[31]

There is considerable disagreement when we attempt to explain why everybody in the United States does not have an equal "piece of the pie." Recent polls show that the vast majority of white Americans believe racial and ethnic inequality is a thing of the past. When inequality is acknowledged, Whites tend to view it as a personal problem. People of color are more apt to see inequality as a problem that is rooted in society and is still very much with us.

People who do not encounter discrimination on a daily basis are more apt to see it as an aberration; it happens but it is rare and relatively inconsequential. In an ABC news segment entitled "True Colors," the everyday activities of a white and a black male were videotaped for two and one-half weeks in a large metropolitan area in the Midwest. Both of these men were "testers," meaning that they were trained in presenting themselves in exactly the same way. One white student's reaction to the video is found in the following perspective:

When it comes to discrimination, I don't think I am as naive as some of my friends. I realize that it still exists in America. Before seeing this video, I assumed that maybe the cameras would catch a few things, like a salesman tailing the black man in a store, or perhaps a few not giving the black man the same friendly service. I was amazed when I saw not one but two car salesmen charging the black man a higher price than the white man for the exact same car. I saw a landlord giving the white man the keys and a welcomed tour of an apartment. The same landlord, however, told the black man this apartment was not available: a blatant lie. When the reporters entered the landlord's office with both the black and white man, they showed the landlord footage of the tape and asked him for an explanation. Although he had obviously just discriminated against the black man, he got upset and replied, "I am not a racist, I got Mexicans, and 'Jewies,' I got 'em all here." Not only was this man extremely racist when telling the black man that there was no apartment available, but he didn't even realize it. It seems to me that some people think that as long as you are not calling Blacks by derogatory names or telling them to their face they cannot do something because they are Black, that they are not discriminating.

—A student's perspective

The use of testers as shown in "True Colors" has yielded similar results in many other cities and suburbs throughout the United States. If you were constantly subjected to the kind of treatment that was documented in this video, what would be its cumulative effect on you? What would be the psychological *and* economic implications?

In gauging the level of the playing field, it is important to ask yourself the following questions:

1. *Are you blaming the individual or society?* When we blame individuals, we find fault with their characters, work ethics, attitudes, or some other individual difference. We assume that individuals are holding themselves back. Blaming society changes the focus from problem people to people with problems. These problems or barriers, which are found in the larger society, act as obstacles or detours. Social barriers might take the form of racism, a concept discussed earlier, sexism, and classism. **Sexism** refers to the thinking that one sex is superior to another and that unequal treatment is therefore justifiable. **Classism** can be defined in the same way, with the focus on social class. Both the individual and societal points of view are shortsighted and incomplete. One assumes total control over one's fate, the other assumes almost a total lack of control. The individual and society are both important and interconnected. Individuals do have the freedom to choose. People are not at the mercy of their environment. On the other hand, inequality does exist. We do not live in a **meritocracy**, a system in which people get ahead *solely* on the basis of merit. Factors that have nothing to do with ability can affect your move up the economic ladder, regardless of your motivation. These factors include who you know, your looks, and other people's preconceived notions about you.

2. *Are you assuming that if one person can succeed, anybody can?* How do you feel when people in the public eye are held up as evidence that anyone can make it to the top? What about when someone compares your school grades with someone else in your family or with a close friend? We are all different and unique, with our own strengths and limitations. A goal that is realistic or obtainable for one person may be out of someone else's reach or vision. Holding up one person as an example that anything is possible is an example of tunnel vision. People, for example, may point to a female CEO or Supreme Court Justice and cite her success as proof of equal opportunity for men and women. We cannot assume that what happens to one person necessarily applies to the entire group. If we focus exclusively on the one or two who "make it big," we may ignore the vast majority who do not. Circumstances vary from person to person and from one field of employment to another. To draw meaningful conclusions, we need considerably more data about the experiences of men and women in general. Moreover, we cannot gather and analyze evidence haphazardly.

3. *Do you see power and privilege as an all-or-nothing proposition?* Part of the problem with the terms *minority* and *majority* is that they create the impression that we are one or the other. When discussing social inequality, majority and minority refer to power, not numbers. **Majority** refers to the group with power and privilege. **Minority** is the group at a disadvantage in terms of power and privilege. In reality, the division between the more and less powerful is not that easy to see. As an example, a student's majority statuses might include being White, male, and upper class. This same student's minority statuses might be that he is gay and has a disability. Depending on the situation, people may consider him a majority- or a minority-group member. It is a mistake to ignore our multiple statuses and their impact on us.

4. *Do you immerse yourself in your own victimization to the point that you cannot see or comprehend the victimization of others?* Victimization can take many forms, including lost opportunities and the loss of self-esteem. People can feel like victims because of their minority and/or majority statuses. Awareness of our own victimization can make us more or less sensitive to the victimization of others. At times, we may use it as an excuse to stop trying. We *can* empower ourselves. Learning from our own experiences and observing how others have resisted victimization can help us think through social inequality. Experiencing what it is like to be a victim may sensitize us to the subtle and not so subtle ways in which our actions victimize others.

Checking Up on Yourself

Many of us shy away from self-examination. We would rather focus on other people and their shortcomings. In a way, it is much more difficult to confront our own prejudices, stereotypes, and ethnocentrism because it requires us to closely examine our assumptions. These assumptions can be difficult for us to see. They are often so embedded in us that we take them for granted.

A good example is the belief that "women, by nature, make better nurses than men." For some of us, this is an absolute truth. The media, school, and family cultivate and reinforce this assumption. It is difficult to step back and look at this commonplace assumption in an uncommon way. What are the sources of this assumption? Are these sources reliable? Historically, why did the nursing profession become predominantly female? How does this assumption affect our thinking and behavior toward male and female nurses? Wrestling with questions such as these is difficult. It also requires **critical thinking**, the ability to freely question and evaluate ideas and information.

Critical thinking is a diversity skill that enables us to recognize our biases and those of others. It can help us understand that our point of view is one of many. Critical thinking can also reveal gaps or inconsistencies in our assumptions. Research has shown that one key factor in reducing bias is the ability to think critically. In general, students who question what they hear from others and think things through show less prejudice than those who simply accept things at face value.

Checking up on yourself requires constant questioning, reevaluation, and self-reflection. Questions, such as those that follow, provide us with valuable insight into our thinking and behavior throughout the day.

1. *Are you more comfortable around certain types of people?* Why? For example, are you uncomfortable doing business with men who come across as aggressive? If so, are you equally uncomfortable around white and black men who act this way? What does this teach you about with whom you are comfortable and with whom you are not? James Box, a paraplegic and founder of a high-tech wheelchair company, suggests that we need to confront our discomfort and wrestle with it. If something "turns us off" or repulses us, we need to examine it for a while and ask questions of others and ourselves until we can figure out why we are uncomfortable.

2. *Do you make snap judgments about people?* When you are walking through a shopping mall, for example, what assumptions do you make based on clothing, hairstyle, and physical features?

3. *Who do you tend to include in your social circle?* Who do you tend to leave out? How might you expand your social circle?

4. *When you communicate, what messages are you sending?* What about your body language? Do you simply assume that people interpret your communication as you intended?

5. *Is your behavior consistent with your thinking?* In *To Be Equal*, Whitney Young addresses the need to do more than use language that is inoffensive. A change of vocabulary, according to Young, is something quite different from changes in behaviors and attitudes.[32]

Self-examination is ongoing. Since our environment is constantly changing, our awareness and understanding needs constantly to keep pace. We need to grow and adapt as our world and life experiences expand. Checking up on ourselves gives us direction. Companies, for example, regularly conduct assessments before they draw up a plan of action. Individuals need to do the same thing. Before we are able to improve and develop skills such as teamwork, leadership, and communication, it is necessary to think through where we are and in what direction we are going. This takes time, commitment, patience, and awareness of self.

Following Through

Diversity consciousness does not refer simply to our awareness of ourselves and others. It extends to how we behave and interact with others. In other words, we need to apply our knowledge and awareness constantly to real-life situations. We learn by doing. For example, hearing your instructor lecture about computers or reading your textbook is not sufficient to develop your computer skills. Think how much more you learn by sitting down at a computer and actually using it time and time again.

We can only develop and refine diversity skills through constant use and self-evaluation. For instance, many of us regard listening as passive. However, we can improve our listening skills through **active listening**, taking a more active role in hearing and digesting what is being said as well as encouraging the speaker. Specific techniques for developing this skill are found in Chapter 5.

It is very important for me to maintain control of my wandering mind. I try to avoid all of the listening traps, such as dwelling on one thought while the person continues speaking or thinking about tomorrow's list of errands. I focus on the one thing the speaker says that enlightens me for the moment. Also, I always carry a note pad and pen so that I will not cause my own frustration by forgetting my own opinion about whatever is being shared. Often, everyone is so intent on being able to speak that no one actually listens for content, but for cues that the end of the last sentence is about to arrive. A lot is missed in that kind of environment.

—A student's perspective

Practicing a diversity skill is not a feel-good activity. There is an element of risk taking. Try not to get too down on yourself or allow others to frustrate you. As time goes by, you will realize that it is worth the struggle.

■■■■ STRATEGIES FOR DEVELOPING DIVERSITY CONSCIOUSNESS

Developing diversity consciousness is an uneven process, meaning that it is very unpredictable and sporadic. There is no magical moment when you develop diversity consciousness and say to yourself, "Ah ha, I got it." You may find the more you learn about diversity, the less knowledgeable you feel. As you grow, you may go from feeling, "I'm not prejudiced" to "maybe I am" to "I am prejudiced."

Ultimately, each of us must take responsibility for our development in this area. The following eight strategies, which revolve around education, self-examination, and networking, can help you move toward that goal.

1. *Expand your knowledge through reading.* Articles, novels, and personal narratives can provide you with realistic and dramatic portrayals of diversity. This is especially true of first-person accounts. These accounts or stories tend to be much more real, intimate, and varied. They remind us that Americans represent many cultures and come from many countries. When we read about history, different accounts emerge. To illustrate, the westward expansion by early European settlers is a different story when told by Native Americans. For them, the expansion meant encroachment, death, and disease.

A number of first-person accounts are included in the Bibliography and Suggested Readings at the end of the book.

2. *Put yourself in a learning mode in any multicultural setting.* Suspend judgment and adopt a childlike kind of inquisitiveness when trying to make sense out of a situation. One of my students compared this to starting over or "wiping the slate clean." She went on to say that her English instructor told her on the first day of class to forget everything that she had learned about English. The instructor was pushing her to relearn the subject matter and undo her bad habits. In a similar vein, each of us has to shed what we know in certain situations. Only then can we look at people and lifestyles as if we were encountering them for the first time.

3. *Remember that your own life experiences are one of many important sources of knowledge.* This applies to everyone. In the book *Women's Ways of Knowing*, women who live ordinary lives are interviewed about how they perceive themselves and the world around them.[33] Many of these women had little respect for their own minds, ideas, and experiences. At work, school, and home, they relied on others to feed them information and felt voiceless much of the time. Despite their own feelings of inadequacy, the interviews revealed that these women were extremely knowledgeable as well as talented.

4. *Move beyond your comfort zone.* Sometimes, learning can be difficult and uncomfortable. However, this is a necessary part of opening up intellectually and emotionally. The company Hoechst Celanese requires its top executives to join two organizations in which they are an "outsider," so to speak. The rationale for this policy was summarized by the CEO: "The only way to break out of comfort zones is to be exposed to other people. When we are, it becomes clear that all people are similar."[34]

5. *Be modest.* A few years ago, Bill Cosby told a graduating class at George Washington University: "Don't ever think you know more than the person mopping a floor." Everybody has something of value to share. Be aware that no matter how much you know or have seen, you can still learn from anyone. This perspective will make you more open to differences and more willing to learn from those around you.

6. *Don't be too hard on yourself if misunderstandings arise.* No matter how hard we try, there will be situations in which we show our lack of knowledge of other cultures. We may do this without even knowing it. The important thing is to acknowledge our mistakes and learn from them.

7. *Realize that you are not alone.* There are other people out there who care about you and will support you as you grow, learn, and wrestle with diversity issues. Surround yourself with these kinds of people.

THINKING THROUGH DIVERSITY:
journal entry
Do you think you can honor and respect diversity without understanding it?

8. *Take advantage of learning opportunities.* Opportunities to learn and grow can arise at any moment. Learning can be triggered by any number of experiences, such as overhearing an insensitive comment, attending a workshop on diversity, or doing something that might seem totally unrelated to diversity. In the next section we describe a range of opportunities available to students.

Some Specific Opportunities for Diversity Education

We are surrounded by opportunities to learn more about diversity. Whether we avail ourselves of these opportunities is up to us. For example, a wide range of diversity education programs and courses are available on most college campuses. If these opportunities are not available, you might suggest them to your instructor or someone in charge of student programming.

Individuals, groups, and entire communities can initiate and participate in diversity education. Eight possible activities follow:

1. *Computer technology.* New uses of technology, such as the Internet/World Wide Web (WWW), distance learning, and teleconferences make it possible to cross cultural boundaries very easily and quickly. Computer simulations are available that allow students to work through self-paced lessons on diversity issues.

2. *Taping.* If you have ever heard or seen yourself on tape, you know that this can be a real learning experience. It is not uncommon to uncover cultural biases that may surprise you.

3. *Courses.* More and more faculty are integrating diversity into their courses. This is true of a wide range of courses, including literature, art, business, math, allied health, student success, and social sciences. If diversity is not the focus of the entire course, it is likely to be discussed in one or more units of a course.

4. *Travel and opportunities for study abroad.* Students who study abroad learn the importance of a world view. This is particularly true of extensive trips abroad which provide opportunities for studying, working, and socializing (see Fig. 4.3).

5. *Racial/cultural awareness workshops.* Academic departments, offices dealing with student affairs, and community groups frequently offer workshops of this nature. Although one two-hour workshop is not going to change your thinking and behavior dramatically, it can deepen your understanding of diversity issues and put you in touch with people who may have similar interests and concerns. In his comprehensive study of undergraduates throughout the country, Astin found that participation in workshops increases students' awareness that (1) discrimination is still a problem and (2) individuals can bring about change in society.[35]

Figure 4.3: *Students visit a museum in Cairo, Egypt. The students, who are spending a semester on board a cruise ship, are enrolled in the University of Pittsburgh's "Semester at Sea" course. Each semester, more than 600 students take classes on board a cruise ship and then experience what they study by visiting countries throughout the world. (Courtesy of the Institute for Shipboard Education, University of Pittsburgh, Pittsburgh, PA.)*

6. *School programs.* Many programs aim at promoting the understanding and celebration of cultural differences. Many colleges offer these programs in connection with Black History Month, International Women's Day, AIDS Awareness Day, and other events. Lectures, dramatic presentations, art exhibits, and field trips are cocurricular activities that can enhance and broaden your education. Additionally, these programs are motivational as well as informative.

7. *Cultural activities in the community.* Plays, movies, art exhibits, museums, and community resources and events provide numerous opportunities to learn about diversity. Sometimes it makes sense to do this as a group so that you can share your thoughts and feelings afterward. With a minimal amount of expense or planning, student groups can rent and watch videos such as *Philadelphia, Beloved, Schindler's List, The Joy Luck Club, Rain Man, Smoke Signals,* and *Hoop Dreams.* This type of experience can break the ice and provide insight into history, culture, and different life experiences. It can also make it easier to talk about a variety of issues dealing with diversity.

Music and art have shown me the common ground between people and what we can do for each other.

—An instructor's perspective

8. *Study circles/groups.* As discussed earlier, study circles are small group discussions that focus on any number of issues, including diversity. The basic idea is that a group of perhaps 8 to 12 people commit to meeting regularly over a period of time. This type of discussion allows people to get to know each other, discover common ground, and take action. Schools, businesses, and communities throughout the country have adopted the study circle concept.

■■■■ A CONTINUING PROCESS

The greater our knowledge increases, the greater our ignorance unfolds.

—John Fitzgerald Kennedy

Diversity consciousness is not something we can develop, store, and then consult periodically. It is not something that "kicks in" at school or work. Rather, it is an unending process. We need to reevaluate our knowledge of ourselves and others continuously as we gain new knowledge. As our thinking changes, so does our behavior. This kind of change requires both time and effort.

As we develop diversity consciousness, a number of positive changes will gradually occur:

- ○ Our thinking will become less rigid and more flexible.
- ○ Our awareness and appreciation of human differences will heighten our ability to see and value similarities.
- ○ We will move from a perspective that centers on ourselves and our immediate environment to one that is more inclusive and global.

It should be clear from this chapter that it is extremely difficult to develop diversity consciousness. For many of us, just tolerating certain differences requires a radical change in our thinking and behavior. In many cases it means unlearning much that we have been taught. Diversity consciousness moves us beyond tolerance. Rather than putting up with differences, it makes it possible for us to understand, respect, and value differences. This kind of personal transformation requires not only time but also commitment.

Education is all a matter of building bridges.

—Ralph Ellison

In the next two chapters we examine two diversity skills: communication (Chapter 5) and teamwork (Chapter 6). As our society becomes more diverse and the larger world becomes more interconnected, it is increasingly important for us to understand the significance of these skills and their relationship to diversity consciousness.

Exercises

IN-CLASS

Exercise 1: The Name Game

Directions for Instructor.
Ask each student to respond to the following questions in writing:
1. Each of us learns about many famous people who have shaped history. Draw on this knowledge and name three well-known people (living or dead) who are:
   a. Upper class
   b. Lower class
   c. Gay and Lesbian
   d. Asian-American
   e. Native American
   f. Female
   g. Male
   h. Disabled
2. Have students pair up. Ask each pair of students to review the names each of them listed for the eight categories. Which categories of people were the easiest to name? Why? Which categories of people were the most difficult to name? Why?
3. As a class, discuss what this exercise reveals about you and your upbringing. Discuss what it reveals about your education.

Exercise 2: Family Stories

The African proverb "a person is a person through other persons" applies to each of us. In particular, it describes our relationship with family members. As we get older, we become more aware of these relationships.

Directions for Instructor
1. Ask each student to think of stories that have been passed down from generation to generation in her or his family. Students should select

one story that has influenced their lives in some way, such as making them stronger or altering how they view what is really important in life. They should try to remember as much of the story as possible.

2. Have students pair up. Each student shares his or her story. Also, the student should explain how the story affects her or him.

3. As a class, discuss the following questions: Is there anything that your stories have in common? In what ways are they different? Why do you think that some family stories are forgotten and others remain with us? What have you learned from these stories?

Exercise 3: Unearned Privileges

Each of us has privileges as well as disadvantages. Many of these relate to different dimensions of diversity, such as race, ethnicity, class, gender, sexual orientation, and religion. In the case of privileges, some are earned whereas others are unearned.

Directions for Instructor

1. Ask each student to list in writing three privileges he or she has that are *earned*. Then list three that are *unearned*. Be as specific as possible. Share these with the class.

2. As a class, discuss which of our privileges—earned or unearned—are easier for us to identify. Why?

OUT-OF-CLASS

Exercise 1: Shifting Perspectives in the Classroom

You are sitting in a college classroom. It is the first day of class. Your instructor, whom you have never met, walks in, introduces himself, and hands each student a course syllabus. Prior to going over the syllabus, the instructor reviews his expectations for classroom interaction.

○ Students should act as if they understand everything and never ask any questions.

○ Students should never raise questions about tests or grades at any time.

○ Students should not look directly at the instructor when he speaks.

Answer the following questions.

1. In general, how did you feel about these expectations? Why do you feel this way? How is your cultural background related to your feelings?

2. Talk to other students who have attended schools outside the United States. How do they feel about the expectations outlined above? How have their educational experiences differed from yours?

Exercise 2: Cross-Cultural Interview and Analysis

Interview. Interview someone who was born and grew up in a country other than your own. This person should be a fellow student or a member of the faculty or staff. When interviewing someone, find a comfortable place to talk. Begin by getting acquainted with each other. Then focus your questions on the following topics related to the interviewee:

- Family background
- Cultural background
- Educational background
- Community in which he or she was raised
- Leisure activities as a child
- Religious background
- Other areas of interest

Analysis. Once the interview is completed, think through how you might have responded to these questions. Compare your responses with those of the interviewee.

1. List some of the major differences in your backgrounds. What are some of the major similarities?
2. Create a poster that represents these differences and/or similarities. Do not use any words; rather, express yourself through images. The images may be drawn by hand or created on the computer. You may include clippings from newspapers and magazines as well as photographs.

Exercise 3: The Challenge of Diversity Consciousness

What do you think will be your most difficult challenge as you work on increasing your own diversity consciousness?

INTERNET ASSIGNMENT

1. Go to your college Web site. Search it thoroughly for courses, programs, and/or activities relative to diversity. Make a list of all you are able to find. (*Note:* If your college does not have a comprehensive Web site, do this using your college catalog.)
2. Go to another college Web site (www.collegeboard.org is a good starting point). Find one that has significantly more or fewer diversity programs, courses, and activities. List these as well.

NOTES

[1]Juan L. Gonzales, Jr., *The Lives of Ethnic Americans*, 2nd ed. (Dubuque, IA: Kendall/Hunt, 1994), 98.

[2]"Women, Men, and Media," in M. Junior Bridge, *Marginalizing Women* (Unabridged Communications, 1996).

[3]National Council of La Raza, *Don't Blink: Hispanics in Television Entertainment* (Washington, DC: Center for Media and Public Affairs, 1996).

[4]Martin Gilens, "Race and Poverty in America: Public Misperceptions and the American News Media," *Public Opinion Quarterly*, 60, 1996, 515–541.

[5]Associated Press, "Number Living in Poverty Drops for 3rd Year in a Row, U.S. Says," *The Sun*, Sept. 25, 1998, 3A.

[6]National Center for Education Statistics, *Digest of Education Statistics, 1997*, NCES 98-015 (Washington, DC: U.S. Department of Education, 1997), 186.

[7]Ibid.

[8]Ibid., 324.

[9]"Facts about Higher Education in the U.S.," *Chronicle of Higher Education Almanac Issue 1998/1999*, XLV(1), Aug. 28, 1998, 38.

[10]Ibid., 5.

[11]Associated Press, "More Women Finish College Than Men," *The Sun*, June 29, 1998, 3A.

[12]Charles Gallagher, "White Reconstruction in the University," *Socialist Review*, 24, 1994, 165.

[13]Cheryl Tan, "For College Students, Degrees of Ethnicity," *The Washington Post*, Sept. 3, 1996, B1.

[14]Morgan Appel, David Cartwright, Daryl Smith, and Lisa Wolf, *The Impact of Diversity on Students* (Washington, DC: Association of American Colleges and Universities, 1996), x.

[15]Roberta Hall and Bernice Sandler, *The Classroom Climate: A Chilly One for Women* (Washington, DC: Association of American Colleges, 1982), 3.

[16]Ansley A. Abraham, *Racial Issues on Campus: How Students View Them* (Atlanta, GA: Southern Regional Education Board, 1990), 2.

[17]Zora Neale Hurston, as found in Dorothy W. Riley (ed.), *My Soul Looks Back, 'Less I Forget*, (New York: Harper Collins, 1993), 81.

[18]Ursula Heigi, *Tearing the Silence.* (New York: Simon & Schuster, 1997).

[19]Jonathan Yardley, "Coping with History," *The Washington Post: Book World*, July 6, 1997, 3.

[20]John Lahr, "Speaking across the Divide," *The New Yorker*, Jan. 27, 1997, 41–42.

[21]Robert Whiting, "You've Gotta Have 'Wa'," *Sports Illustrated*, September 24, 1979, 60+.

[22]Moshe Rubinstein, *Patterns of Problem Solving* (Englewood Cliffs, NJ: Prentice Hall, 1975).

[23]Malcolm X, *The Autobiography of Malcolm X* (New York: Ballantine Books, 1965).

[24]Carter Woodson, as quoted in Dorothy W. Riley, ed., *My Soul Looks Back, 'Less I Forget: A Collection of Quotations by People of Color* (New York: Harper Collins, 1995), 189.

[25]Emory Bogardus, "Measuring Social Distance," *Journal of Applied Sociology*, 9, Mar./Apr. 1925, 299–308.

[26]Amy Maddox, "Underneath We're All the Same," *Teaching Tolerance*, Spring 1995, 65.

[27]John H. Griffin, *Black Like Me.* (New York: NAL/Dutton, 1999).

[28]W. E. B. Dubois, *The Souls of Black Folk* (New York: Fawcett, 1961).

[29]George Pillsbury, as quoted in John Sedgwick, *Rich Kids* (New York: William Morrow, 1985), 120.

[30]Martin Luther King, Jr., *Where Do We Go from Here: Chaos or Community?* (Boston: Beacon Press, 1968).

[31]Peggy McIntosh, *White Privilege and Male Privilege* (Wellesley, MA: Wellesley College Center for Research on Women, 1988), 7.

[32]Whitney Young, *To Be Equal* (New York: McGraw-Hill, 1966).

[33]Mary Belenky, Blythe Clinchy, Nancy Goldberger, and Jill Tarule, *Women's Ways of Knowing* (New York: Basic Books, 1986).

[34]Fay Rice, "How to Make Diversity Pay," *Fortune*, Aug. 8, 1994, 82.

[35]Alexander Astin, "Diversity and Multiculturalism on the Campus: How Are Students Affected?" *Change*, Mar./Apr. 1993, 47.

5

COMMUNICATING IN A DIVERSE WORLD

chapter objectives

Upon completion of this chapter, you will be able to:

○ Explain how **communication** and culture interrelate.

○ Discuss the effects of **electronic communication**.

○ Explain the relationship between diversity consciousness and communication.

○ List and give examples of barriers to effective communication.

○ Define and give examples of "**hot buttons**."

○ List the ground rules for difficult dialogues.

○ Describe strategies for communicating inclusively.

> *I think that people within my culture and from other cultures may mistake my lack of eye contact for dishonesty. I feel that staring into someone's eyes lets them see into my soul so instead I focus on something else when speaking. This way is more comfortable for me. I find that when I try to give eye contact, I often end up focusing on some other feature of the individual's face. I think that I offend many people when I don't look them eye to eye.*

> —•—

> *I usually fold my arms and I don't walk around smiling. People always comment to me "Is it that bad?" or "Smile; there is nothing to be sad about." I have been told that I look unapproachable because of my stance and facial expressions, but I think I am one of the most approachable people on the streets.*

> —•—

> *One day, a man called my house taking a survey and he started asking me questions. Before I got a chance to tell him my race, he was already writing down that I was White. I interrupted and told him that I was Black and he apologized and told me that I sound White. I was wondering what do Whites sound like.*

> —•—

> *A communication style I have that other cultures may find offensive is my openness about personal feelings or experiences. I have to be careful not to overwhelm people with "too much information" about a certain subject. This tends to make many people feel uncomfortable. I have learned to think before I speak; however, it is sometimes difficult.*

> —•—

> *When I smile, there are men who think I'm "coming on to them." All I'm trying to do is be friendly.*

> —Students' perspectives

Communication takes place whenever meaning is attached to a message. The meaning may be intended or unintended. By developing our diversity consciousness and in particular, our communication skills, we become more aware of the messages we are sending and receiving. This empowers us and enriches our lives. On the other hand, poor communication skills can make it difficult for us to achieve our goals and can alienate, confuse, and hurt others.

■ COMMUNICATION AND CULTURE

Communication and culture interrelate. Each of us communicates a certain way because of our upbringing. Because of our individual and cultural backgrounds, we attach specific meanings to what people say and do. These meanings may vary within and between cultures. As our work, school, and community environments become more multicultural, it is increasingly important to become more conscious of our cultural differences as well as our similarities. This enables us to communicate more effectively and helps us understand and respect each other.

Communication is the process by which people transfer information, ideas, attitudes, and feelings to each other. The word *communicate* comes from the Latin verb *communicare*, which means to share. When people use and share symbols with others who can understand their meanings, they are communicating. A **symbol** is any thing that represents something else. Symbols take many forms. Spoken and written words probably come to mind, but we also communicate with nonverbal symbols. Examples of nonverbal communication, or what we refer to as body language, include gestures, facial expressions, body positioning, touching, and eye movements.

People throughout the world send messages by a vast array of body language. In *Gestures: The Do's and Taboos of Body Language Around the World*, author Roger Axtell discusses **kinesics**, the study of body movements as a means of communication. He cites studies by a number of researchers, including Mario Pei and Ray Birdwhistell. Pei estimates that humans can produce approximately 700,000 physical signs. According to Birdwhistell, the face alone is capable of 250,000 expressions.[1] By studying the kinesics of different cultures, anthropologists have determined that people from different cultures may signal each other in very different ways.

Body language throughout the world is culturally specific. If a gesture is **culturally specific**, it may mean one thing to one culture but something quite different to another. When he was vice-president of the United States, Richard Nixon learned this lesson the hard way. On a goodwill tour of Latin America in the 1950s, he stepped off his airplane and was met by a cheering crowd. He responded by flashing the "A-OK" sign, his thumb and forefinger forming a circle. The crowd immediately began to boo and show their disapproval. The next day, large pictures of Nixon making the gesture made the news from Mexico City to Buenos Aires. The gesture generated so much attention because in this part of the world, it means "screw you."

Communication allows us to dialogue and feel a sense of togetherness. Also, it can illustrate our differences and drive a wedge between us. This is especially true of intercultural communication. **Intercultural communication** refers to a process whereby people from one culture interact with people from another. Misunderstandings can also occur between people who may be different in other ways. Maybe they have different styles of communication. Perhaps differences in gender, age, marital status, or social class make it difficult to connect with someone.

Miscommunication often results because we attach different meanings to the same symbol. As an example, Nike marketed some of its products a few years ago by displaying their logo, the word "Air," in stylized letters. They soon discovered that the logo resembles the Arabic word for Allah. Under threat of a worldwide boycott of its product by Muslims, Nike agreed to recall and stop selling any shoes with this logo. Muslims did not object to this logo on caps and tee shirts. However, they felt that its appearance on shoes was a sign of disrespect. By communicating a totally different message than they intended, Nike learned a costly and important lesson. According to one spokesperson for Nike: "Our company has to be more vigilant and work more with communities on issues of sensitivity."[2]

▥ MEN AND WOMEN, DIVIDED BY LANGUAGE

Deborah Tannen is a professor of *linguistics*, the science of language. In her research, Tannen has focused on the different communication styles of men and women. She has written extensively on this subject. Her books, entitled *You Just Don't Understand, That's Not What I Meant*, and *Talking from 9 to 5*,[3] offer some examples of gender differences:

- Men engage in report talk, women in rapport talk. *Report talk* is a way of showing one's knowledge and skill. *Rapport talk* allows one to share with others and develop relationships.

- When making requests, women tend to be indirect. A female supervisor might ask: "Could you do this by 5 P.M.?" Something more direct and to the point is more typical of a male supervisor: "This needs to be done by 5 P.M."

- Women have a greater *information focus*. They do not hesitate

to ask questions in order to understand something. Men have more of an *image focus*. Even though men may be unclear about an issue, they may forego asking questions, to preserve their image or reputation.

- Women often say "I'm sorry" to express concern about something. Men, on the other hand, may interpret this to mean that women are accepting blame or responsibility. This is not at all what women have in mind.

- People tend to judge men for what they say and do, women by how they look and dress.

Tannen makes the point that these differences do not apply to all men or women in all situations. By realizing that differences such as these may exist, we lessen the chances of miscommunication and conflict.

Most of us think of ourselves as literate. Because of our educational background, we can read and write. But we are literate only in a particular cultural environment. In another setting within our society or abroad, we may have no idea how to communicate ideas and feelings.

There are a lot of beautiful, favorite places in any language in which you feel yourself at home. In English, I don't have such a place yet. All phrases come out from my mouth, rough and heavy...the words fall with plops on the floor, like ugly frogs. And I am so waiting for the butterfly.

—A student's perspective

Imagine sitting in a classroom at Gallaudet University in Washington, DC, the world's only accredited four-year liberal arts university for deaf and hard of hearing people. In *Seeing Voices: A Journey Into the World of the Deaf,* Oliver Sacks describes his first visit to Gallaudet. "I had never before seen an entire community of the deaf, nor had I quite realized (even though I knew this theoretically) that Sign might indeed be a complete language—a language equally suitable for making love or speeches, for flirtations or mathematics. I had to see philosophy and chemistry classes in Sign...I had to see the wonderful social scene in the student bar, with hands flying in all directions as a hundred separate conversations proceeded."[4] (See Fig. 5.1.)

Figure 5.1: *Students at Gallaudet University communicate with each other about their weekend plans. (Courtesy of the Office of Public Relations, Gallaudet University, Washington, DC.)*

Linguistic diversity refers to the many languages spoken in the United States and throughout the world. Some people speak only one language, while others speak more than one. We refer to people who are able to speak two languages fluently as **bilingual**, and those capable of speaking more than two as **multilingual**. Language differences and the way we view these differences affect our achievement. Although proficiency in English is critically important, more and more research shows that fluency in more than one language can increase one's chances for success. Many colleges offer programs for English as a Second Language (ESL) students. These programs serve immigrants, refugees, foreign students, and other people who need to improve their English skills.

Students or teachers who speak a language other than English may encounter **linguicism**, a relatively new term that refers to discrimination based on language. How do you feel when you enter a particular class for the first time and you are met by an instructor or teaching assistant who is bilingual and speaks English with an unfamiliar accent? When you are in a group with a number of ESL students, do you take the time to listen carefully and encourage full participation from everyone? Do you accept responsibility for making sure that you understand what is being communicated?

Some students are apt to view situations such as these as problems rather than challenges. Although communication with the aforementioned teacher or students might be difficult for a period of time, persistence as well as good listening skills can help a great deal. Also, consider what they have to offer. Studies show that people who speak more than one language have higher levels of *cognitive flexibility*, meaning they can adjust more easily to different situations. Someone who is bilingual or multilingual may be better able to share a variety of world perspectives.

ELECTRONIC COMMUNICATION

Electronic communication is the imparting or interchange of information through technology, such as phones, satellites, or the Internet. The capabilities of electronic communication are expanding rapidly. As more and more people throughout the world learn to use new technologies, new communication problems arise.

Since Internet communication relies primarily on text, such as e-mail, chat rooms, and news groups, people cannot rely on other cues, such as tone of voice or gestures. We do not necessarily know anything about who is sending the message and his or her position, cultural background, or even the person's mood. Lack of familiarity with certain rules of etiquette may also result in misunderstandings. For example, Internet etiquette defines communicating in all capital letters as YELLING. Some people, who like using "all caps" because they find it easier, do not realize that they may be offending others.

What are the possible effects of Internet communication? Some see this form of communication as a vehicle for breaking down barriers and promoting the diffusion of language and culture in general. **Cultural diffusion** refers to the spread of objects and ideas from one culture to another. Each year, the Internet is becoming more multicultural. Computer companies and software designers are developing a universal system to accommodate all of the world's languages. This allows any computer user to enter information in his or her own language. New software allows for instant translation of Web pages written in any foreign language.

Others view the impact differently. According to former Brown University president Vartan Gregorian, "What is being created is...the ability to retreat to small communities of the like-minded, where we are safe not only from unnecessary interactions with those whose ideas and attitudes are not like our own, but also from having to relate our interests and results to other communities."[5] News groups and chat rooms allow people with similar interests or agendas to gravitate to each other. This can have positive or negative consequences. As an example, the Net can bring together people who are looking for support and current information about a particular disease or disability. It can also serve as a safe haven for hate groups. Therefore, electronic communication is a tool we can use to access other perspectives and worlds or isolate ourselves even further.

✖ E-MAIL HUMOR

Many employees converse casually by e-mail each day. In many instances, they mistakenly assume that their messages are private. Consequently, they often say things they would not communicate in writing or discuss in public. This includes racist, sexist, and other derogatory messages. Many companies routinely save all e-mail messages. These saved messages are now being used to sue companies.

Experts say that e-mail is a matter of official record. It is no different than a memo written on company letterhead. Consequently, jokes circulated through a company's e-mail system may constitute evidence of discrimination. Companies are responding by creating policies regarding e-mail usage.

Computer technology is transforming electronic communication in educational settings as well as the workplace. College professors use the Internet and Web pages to post syllabi, class notes, related links, and other necessary information. Employees can work at home or any other location. Unlike the office setting of the past, they communicate by fax, e-mail, pagers, and in a variety of other ways with anybody at any time from any location.

Business and educational publications describe the effects of communicating via computers using terms such as *empowerment* and *inclusiveness*. There are a number of reasons for this. When conferencing through the Internet, for instance, a person with relatively little status can be empowered. This same person's status may be much more of a consideration in a face-to-face meeting. In face-to-face groups, higher-status people tend to talk more, and what they say is assumed to be more important. On the other hand, numerous research studies show that the flow of communication online is more evenly distributed and respected, regardless of who occupies what status.

In their book, *Connections: New Ways of Working in the Networked Organization*, Sproull and Kiesler describe a study of decision making by college students: "When pairs of graduate students and undergraduates met face-to-face to decide their joint project, the pairs were likely to choose the topic preferred by the graduate student." When the decision was made via computers, each person's choice was equally likely to be chosen.[6]

In college, online courses offer a number of advantages. Students who are for any reason unable to attend school physically can still take courses. In general, students taking online courses have more time to ask and respond to questions. Moreover, they can communicate through writing, graphics, images, and sounds. Learning is asynchronous, meaning students can interact in the "classroom" at any time. Consequently, they never have to miss a class. The identity of the communicators remains hidden or anonymous. As a result, people may ask questions online that they would not ask face to face. People may project themselves in any way they want. In this kind of communication, race, gender, and other dimensions of diversity become less relevant. The message is more important than the messenger.

DIVERSITY CONSCIOUSNESS AND COMMUNICATION

As discussed in Chapter 4, the development of diversity consciousness occurs in six areas. These areas help us understand the communication process. For example, if we are to communicate effectively, we need to have a sense of who we are individually and culturally. Additionally, we need to broaden our perspectives and develop an understanding of people from a variety of backgrounds. Finally, we need to apply and improve those skills that allow us to connect with others.

Knowledge of languages helps us to extend our circle of friends.

—A student's perspective

Areas of Development: Diversity Consciousness and Communication

Your communication skills will improve as you become more conscious of diversity. As discussed earlier, there are six areas of development: (1) examining yourself and your world, (2) expanding your knowledge of others and their

Diversity Consciousness: Opening Our Minds to People, Cultures, and Opportunities

worlds, (3) stepping outside of yourself, (4) gauging the level of the playing field, (5) checking up on yourself, and (6) following through. Each of the areas, and its implications for effective communication, are discussed below.

Examining Yourself and Your World

Before we begin to make sense of communication outside our culture, we need to develop awareness of our own communication style and why we communicate the way we do. Our individual and cultural backgrounds profoundly influence the way we communicate. The most obvious example is the language we learn and use. It is easy to take our own language for granted and assume that everybody interprets words and gestures in the same way. What about the words *you* use? If you are majoring in computers, your vocabulary consists of terms such as *gigs* and *megs*, *operating systems*, *hardware*, and *software*. When you use these terms with people who are not familiar with computers, how do they react? In general, is communication between people who are and are not computer literate problematic?

Even material culture can be interpreted in many ways. **Material culture** is that which we create and can see, touch, or feel. Consider the clothes you wear. What do they communicate to different people in different settings? How are they connected to your culture? For example, what does a pair of $70 jeans symbolize? Does it symbolize the same thing to people of varying ages? Sometimes, we are ineffective communicators because we fail to realize that everyone does not share our interpretation(s). Furthermore, we may find it difficult to examine our own ways of communicating.

In her book *Ways with Words*, Shirley Brice Heath describes a technique that students can use to stand back and look at themselves. She suggests that students put themselves "under a microscope" and take the role of an **ethnographer**,[7] a person who spends time living with people in order to research their customs. Using this method, students assume the role of a neutral observer and observe their own communication systematically. They record even the smallest details and try to discover patterns. As an ethnographer, you might focus on how you communicate with others in the classroom. What about the tone and volume of your voice? How might your body gestures influence how your message comes across to others? How do you react to lectures, discussions, and group work in class?

Expanding Your Knowledge of Others and Their Worlds

Do we even recognize the presence of others and their capacity or right to communicate? Sometimes, we view women, men, children, lower-class persons, and people with disabilities as unable to speak for themselves in certain situations. Raymond Bingham, a white male nurse, recounts the assumptions he made one morning while working in a newborn intensive care unit. A child with a heart defect needed emergency surgery. The nurse vividly recalls meeting the child's father for the first time. He was "a large black man, with unkempt clothes, somewhat slurred speech, and at 8 o'clock in the morning a hint of beer on his breath."

The nurse's first impression was not to expect too much from this man. He was soon proven wrong. The father showed a lot of caring and compassion for his son. When he needed to explain the procedure to the child's mother on the phone, he gave a complete and thorough description of the surgery and why it was necessary. Finally, the nurse remembers the father sitting at the child's bedside and crying. Toward the end of his shift, the nurse reflected back on this experience. "This man, of whom I had thought so little at first glance, who had been so strong, so calm, so resolved throughout a tumultuous day, who had so many things to worry about and take care of…had handled them all."[8]

THINKING THROUGH DIVERSITY :

journal entry

If you and other students sit in the same classroom, read the same assignments, and hear the same lectures, are all of you receiving the same education? Might each of you interpret the same lesson differently because of the social worlds in which you live?

It is important to be aware of different communication styles and what kinds of misunderstandings can result from them. How do you react to these differences? Do you listen intently and try extra hard to understand? Are there times when you refuse to accommodate or even acknowledge differences? When you go to school or work, are you likely to encounter cultural differences? What do you assume when:

- *People converse with their faces only a few inches apart?* Among some cultures, this is the norm. In others, people like to keep their distance and are uncomfortable if someone stands closer than a couple of feet.
- *A student or a co-worker takes a long time to answer a question?* According to researchers who study language, short wait times put some people at a disadvantage. For example, the cultures of many Native Americans emphasize deliberate thought. Before making a decision, they learn to consider all possible implications.
- *People do not look at you when you talk to them?* Among many African, Asian, and Latin American cultures, it is rude to establish direct eye contact with elders or people in authority.
- *People talk informally for a period of time before "getting down to business"?* In many cultures, this is considered good manners. Many Middle Easterners, for example, see this type of "small talk" as a necessary part of business. Many Asians view the process of getting to know each other as important as the message itself. To many American businessmen and women, it is simply a waste of time.
- *People answer a question with "yes"?* In many East Asian cultures, it is rude to answer a question in the negative. In such situations, people may say "yes" even though they mean "no." It is a way of showing respect or "saving face," saving someone from embarrassment.

○ *You see two people verbally challenging each other?* If your cultural background is Greek, Italian, or Israeli, you might view it positively, as a sign of intimacy. If you were from certain Hispanic or Asian cultures, you would probably view this kind of verbal sparring differently. Since expressing anger in this way is frowned upon, you might consider it more appropriate to repress feelings and simply smile or change the subject.

When you meet people on the way to class, on the street, in a store or wherever, they say "Hi" plus they ask "How are you doing?" or "How are you?" even if you are a complete stranger to them. I like when they say "Hi" to me, but what really doesn't make sense is that they add "how are you feeling?" even though they don't care whether I am well or not. I feel like Americans ask this just because they are obliged to do it. In fact, if I answered "I am not OK," nobody would care. In a certain way, this is like a movie where the actors have to say what is written in the script. To the question, you feel obliged to answer you are well no matter whether it is the truth or not. Considering this point, I prefer Italians who just say "Hi" or nothing to the people they have never met before. They don't even think to ask about their health. It could appear colder, but it is certainly less hypocritical.

—A student's perspective

✠ INTIMATE TALK AMONG COLLEGE STUDENTS: SOME GENDER DIFFERENCES

Recent research has taken a look at the degree to which male and female college students "open up" in intimate relationships. In one study, 360 college students attending universities in the South and Midwest were surveyed. The study suggests that female students:

1. Tend to disclose much more than men.
2. Are more apt to open up and discuss previous love and sexual relationships.
3. Are more likely to communicate to their partner how they really feel about them.
4. Are more apt to express what they want for the future of a relationship.

These findings are consistent with other research which shows that women tend to be more relationship-oriented than men.[9]

You cannot be familiar with all variations in communication. Furthermore, you cannot assume that all people from a given culture will communicate in the same way. However, it is important to be open to the possibility that communication differences exist. Keep in mind that despite our differences, we all want people to listen to, acknowledge, and respect us.

Stepping Outside of Yourself

It would help if everyone could experience what it is like to be a minority for a while, to learn what it is like.

—A student's perspective

One of the most important skills needed for effective communication is the ability to process and understand the other person's point of view. This skill allows you to step outside of yourself and become more open and sensitive to others, although it does not necessarily mean that you will fully comprehend or agree with their thoughts and feelings. Certain experiences may teach students the importance of putting themselves in the shoes of friends, family, and others.

Ashley is a college sophomore whose best friend is dealing with an unwanted pregnancy. Even though Ashley has never been in this situation, she can "feel her friend's pain" and this helps her know what to say. Judah, a community college student, writes about how he works with a number of people with severe cerebral palsy. Since some cannot communicate verbally, he finds it helps to "put his mind into theirs" and rely on other physical cues. Ernestine, an older female student who has a household of daughters, explains how she struggles with their thinking about life. They have watched many of their friends die violently. As a result, her daughters prefer to focus on the present and not think about the future. Says Ernestine, "I try to imagine going to countless funerals of classmates and soulmates and babies, all because somebody dissed them or stepped on their shoes or looked at them the wrong way." These three students—Ashley, Judah, and Ernestine—are more effective communicators because they have the ability to step outside of themselves. They are not locked into their own way of thinking.

When people try to understand a variety of perspectives, it opens up lines of communication. People are more willing to share when they sense that others are really listening and not judging or comparing. Also, stepping outside of yourself can make you more aware of your own thoughts and feelings. In *I Know Why the Caged Bird Sings*, Maya Angelou talks about the development of this kind of self-awareness. "I had gone from being ignorant of being ignorant to being aware of being aware."[10] This revealing, empowering process is not easy. Yari, a college student, describes what it is like to really let herself go into the "inner world of another person." "It is one of the most active, difficult, and demanding things I do. And yet it is worth it because it is one of the most releasing, healing things that I have any occasion to do."

Gauging the Level of the Playing Field

On the surface, this area of development does not appear to relate to communication. What do concepts such as status and inequality have to do with language? Ask yourself whether you address your teacher differently than you do a fellow student. What if you were angry? Would you show that anger differently? As an employee, do you communicate any differently with your coworkers than with your supervisor? The relationship between the speaker and the receiver influences communication. One aspect of this relationship is status and power. **Status** refers to one's position. **Power** is the ability to influence people. Our interaction with others takes the form of an equal or unequal status relationship. In the classroom, an unequal status relationship exists between teachers and their students. Simply put, teachers have more authority because of their position. In another setting, this relationship might change and so might the communication between teacher and student. (see Diversity Box: Communication on the Court and in the Classroom).

▓ COMMUNICATION ON THE COURT AND IN THE CLASSROOM

As a new, young instructor teaching sociology at a predominantly black college, I remember numerous times when I was the only white person. This often occurred when I walked into a classroom, ate in the cafeteria, or worked out at the gym. One day, I remember going over to the gym to play some basketball. There were pickup games at each of the six baskets. I was the only white person in the gym. No one knew me since I had only been teaching a few weeks and none of my students were present. When there was a break in the action, I started to take some shots at one of the baskets. Someone suggested that we pick sides. I got picked last. After a few minutes, I heard someone yell, "Hey, white boy!" Obviously, it was not difficult to figure who was being singled out by that comment. I tried to ignore it but he kept repeating "Hey, white boy!" "Hey, white boy!"

I still remember that day as if it was yesterday. Even though I was 24 years old, it was the first time in my life I can remember my race being held against me. This experience also helped me understand the different dynamics on the basketball court and in the classroom. On the court, we were pretty much equals, especially since the other players assumed that I was just another student. Our age, class, and lifestyle did not matter. The student who called me "white boy" was treating me like he would any other young adult white male. Once in the classroom, however, the relationship as well as the communication changed. It was considerably more difficult to be open and honest because I was the teacher and they were the students. This was particularly evident when we talked about controversial and emotional issues such as race and social inequality. There was an unwritten script that each of us followed. Consequently, it was difficult for us to be spontaneous and communicate our true feelings.

journal
entry

A college professor refers to his secretary as "hon," which is short for "honey." He views this as a loving, affectionate term. She considers it demeaning and disrespectful. Nevertheless, she has never told him how she feels about being called "hon," perhaps because the professor is her boss. Do you think it is appropriate to address anyone in this manner in the workplace? Why or why not?

Differences in power and status can be an obstacle to effective communication. With effective communication, the receiver interprets the message just as the sender intends. Those with less power are often ignored during the communication process. For example, we tend to listen and assign more importance to what an adult says than to what a child says. In the classroom, we want to know what the teacher thinks is important. What students say typically carries less weight. Students who sense they lack power may feel that their input is not as important. However, everybody has something important to offer. Take advantage of opportunities to hear and learn from others, regardless of their credentials or titles.

One technique used in diversity training is to instruct people in a group to completely ignore each other's titles and degrees. The idea is to focus on the message rather than the messenger. Although this technique sounds promising, it is extremely difficult to put into practice in everyday life. Actually, children are more effective communicators in this sense. Unlike adults, they do not get so caught up with the trappings of power.

Every opinion, every voice deserves to be heard. And it is a rare gift indeed to hear voices that are so very different from my own.

—A student's perspective

Checking Up on Yourself

The problem with communication is the illusion that it has been accomplished.

—George Bernard Shaw

Effective communication requires constant practice and self-examination. To improve our communication skills, we need to be open to *feedback*—people's responses to us. Otherwise, we do not know when we are relating well to others.

What letter grade would you give yourself for your ability to communicate in a multicultural setting? Why?

Despite our knowledge and sensitivity, misunderstandings will occur. Often, we are not even aware of a problem. Therefore, it is important to ask constantly for feedback from others. To illustrate, Michelle, a study group leader, uses several techniques to ensure that she is not simply "talking at" students in her group. As much as possible, she engages each student in a dialogue. She focuses on their body language as well as what they say. Furthermore, she is learning to provide more and more wait time. This encourages more thorough and thoughtful questions and answers from a larger number of people.

In any given situation, ask probing questions of yourself. This enables us to go deeper and examine what messages we send and receive. However, try not to get so caught up with analyzing yourself that it interferes with your ability to listen. Think through the following questions:

1. *Am I considering my entire audience?* This includes people who will hear the message either directly or indirectly. At work, for example, your supervisor may eventually receive your message through someone else. Consider the personal and cultural characteristics of your entire audience. Also, think about how much they know and how they may feel about the subject matter.

2. *What is the situation?* What influences outside and within this particular setting might have an impact on communication? What cultural differences may exist? Is the setting formal or informal? Elijah Cummings, a U.S. congressman, talks about how he communicates differently depending on the situation. When he is in the halls of Congress, he uses what some might refer to as "paycheck" or "edited" English. But when he is back home, he communicates more informally.

3. *What options are available to me?* In other words, what form or forms of communication might I use? Your message might be written, oral, visual, or a combination of these.

4. *What is the specific purpose of the communication?* Perhaps the purpose you have in mind is not shared by others. As an example, Westerners tend to emphasize the end product of communication, the message. On the other hand, many Asians place more importance on being together and getting to know each other.

5. *What feedback am I receiving regarding the messages being sent (content) and how they are sent (style)?* Tone of voice, volume, pauses, facial expressions, and gestures can be just as meaningful as words themselves.

6. *What might I do differently to communicate more effectively?* For example, what can I do to listen more actively? How can I communicate more inclusively? Toward the end of this chapter, some specific suggestions are offered.

7. *Am I using language that might be viewed as offensive?* Sometimes offensive terms or phrases, called *hot buttons*, impair communication. Hot buttons are discussed in more detail later in this chapter.

A friend of mine at work told me a story about how she was home alone and two black guys came to the door selling something. Later I started wondering why she felt she had to use the word black.

In my work environment, I work with people of many cultures. When I don't understand what is being said or what is meant, I ask questions to make sure that I understand instead of assuming.

—Students' perspectives

Following Through

Many educators and businesspersons encourage us to communicate in a variety of styles. A teacher who is very task-oriented might find that her relationship with students improves if she engages in a little chitchat before the start of class. An employee might experiment with different ways of listening. For example, he might try to give more feedback when others are talking. He might find that nodding his head, using facial expressions, and making "listening noises" such as "hmmm" and "oh" allow him to show others that he does care. Constant practice allows people to develop and refine their communication skills.

THE IMPORTANCE OF COMMUNICATION

As students, you observe the value of good communication skills on a regular basis. Why do you like some teachers more than others? Most teachers are well liked because they "know their stuff" and they relate well to students. Relating well has to do with communication skills.

When people talk about the power of communication, what does that mean? Think of the last time you:

- *Heard a dynamic and charismatic speaker address a large audience.* The message conveyed by that person will probably remain with you for the rest of your life.
- *Had an extremely difficult time communicating with someone who is very close and important to you.* How did that make you feel? How did that affect your relationship?
- *Were part of a team whose members could not communicate very well.* How did this affect your ability to function as a team?

○ *Felt hurt by what a teacher, student, or administrator said.* This kind of remark can poison your relationship with someone. At the very least, it can be difficult to forget. It can also make you view that person or even yourself in a different light.

▓ THE POWER OF LANGUAGE

Even one word can stick with us for a long time. Indeed, it can be the only thing that we remember about an event that took place a long time ago. In the following poem entitled "Incident," the lingering impact of a single word is described by Countee Cullen.

Once riding in old Baltimore,
    heart-filled, head-filled with
    glee,

I saw a Baltimorean keep
    looking straight at me.
Now I was eight and very small,
    and he was no whit bigger,
and so I smiled, but he poked
    out his tongue, and called
    me "nigger."
I saw the whole of Baltimore,
    from May until December;
of all the things that hap-
    pened there that's all that I
    remember."[11]

Words are powerful and have physical impact on the receiver. They assault and abuse if used offensively.

—A student's perspective

To a large degree, your success in all realms of life is dependent on your ability to communicate effectively. Whenever you encounter someone at school or work, you communicate something even if you say nothing. Each encounter poses a challenge. When communication is ineffective, mutual understanding and joint action are highly unlikely. On the other hand, when communication is effective, your chances for relating well are that much greater. Teaming, networking, and learning are easier and more rewarding if you can communicate effectively with different people in all kinds of situations. Consequently, many businesses report a need for employees with good communication skills (see Fig. 5.2, next page).

Once a human being has arrived on this earth, communication is the largest single factor determining what kinds of relationships she or he makes with others and what happens to each in the world.

—Virginia Satir

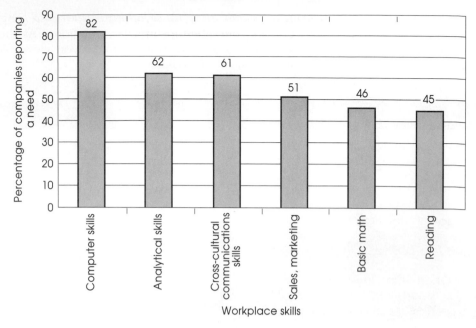

Figure 5.2: *Workplace training skills. This information comes from a survey by the American Society for Training and Development. Companies were asked what kind of training their employees need. Although computer training is what companies cite as most needed, training that targets communication skills ranks high as well.*[12]

■■■■■ BARRIERS TO EFFECTIVE COMMUNICATION

There can be any number of barriers to effective communication, particularly when we communicate across cultures. These barriers include cultural biases, lack of awareness of cultural differences, language differences, ethnocentrism, and inactive listening.

1. *Cultural biases.* In some situations, we make certain unwarranted assumptions about the person or persons with whom we are communicating. In a film on cross-cultural communication, two people are shown interviewing for a job. Both answer the questions in exactly the same way. However, one of the interviewees talks with a noticeable accent. After hearing both interviews, the narrator of the film poses the question, "Who would you hire?" Too often, a person with an accent is assumed to be less intelligent or less qualified.

*Personally, when I have had the occasion of speaking with students
from other cultures I have found myself focusing on how they differed from*

Diversity Consciousness: Opening Our Minds to People, Cultures, and Opportunities

*what I felt normal for me. While focusing on differences, I was really miss-
ing the point of what was being said. I found myself making a judgment on
the person speaking based solely on his culture.*

><Om ><Om ><Om

*Having another language is treated like it's a disease. If you're in
America, it is assumed that you ought to automatically speak THE language—
that is, English.*

—Students' perspectives

2. *Lack of awareness of cultural differences.* If you are communicating
with someone from a different culture, the two of you may interpret the same
symbol differently. Several examples follow.

- ○ What does holding your thumb up mean to you? If you are in the United
  States, most people would probably interpret this gesture to mean
  "okay." However, in another country, you might interpret this differently.
  In his book *Cultural Diversity in the Workplace*, George Henderson
  examines various meanings that people attach to this gesture in different
  parts of the world.[13] In Japan, it means money. In Ghana and Iran, it is
  a vulgar gesture, similar to raising the middle finger in the United States.

- ○ When a teacher asks a question of the entire class and there is a long
  period of silence, what does this mean to you? Does it make you feel
  uncomfortable? In most college classrooms, silence is viewed as something to fill up. This is a reflection of our cultural upbringing.
  According to George Henderson, many Native American cultures
  admire a person who has the ability to remain silent. Many Asian students learn to listen to what is not said as well as to what is said. Zen
  Buddhism, which is influential in many parts of Asia, reinforces this
  lesson. According to a Zen proverb, "He who knows does not speak
  and he who speaks does not know."

- ○ During an argument, how do you feel when other students all try to talk
  at once? In *Aspects of Ethnicity: Understanding Differences in Pluralistic
  Classrooms*, Wilma Longstreet describes how different students react
  during a heated debate in a seminar.[14] When a number of black students start talking at the same time, the rest of the class remains quiet.
  After a few minutes, the black students appear angry. They want to
  know why the rest of the class is no longer talking. The white students
  explain that they are waiting for their turn in the discussion. Meanwhile,
  the Asian students express a need to think and reflect for a moment
  before talking.

3. *Language differences.* Communicating in an unfamiliar language can be
challenging. For example, some businesses cater to customers who speak a
variety of languages. When people try to communicate in a language other than

their own, the results can be amusing. The following attempts to communicate in English did not come across as intended:

- ○ "Our wines leave you nothing to hope for." (from a restaurant menu in Switzerland)
- ○ "Ladies are requested not to have children at the bar." (from a bar in Norway)
- ○ "Fur coats made for ladies from their own skins." (from a Swedish furrier)[15]

4. *Ethnocentrism.* Ethnocentrism shows itself in the language we use. When we talk about the *cultural deprivation* of a group of people, what does this mean? This once commonly used term implies more than just difference. According to this label, anyone who does not share a certain way of life is assumed to be at a disadvantage. Another example of ethnocentric language is the way we fail to differentiate between *arrival* and *discovery*. A few years ago, many people celebrated the 500th anniversary of Columbus's *discovery* of the "New World." This touched off a heated public debate because Native Americans lived here long before Columbus *arrived* in 1492.

5. *Inactive listening.* Poor listening skills can make it much harder to communicate across cultural boundaries. Listening intently and actively helps to overcome misunderstandings and maximize effective communication. Later in this chapter, we examine specific skills that promote active listening.

▪▪▪▪ HOT BUTTONS

I was grocery shopping one day when an elderly woman called me a "nigger." All of the hate and venom was there. I didn't know what to do. I thought of going to the manager and demanding that he do something. But what could he do? I wanted the world to stop and pay attention to me because I had just been assaulted! I did my shopping in stunned, confused, and angry silence. Now I am sorry I didn't tell management in the store this happened while I was buying their groceries. I may not have gotten validation, but I would not have kept it quiet.

—A student's perspective

Hot buttons refer to language that triggers negative reactions from people who view it as insulting and derogatory. Hot buttons are not the same for everyone. What is insulting and derogatory to one student might be perfectly acceptable to another. Similarly, a supervisor might consider a sexist joke "just playing around" or "part of the territory." An employee might view that same joke as threatening, serious, and possibly grounds for a lawsuit.

For some, the issue of hot buttons is one more example of *political correctness* being taken too far. There are those in the workplace who complain that they feel like they are "walking on eggshells" all the time. They maintain that they cannot be themselves. Others make the point we are simply talking about being respectful of others. Regardless of where you stand on this issue, it is important to understand how powerful language is. Saying something offensive can jeopardize communication and create mistrust and hostility.

Good intentions are not enough. A fellow teacher shared with me how his students became visibly upset in class when he referred to a few of them as "you people." He was completely taken aback by their reaction. After all, he did not mean anything negative by it. He explained "you people" was directed at certain students who did poorly on a test; it was meant to motivate them to do better. Only later did he find out the negative connotations of this hot button. Some students said it made them feel inferior and different. One student compared it to being called "you dog" or "you good-for-nothing."

No matter how hard we try, periodically, each of us will use language that may take the form of a hot button. It is important to learn from our mistakes and accept responsibility for what we say and do.

Using appropriate language is not something we can easily turn on and off. It always helps to think things through before and after communicating. For instance, change a key word in a phrase and see if it still applies. Suppose that you read an article about "*the* gay lifestyle." Ask yourself, would it make sense to talk about "*the* heterosexual lifestyle?" Someone might consider the phrase "I don't think of you as Latino" a compliment. Change it. Would someone say "I don't think of you as White?"

Another point to consider is the history of a phrase or the context in which it is used. Comparing a hard-driving boss to a slave driver serves to trivialize a period of history that is very painful to some. This same kind of reasoning may apply to fans mimicking "tomahawk chops" and "war chants" at sports events. Whether these actions honor or slight Native Americans is currently the subject of much debate.

Another example is marketing. Sports teams have adopted names and mascots such as Redskins, Redmen, or Red Raiders (see Fig. 5.3). Because of efforts by Native American activists, many of these teams at the high school and college level have changed their names. This controversy is by no means limited to sports teams. A case in point is a company in New York that sells a malt liquor under the name Crazy Horse. The bottle features a Native American in headdress. While the makers of this product argue they are simply capitalizing on a clientele that identifies with the "Old West," others feel that it is one more example of how Native Americans have been dishonored and dehumanized throughout American history. One state lawmaker, who tried to ban Crazy Horse malt liquor in Minnesota, suggests that this debate illustrates a double standard. "Everybody would understand how insulting it would be to have, say, a Martin Luther King Jr. dark ale or a Golda Meir dark stout. But when it comes to Native Americans, somehow it's a different thing."[16]

JUNEAU JEWS
OREGON ORIENTALS
NIAGARA NEGROES
ARKANSAS ARABS
LOUISVILLE LATINOS
CLEVELAND INDIANS

Figure 5.3: *(By permission from the Los Angeles Times Syndicate.)*

journal entry

THINKING THROUGH DIVERSITY:
How do you feel when fans mimic "war chants" and "tomahawk chops" at sports events?

What Not to Say

In the early 1970s, Sheila Rush and Chris Clark authored the book *How to Get Along with Black People*. The authors cited a number of clichés that were extremely objectionable to Blacks. Interestingly, many of these clichés are still commonplace today.

- "What do you people want?..."
  Rush and Clark: "It assumes that Blacks must want something different from what white people want." When used in this context, the word *you* can be seen as degrading and dehumanizing.
- "A credit to his race..."
  Rush and Clark: "The phrase assumes that Blacks need crediting or something to balance their dark doom. To become a 'credit,' one must be compliant." It is also interesting to note when this phrase is or is not used. Have you ever heard a white male referred to as a credit to his race?
- "It's for your own good..."
  Rush and Clark: "It implies that Blacks don't know their own best interests—and that's insulting." This comment is frequently directed at women, too.
- "But the Irish (Jews, Italians, Cubans) did it, why can't you?..."
  Rush and Clark: "The implication, of course, is that if Blacks had worked harder, their fate would have been different....No group ever worked harder in the service of building America. (Remember slavery?) So why are Blacks still 'last'? For all but the fairest Blacks, the possibility of melting in the great American pot did not exist. Blacks could never get lost in the crowd..."[17]

◼ DIFFICULT DIALOGUES

I remember the day O.J. was acquitted. That same day, I had called a local radio station. A conservative talk show was on. The only thing I wanted to say was that until black people and white people, or just people in general, start talking there will always be racism. I was really upset and the talk show host made a fool out of me on the radio. For days after that, he made comments about me...like "her name's Utopia (he didn't think that was my real name); she must live in a utopia."

I cried that whole weekend. On Monday I went to school. I attended a predominantly white school. In most of my classes, I was the only Black. I remember walking into class and sharing with them what happened to me. I then said "I don't know if white people don't understand or they don't want to understand." I was just sitting there crying and that was the first time they all paid attention to me and listened to everything I had to say. That was the first day I felt I made a breakthrough with white people. I realized that it's possible that we can communicate, we can talk, and we can listen. Maybe not necessarily always agree but respect what each other has to say. That was the first year I even allowed myself to have white friends.

—A student's perspective

Difficult dialogues are sometimes necessary. If we handle them well, these kinds of discussions can bring issues out into the open and "clear the air." A study cited earlier illustrates the importance of dealing with student concerns about prejudice and discrimination. Of those minority students surveyed at five colleges in the eastern United States, one-fourth said that acts motivated by prejudice interfere with their ability to study.[18] If one considers co-victimization, the numbers are apt to be much higher. **Co-victimization** means that you can feel the pain of victimization even if people do not attack or victimize you directly. Anyone who has been through difficult times with a good friend knows how their lives are affected as well.

Despite the importance of opening up and engaging in difficult dialogues, people rarely do it. This is the case in classrooms, offices, and even on a national level. According to Cornel West, author of *Race Matters*, our society has never had an open and honest discussion about race.[19] The same can be said about other diversity issues. When a group of college students were asked to explain why these kinds of dialogues are so rare, they offered the following perspectives.

I don't want to be told that I'm the cause of someone else's pain and suffering.

Many people fear that if they open up and share their innermost feelings, they will be called racist, sexist, or homophobic.

People are afraid that they're going to say something that is really going to demoralize another person or demoralize themselves.

People fear being perceived as a complainer. They fear that their concerns won't be addressed, that people won't listen.

I don't want something I've said to be taken the wrong way.

—Students' perspectives

Some of the reasons for the lack of dialogue may have more to do with the social setting than with the person. According to a report entitled *Racial Issues on Campus: How Students View Them*, many college students cite a lack of opportunity to voice their concerns. Many of these students, who attended 20 predominantly white and 20 predominantly black campuses, felt a sense of alienation and isolation. They had concerns about campus climate and personal experiences but few formal opportunities to address them.[20]

Often we reserve difficult dialogues for friends and family. This is because we feel that we know and trust them. In all likelihood, we will not risk opening up elsewhere unless we also feel a certain level of trust. However, the development of trust requires considerable time and effort. In my classes, my students and I have worked very hard to get to the point where we can talk about race, gender, social class, and other issues related to sociology. This process starts on the first day of class with each of us sharing some of our personal background. Our comfort level with diversity increases as we discuss its relevance throughout the semester. Although students do not always agree, they learn to respect each other's opinions.

In my classroom, we use the following nine ground rules, particularly when we engage in difficult dialogues.

Nine Ground Rules for Difficult Dialogues

1. If someone pushes a "hot button" of yours, it's okay to let the group know what it is and how it makes you feel.
2. Be as open and honest as you feel you can be. Try to move outside your comfort zone.
3. Respect each person's right to be heard.
4. Realize that we are all teachers and learners.
5. Be an active participant. Remember that we participate in different ways.

6. Listen even when you do not want to listen.

7. Do not judge another person's feelings.

8. Focus on the behavior rather than the person.

9. Do not ask people to be spokespersons for their groups.

People don't get along because they fear each other. People fear each other because they don't know each other. They don't know each other because they have not properly communicated with each other.

—Martin Luther King, Jr.

COMMUNICATING INCLUSIVELY

There is a growing body of literature on multicultural or inclusive communication. As the world grows smaller and our society becomes more diverse, employers will increasingly view people who lack skills in this area as liabilities. Communicating in a way that makes people feel included rather than excluded is not a lesson that can be taught in a matter of minutes. It requires commitment and practice. The following 11 strategies provide a good starting point. Rather than focus on all of these at once, it might be helpful to focus on one or two strategies at a time.

1. *Address people the way they want to be addressed.* Many Native Americans identify with their tribal background. Consequently, they may prefer being called Navaho or Sioux rather than Native Americans. Do not judge a person's preference. Simply respect it. Also, keep in mind that different people within a group may want to be addressed differently.

2. *Keep an open mind.* People can view the same thing differently. Be open to the "different lens" through which people view the world. Also, be willing to question your own assumptions and learn from the feedback you receive from others.

3. *Listen actively.* Active listening skills require practice (see Diversity Box: Active Listening Skills Checklist). Often, we are so intent on getting our point across that we do not listen to what others are saying to us. Pay careful attention to what people are saying and how they are saying it. For instance, we can learn something from inflections in a person's voice, and even from pauses. Remember to focus on body language. According to research, most of what we communicate during a conversation is nonverbal.

⊞ ACTIVE LISTENING SKILLS CHECKLIST

- Do you listen intently even when you disagree with someone?
- Do you listen intently even when you have a difficult time understanding someone?
- Do you hear only what you want to hear?
- Are you aware of verbal and nonverbal messages?

- Do you restate, summarize, and question to promote understanding?
- Do you provide positive feedback through body language and "listening noises"?
- Do you give people time to respond?
- Are you just quiet sometimes?

4. *Check understanding.* Instead of assuming that someone understands you, assume just the opposite. Ask questions that might pinpoint possible problems. "Is this clear?" "Do I need to explain further?" "What do you think I have been saying up to this point?" Repeat these questions continuously. When you are the receiver of information, ask questions, too. "Is that idea like...?" "Are you suggesting that...?" "Can you give me an example of...?"

5. *Do some research.* Businesspersons who are traveling abroad or venturing into unfamiliar markets at home often ignore this sort of preparation. The Internet can provide a wealth of current information. College libraries or ethnic organizations in your community may be other valuable resources.

General Motors is one company that did not do its homework. When the Chevy Nova was introduced in South America, the company could not explain the car's sluggish sales. Eventually, General Motors was forced to change the name of the model to Caribe after finding out that "No va" means "it doesn't go" in Spanish. Another company, Coors, discovered too late that its slogan "Turn It Loose," when translated into Spanish, meant the beer that would make you "Get the Runs."

6. *Think through what you are going to say before you say it.* When you talk about others, do you refer to them by their race, ethnic background, social class, gender, or some other distinguishing characteristic? If so, ask yourself why.

7. *Avoid slang.* Telling someone that she has "phat" clothing can lead to misunderstanding. To my teenage daughter, it means awesome or good. To one of my colleagues at work, it might mean something insulting.

8. *Avoid ethnic jokes.* This is a serious matter, especially in the workplace and at school. To some, ethnic jokes or ethnic humor in general may be acceptable. This is particularly true of self-directed ethnic humor. However, you cannot assume or predict that people will interpret something the same way you do. Jokes are usually made at the expense of others. Think through how you should react if someone decides to tell an ethnic joke in your presence.

9. *Use as many different styles of communication as possible.* Visual aids can help. You might want to write something down or spell difficult words if simply saying something does not seem to be working. If you do not understand what someone is saying, do not simply smile and nod your head. Let them know politely.

10. *Do not assume that you can or should ignore differences.* The problem lies in the value judgments we attach to individual or cultural differences, not in the differences themselves. For example, noticing someone's accent does not make you prejudiced. Having negative thoughts about the accent does.

The poem "For the White Person Who Wants to Know How to Be My Friend" suggests how we should and should not respond to cultural differences.

> *The first thing you do is to forget that I'm black.*
> *Second, you must never forget that I'm black.*
> *You should be able to dig Aretha,*
> *but don't play her every time I come over.*
> *And if you decide to play Beethoven—don't tell me*
> *his life story. They make us take music appreciation too.*

—Pat Parker[21]

Acknowledge each other's differences and move past them; just don't move too fast.

—A instructor's perspective

11. *Be conscious of how fast you are talking.* If you were raised in one region of the United States and now live in another, you may know how difficult it is to adjust to differences in pronunciation and terminology. Generally, it helps to slow down a little. Repeat yourself if necessary.

In this chapter we have addressed the importance of effective communication. Moreover, we have examined the interrelationship of diversity consciousness and communication. Communication is a diversity skill that we learn, develop, and refine throughout the course of our lives. As we become more conscious of diversity, our communication skills will improve. This will open up a myriad of possibilities and opportunities in our ever-changing world.

Exercises

IN-CLASS

Exercise 1: Active Listening

Directions for Instructor.
Divide students into pairs. One student in each pair tells the other student about a problem at school or work that he or she is experiencing. The problem should not be too complex. The time limit is 1 minute. The listener may ask for clarification but cannot say anything else. In addition, the listener may use "listening noises" or body language. Notes may not be taken. After the speaker finishes, the listener gives feedback on exactly what he or she heard. When necessary, the speaker can correct and help the listener remember exactly what was said. Repeat this process with the listener and speaker exchanging parts.

Analysis. What did you learn from this experience? Were you more comfortable taking on the role of the speaker or the listener? Why? Did you have a difficult time tuning in and remembering what your partner said? If you did this again, what might you do differently to be a better listener?

Exercise 2: Responding to Hot Buttons

Directions for Instructor.
Form groups of three to four students. Ask students to read the following five scenarios. Each group member should then pick one scenario and act out how he or she would respond. Afterward, the group discusses the appropriateness and effectiveness of each student's response, using the "Nine Ground Rules for Difficult Dialogues" (see pages 150–151).

○ You are at work. Your boss calls you "honey," but you prefer that he call you by your first name or as Ms._____(last name). You explain this to your boss as tactfully as possible, but he laughs it off. You don't want to offend your boss, but you don't feel that he understands how strongly you feel about this. How do you respond?

○ You are a middle-aged male who works in an office. A co-worker whose desk is next to yours makes a habit of cornering you one-on-one and sharing his latest joke. Most of the jokes are aimed at women and have sexual overtones. Initially, you try to humor him but you are growing increasingly uncomfortable with this situation. You try to avoid this person, but it is not working. You feel that you must say something to him or your supervisor. How do you respond?

○ You are at a party with a group of students that you do not know really well. You are watching a professional football game and one of the students makes a racist remark about one of the players. No one laughs but nothing is said. How do you respond?

○ You and your friend are using the photocopying machine in the library. You accidentally copy the wrong material. Your friend, realizing the mistake that you just made, says: "You're such a retard." How do you respond?

○ You and 40 co-workers are participating in a "diversity workshop." After lunch, the workshop facilitator divides the participants into smaller groups. She then asks group members to discuss any prejudices they might have. Midway through the exercise, one member of your group complains: "This discussion is a waste of my time. I don't see color. I'm colorblind." How do you respond?

OUT-OF-CLASS

Exercise 1: Ethnic Jokes

Imagine that you and other employees at work correspond by e-mail. You have just received the following message on your computer:

> This one was priceless...I'm still laughing. Enjoy! This is a letter from a Cajun mother to her Cajun son:
>
> Dear Son,
>
> I'll try not to write too fast because I know you read kinda slow. After you got married and moved out of our home, we decided we had to do likewise. Your pa read somewhere that most accidents happen within 20 miles of our home. We figured we didn't want to take a chance. I won't be able to send you our new address for a while. The Cajun family that used to live here took the numbers off the house when they moved. I guess they didn't want to have to change their address.
>
> You know the coat we were going to send to you. I still have it. Yesterday, I put it in a package, put some stamps on it, and took it to the Post Office. They told me that they couldn't send it because there was not enuff postage. They said it was too heavy. So I've decided to remove the heavy buttins on the coat so that the package won't weigh so much. I'll bring the buttins with me next time we visit you. And I'll try to remember to bring you some new shoes. I get worried about you walking around in bear feet all the time. You can save these shoes and use them if your feet wear out.
>
> Just wanted to let you know that your Uncle Tom is no longer with us. He accidentally fell in a vat full of whiskey. Two men who saw what happened tried to pull him out but he couldn't bring himself to stop drinking. He wouldn't come up for air and ended

up drowning. When the coroner cremated him, he ended up burning for days because of all that alcohol in him.

Say hi to your wife for me and pa.

Love, Ma

After reading this, you decide to respond by sending an e-mail message to the sender of this joke. Type your response.

Exercise 2: Creating an Action Plan

Imagine that you are the director of student affairs at a small liberal arts college in the Midwest. During a staff meeting, the president of the college shares a number of complaints from gay students. The complaints allege that many gay students encounter prejudice and discrimination both on campus and among townspeople. The students feel that these problems are college-wide and need to be addressed by the president and her staff as well as by community leaders.

The president asks you to create an action plan. She feels that the college needs to open the lines of communication and encourage an open and honest dialogue on this issue. Develop a two-page typewritten summary of what you propose. Include the rationale behind your action plan.

 INTERNET ASSIGNMENT

1. Go to an Internet job search Web site such as www.careers.com or www.helpwanted.com. Using the Web site's search feature, find jobs related to your present or future career. Then find job descriptions that specify communication skills you will need. Print at least three of these job descriptions.

2. Write a paragraph summarizing what you found.

NOTES

[1]Roger E. Axtell, *Gestures: The Do's and Taboos of Body Language Around the World* (New York: Wiley, 1991), 10.

[2]Alice Reid, "Mosque's Children Await Playground," *The Washington Post*, Nov. 22, 1998, B4.

[3]Deborah Tannen, *You Just Don't Understand: Men and Women in Conversation* (New York: William Morrow, 1990); *Talking from 9 to 5: How Women's and Men's Conversational Styles Affect Who Gets Heard, Who Gets Credit, and What Gets Done at Work* (New York: William Morrow, 1994); *That's Not What I Meant* (New York: Ballantine Books, 1992).

[4]Oliver Sacks, *Seeing Voices: A Journey into the World of the Deaf* (Berkeley, CA: University of California Press, 1989), 127.

[5]Glenn McNatt, "Instant Communication Is Changing Our Very Form of Government," *The Sun*, Feb. 9, 1997, 5E.

[6]L. Sproull and S. Kiesler, *Connections: New Ways of Working in the Networked*

Organization (Cambridge, MA: MIT Press, 1991), 61.

[7]Shirley Brice Heath, *Ways with Words* (Cambridge: Cambridge University Press, 1983).

[8]Raymond Bingham, "Leaving Prejudice Behind," *The Washington Post Health Section*, Sept. 6, 1994, 9.

[9]D. Knox and C. Schacht, *Choices in Relationships* (Belmont, CA: Wadsworth, 1997), 134–135.

[10]Maya Angelou, *I Know Why the Caged Bird Sings* (New York: Bantam Books, 1993).

[11]Countee Cullen (ed.), *Caroling Dusk* (Secaucus, NJ: Carol Publishing Group, 1993), 187.

[12] Kristin Downey Grimsley, "Training in the Theater of the Real," *The Washington Post Business Section*, Mar. 24, 1997, 12.

[13]George Henderson, *Cultural Diversity in the Workplace: Issues and Strategies* (Westport, CT: Praeger Publishers, 1994).

[14]Wilma Longstreet, *Aspects of Ethnicity: Understanding Differences in Pluralistic Classrooms* (Williston, VT: Teacher's College Press, 1978).

[15]Charles Goldsmith, "Look See! Anyone Do Read This and It Will Make You Laughable," *The Wall Street Journal*, Nov. 19, 1992, B1.

[16]Michael Fletcher, "Crazy Horse Again Sounds Battle Cry," *The Washington Post*, Feb. 18, 1997, A03.

[17]Sheila Rush and Chris Clark, *How to Get Along with Black People*, copyright ©1972, Third Press, Joseph Okpaku Publishing Co., Inc., reprinted by permission of Okpaku Communications Corporation, New Rochelle, NY.

[18]Howard Ehrlich, *Campus Ethnoviolence: A Research Review*, Institute Report 5 (Baltimore: National Institute Against Prejudice and Violence, 1992), 8.

[19]Cornel West, *Race Matters* (New York: Vintage Books, 1993).

[20]Ansley Abraham, *Racial Issues on Campus: How Students View Them* (Atlanta, GA: Southern Regional Education Board, 1990).

[21]Pat Parker, *Movement in Black* (Ithaca, NY: Firebrand Books, 1978), 68.

6  TEAMWORK

Upon completion of this chapter, you will be able to:

○ Explain the importance of **teams** today.

○ Explain the relationship between **teamwork** and success.

○ Discuss the meaning and challenges of **virtual teaming**.

○ Define **leadership**.

○ List strategies for building high-performance teams.

○ List and give examples of obstacles to teamwork.

○ Define **conflict** and **conflict management**.

○ List and briefly explain the approaches to conflict management.

The scene: *You are a surgeon in a hospital emergency room in a large city. A patient arrives by ambulance. He is a young child who appears to have a disability. The child's breathing is heavy and he has a fever of 104 degrees. Because he is so anxiety-ridden, he can hardly talk. He seems to be complaining about his stomach. His parents, who recently immigrated from Cambodia, are unable to say more than a few words in English. The doctor who is the resident in charge is a Filipino woman born in the United States in 1940. The anesthesiologist is multiracial and hearing impaired. In a few minutes, the radiologist will arrive. She is an African-American woman who plans on retiring in a few months. Also present is the registered nurse, a 29-year-old of German and French descent, and a nursing assistant, a young Nigerian man who just completed his education. You and other members of this team must deal with this emergency.*

▬▬ TEAMS TODAY

The multicultural setting described above requires people from vastly different backgrounds to work as a high-performing team in a pressure-packed situation. If each of these health professionals is not committed to the team and to the task at hand, their effectiveness as a group will be undermined seriously. Additionally, each professional needs to be able to relate effectively to people who have different beliefs, communication styles, learning styles, educational levels, and cultural backgrounds. Situations like this, which require working together in the midst of diversity, are commonplace today (see Fig. 6.1).

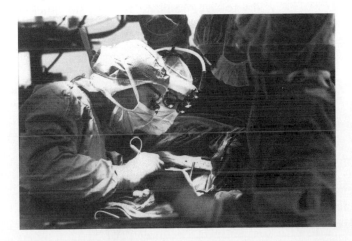

Figure 6.1: *Surgical team at Johns Hopkins Hospital. Their ability to work together under pressure can mean the difference between life and death. (Courtesy of the Office of Communications and Public Affairs, Johns Hopkins Medical Institutions, Baltimore.)*

Most people think of sports when teams are mentioned. However, athletics is only one of many areas in which you find teams. A **team** is simply a number of people who are involved in a cooperative effort. Each of us belongs to many teams. Sometimes we are put on teams and have no choice in the matter. At other times, we may join voluntarily or even create new teams. Your professor might put you on a team in class. As a college student, you may choose to form study groups or join support groups. These groups also constitute teams. You may be asked to join a variety of groups, such as those dealing with student government or your academic major. Additionally, there are numerous teams in the workplace and in the community. These teams might focus on your responsibilities at work, recreational interests, and community activities. The key thing to remember is that you cannot avoid teams—they are part of everyday life.

People have a tendency to want to work with people who are similar to them. However, most teams are made up of individuals who are different in any number of ways. As stated repeatedly in this book, diversity means more than differences in race and gender. When talking about teams in the workplace, the concept of diversity includes many other differences, such as age, personality, learning style, leadership style, job position, and tenure. Your success on any job-related team will depend in part on your ability to relate to all kinds of people. As a team player, you will be able to contribute more. You and your organization will reap the benefits.

Interest in teamwork has grown significantly in recent years. Organizations are becoming more team oriented, flexible, and collaborative. Businesses are using teams to improve marketing, customer service, and productivity. Employees who worked by themselves are now being organized into teams. The composition of these teams is also becoming more diverse. As businesses reorganize, restructure, and downsize, people increasingly find themselves on teams with others who differ markedly in terms of their employment and educational backgrounds. Because of demographic changes, cross-cultural work groups are becoming the norm rather than the exception.

Technology and globalization are also altering the composition of teams. Technological advances are making it possible for teams to overcome geographical barriers in an instant. The ability to communicate clearly and quickly and to work together from anywhere in the world at any time provides teams with a distinct competitive advantage.

One hand cannot applaud alone.

—Arabian proverb

Teamwork at School

Teamwork, the coordinated effort by members of a team working toward a common goal, has been found to be an effective way of improving academic achievement. It has been shown that studying in teams can improve your grades. At the University of California, many freshmen, especially African-American and Latino students, were having difficulty with the calculus course for engineering, math, and physics majors. These students who were struggling with calculus were generally hard-working, highly motivated, and smart. A wide range of remedial programs and tutorial services were provided, but none of them worked.

Uri Treisman, a faculty member, identified the students who were having problems. He surveyed faculty and interviewed students and their families. He discovered that these students were generally "academic loners," meaning that they struggled with calculus by themselves. On the other hand, groups with higher grades, such as the Cantonese-speaking students, studied differently. They regularly studied two to three hours each day by themselves *and* then studied in groups to tackle more difficult problems.

Using this approach, a model program was created for all students which was eventually adopted by many other colleges. Students in need of help were still given difficult problems to solve. They were instructed to solve as many problems as possible on their own. When they got stuck, they were expected to solve the problems in small groups. Also, they were asked to explain their solutions to other members of their study group so that everyone could understand.

The grades at the end of the semester indicate that students who study in groups do much better than those who do not. Those in study groups are more apt to stay in school and not drop out. Why? Working on teams enables students to spend more time practicing how to solve problems. Students also know that they need to understand the problems completely in order to teach other students. These students, working in small groups, could motivate and support each other, move at their own speed, and relate to each other.[1]

Besides increasing student achievement, numerous studies show that teamwork among students is one of the most effective ways of breaking down cultural barriers. In one research study, students were asked to name six of their friends at school. Those in traditional classes, which emphasized competition rather than cooperation among students, named 10 percent outside of their race. Those in classes that promoted cooperative learning, named 38 percent.[2] Another study by Elliot Aronson illustrates the benefits of a teaming technique called the jigsaw method.

▨ THE JIGSAW METHOD

Elliot Aronson was asked to devise an educational plan that would reduce interracial tensions among students attending public schools in Austin, Texas. Aronson developed a cooperative learning technique, the jigsaw method. Classes were divided into teams of six students. Students in each group were racially and academically mixed. Each day, individuals in each group were assigned one of six subtopics. After learning about

continued

that segment of the lesson, each student taught the other group members. The results showed a decrease in prejudice and an increase in self-esteem among students in the jigsaw groups. The academic test scores of minority students in these groups also improved. What seemed to make a difference was these students had to work and fit together like pieces of a jigsaw puzzle. If they were going to do well on the tests, they had to pay attention and support each other. In the process, they learned not only the subject matter but also some valuable lessons about each other.

Carlos, one of the students in Aronson's study, had learned to be quiet in school because he was not very articulate in English. In his jigsaw group of five students, Carlos' experiences were different. "It began to dawn on the students that the only chance they had to learn about Carlos' segment was by paying attention to what he had to say. If they ignored Carlos or continued to ridicule him, his segment would be unavailable to them and the most they could hope for would be an 80% score on the exam—an unattractive prospect to most...And with that realization, the kids began to develop into pretty good interviewers, learning to pay attention to Carlos, to draw him out, and to ask probing questions. Carlos, in turn, began to relax more and found it easier to explain out loud what was in his head. What the (students) came to learn about Carlos is even more important...they began to appreciate...Carlos. After a few weeks, they noticed talents in him they had not seen before."[3]

Research findings that point to the educational and social benefits of teamwork begin to make sense when we think about the relationships we develop in school. Typically, we learn more about each other in small group settings: an athletic team, a close circle of friends, or maybe a committee of some sort. Our learning increases when we depend on each other. We pay more attention to each person's talents and preoccupy ourselves less with differences that are irrelevant to the purpose of the team.

Politician Jack Kemp often talks about the lessons in human relations that he learned playing quarterback for 13 years in the National Football League (NFL). John Mackey, who played against Kemp, remarked, "the huddle is colorblind." This was just another way of saying that when the quarterback gets in the huddle, the race of his teammates is the last thing on his mind. What matters is whether his offensive linemen, receivers, and running backs do their jobs and keep him from getting sacked or hurt.

Teamwork in the Workplace

Teams, particularly those made up of people from diverse backgrounds, are proliferating in the workplace. The accent on teamwork in the workplace is a surprise to many students. In college, the focus is typically on individual success and competition. According to Judy Blair, Vice President of Recruitment and Career Development for American Management Systems, the teamwork focus "is often an adjustment from school where achievement tends to be individual and aimed at getting the best grade....Although individual contribution matters in the workplace, the teamwork element is also key. Someone may be responsible for a particular aspect of work on a project, but collaboration and cooperation with others on the project is key."[4]

Teamwork is not sold as a technique for promoting human relations. Rather, it is viewed as good business. Many companies utilize **total quality management** (TQM), an approach for continuously improving the performance of every member of an organization. The idea behind TQM is that for organizations to compete effectively, employees must commit to and participate in the effort to improve quality. This includes employees at every level and in all areas of responsibility. One of the principal components of TQM is teamwork and the role it plays in the continuous improvement of a company's product or service. As more and more companies expand globally, teamwork is being sold as a means to increase productivity and profits. The idea of bringing the world closer together through teamwork is an effective marketing strategy. For example, Ford's home page for its Web site champions its worldwide connections, and Boeing refers to itself as "people working together as one global company for aerospace leadership."

Research findings point to the benefits of teamwork. A number of academic studies show teams with members from diverse backgrounds are more creative and innovative. At the University of North Texas, business students were divided into teams for a period of 17 weeks. Teams made up of students who were culturally and racially diverse were pitted without their knowledge against teams who were all White and much less diverse. During the first few weeks, the all-white teams sprinted ahead. But by the end of the competition, the more diverse teams were being more creative and flexible in the way they attacked and solved work-related problems. Larry K. Michaelsen, one of the three professors who conducted the experiment, commented: "Cultural diversity in the U.S. work force has sometimes been viewed as a dark cloud. Our results suggest that it has a silver lining."[5]

Teams are not always necessary or desirable. Some tasks lend themselves to individuals. It may not make sense to form a team if time is a concern and the task is clear-cut and relatively simple. However, many tasks in the workplace are too complex and too demanding for one person. Moreover, some jobs require more cooperation than others. The same is true of sports and other activities. A long-distance truck driver does not need to possess the same teaming skills as a police officer, an airline pilot, or a member of the surgical team mentioned earlier in the chapter.

Employees who hoard information and are unwilling or unable to work together waste time and money. On the other hand, employees who thrive in a work environment of teamwork and information sharing are highly valued. From top management to workers in offices and factories, people who are

Figure 6.2: *The power of synergy. Each year, more than 1000 plebes (freshmen) at the U.S. Naval Academy team up to retrieve a cap placed at the top of the 22-foot Herndon Monument. Since the monument is covered with 200 pounds of lard, it often takes hours for the plebes to scale it. (Courtesy of the Office of Media Relations, U.S. Naval Academy, Annapolis, Md.)*

adept at working in teams can pool their talents and be more productive. This is called **synergy**, the concept that members of a team interacting cooperatively will accomplish much more than if they act alone (see Fig. 6.2). In his book *The Seven Habits of Highly Effective People*, Stephen Covey uses this word to describe a problem-solving approach that is better than compromise. According to Covey, synergy makes it possible for one plus one to equal more than two.[6] Think of a time when you and other people were able to brainstorm about an issue or problem. What you came up with as a group was in all probability more creative and useful than anything originally proposed by a single person.

For years, Ford Motor Company used a straightforward process to design, build, and sell cars. The designers submitted their sketches to the manufacturing departments. The cars were then built and sent on to the sales department. Ford decided that it needed to take a different approach to create a new and competitive midsized car. They put the designers, manufacturers, and salespeople on one team. Each person was asked to describe his or her ideal car and submit a "wish list." The end product of this team effort was the Taurus, one of Ford's best-selling models.

Virtual Teaming

Computer technology is revolutionizing the concept of teaming. In today's world, virtual teams are enabling more people to link together at an accelerating rate. In their book *Virtual Teams*, Lipnack and Stamps contrast conventional and virtual teams. The authors describe a **virtual team** as a group of people that work "across space, time, and organizational boundaries with links strengthened by webs of communication technologies."[7] Virtual teaming allows our individual and group creativity to flourish by enhancing our ability to express ourselves. It can also significantly increase our ability to draw on the talents of a culturally diverse and geographically dispersed group of people. At the same time, the diversity of the group is often difficult to gauge unless it comes out in the course of communication or face-to-face interaction. When we communicate on the Internet, individual characteristics such as appearance, religion, and social class may be kept invisible.

According to research in the field of communications, the physical distance of team members and their use of electronic media can affect relationships. Sproull and Kiesler found that relationships via computers tend to be more democratic.[8] This is particularly true when people communicate anonymously. The message, rather than who is sending it, becomes the focal point. This encourages more input from people with diverse backgrounds and positions. One drawback of virtual teaming is that members tend to ignore each other's individual needs. When communicating from geographically disperse locations, desensitization to the values, goals, and competencies of individuals can occur easily.

Teamwork on a virtual team poses a number of challenges. Everything that can go wrong in a face-to-face team can also be a problem in a virtual team. A lack of trust, miscommunication, and conflict are even more problematic. Unfortunately, a good deal of training dealing with computer technology ignores the interpersonal dynamics of virtual teaming. This reinforces the idea that computers are tools for individuals, not groups. For members of a virtual team to be successful, they need to learn how to share their beliefs, knowledge, and skills. When communicating across distances, keep in mind the following strategies:

1. Share and clarify your group's mission and goals.
2. Openly discuss the challenges of virtual teaming and communication.
3. Be aware of the value of communication with other locations and invite feedback from them.
4. Identify and discuss differences. These differences may be cultural, organizational, or geographic.
5. Take advantage of any opportunities to meet face to face. This will personalize and reinforce relationships.
6. Seek and share knowledge. Do not hoard it. Hoarding delays results and works against synergy.

▣ A VIRTUAL WATER COOLER

American Management Systems (AMS) describes itself as an international business and information technology consulting firm. It has thousands of people working on hundreds of projects in more than 50 offices worldwide. One of the ways in which AMS encourages the sharing of knowledge, experiences, and ideas is through *knowledge centers*. Throughout Europe and North America, there are knowledge centers or virtual AMS communities connected by interest and expertise. Each of these communities has a home page which serves as a "virtual water cooler." As with face-to-face interaction around a water cooler in a traditional office setting, this home page provides the opportunity to chat and exchange knowledge about almost anything. Access to the knowledge centers may begin with a call to the "AMS-Know" hotline. The hotline can answer questions eight times faster than consultants do by themselves. According to Sue Hanley, director of the knowledge centers, the hotline handled about 6000 calls in its first year of operation and saved the company $500,000 in research expenses.[9]

AMS bases its high-tech approach to teamwork on the premise that their collective intellectual capital is more powerful than any one person's knowledge. Hanley says: "Our technology and communities allow us to communicate without regard to geographical boundaries. We are able to leverage the knowledge of a diverse population, people who have interests and expertise in common, but who are often otherwise dissimilar in terms of culture, industry expertise and often language."[10]

DEVELOPING TEAMWORK SKILLS

```
journal
entry
```
THINKING THROUGH DIVERSITY:

Given your plans for the future, how would developing teamwork skills benefit you?

As part of your education, have you been taught how to work with people who commit themselves to a common purpose? Is your education providing you with opportunities to develop and practice teaming skills? Many employers believe that there is a mismatch between the skills that students need when they enter the workforce and those they learn in college. This is particularly true in the area of interpersonal skills. Teaming, teaching others, negotiating, and managing people with diverse backgrounds are essential in today's workplace, although they are not always emphasized in the college classroom.

Interest in training related to teamwork has grown with the realization that working together does not necessarily mean working *together*. Good intentions or even a common purpose are not enough. Nor can we assume that people understand teaming is a process that requires education and experience. A variety of educational and training programs exist to help people learn and develop teamwork skills. Some examples follow:

1. One college program forms teams of engineering and business students to work in the classroom and at job sites on real-life problems. The program is based on the idea that students will be collaborating on teams in the workplace. Many of these teams will be cross-functional, meaning that people with different areas of expertise, backgrounds, and job functions will be working together.

2. Marines, from raw recruits to senior officers, go through a three-day test. The test emphasizes values, morality, and above all, teamwork. Marines are evaluated on their ability to work continuously as a team for 54 hours; they stand or fall as a group.

3. Companies are spending more time and money on team building exercises outside the workplace. In business, programs such as Outward Bound teach the importance of teamwork and communication through physical challenges such as rock climbing and white-water rafting. These experiences help employees see each other without their titles. They also make it necessary to work as a single unit. For example, employees who might not trust each other have to help each other and work together in a rock-climbing exercise. If they do not, someone will get hurt. Ideally, this kind of teamwork will carry over into the workplace.

4. Airlines have crew resource management (CRM) training programs. CRM focuses on promoting teamwork among cockpit crew members by improving their communication. Crews are put through various flight exercises in aircraft simulators. The trainers videotape and analyze the interaction of crew members and their ability to respond to emergency situations. The possibility that a number of airline crashes have resulted from certain commands being misinterpreted or ignored by the captain or the rest of the crew has provided the impetus for such training.

◼◼ DIVERSITY CONSCIOUSNESS AND TEAMING

Diversity consciousness develops over time. As our awareness and understanding of diversity grows, we become better able to deal with team members, who in all likelihood will have a wide variety of values, personalities, behaviors, and talents. Therefore, we are in a position to contribute more to a team.

Every team is diverse. In any team, group members vary in background, knowledge, and attitudes to some degree at least. People may even view the concept of team building differently. What is the role of an effective team member? Does it mean being assertive and outspoken or agreeable and a good listener? Is it necessary to build trusting relationships among members before any action can be taken? Is it OK to "rock the boat" or is maintaining harmony of utmost importance? How you answer these questions may depend on your personality or cultural background or even the setting.

Picture yourself in a class of students. You are put in groups at the beginning of the semester. Prior to each test, time is set aside in class so that each group can review the material. Although some students may prefer to defer to other group members, your instructor has made it clear that she wants everybody to be part of the discussion.

How you respond may have a lot to do with your personality, the way you were raised, your cultural background, and the other people in your group. Some group members may find this experience very traumatic because they are not comfortable in small group settings. A young female, raised to believe that women should be seen but not heard, may struggle with her role in the group. A group member from Japan or Laos might stress the importance of being courteous and cooperative. On the other hand, team members who were born and raised in the United States may be more apt to speak their minds, even if it results in conflict and confrontation.

⊞ CLASSROOM BEHAVIOR AMONG HMONG ADULTS

The Hmong are the largest ethnic minority in Laos. Many Hmong refugees resettle in the United States. When Hmong adults participate in American basic education, their cultural background affects their classroom behavior. Through participant observation, a researcher from the

University of Wisconsin was able to study a class for nonliterate and low-literate Hmong adults.

According to the researcher, these Hmong students view classroom work as a cooperative activity. They are constantly in touch with each other and are hesitant to be singled out as being more able than their peers. The stronger students help the weaker students. Students check each other's books, papers, and worksheets. Interestingly, there is no competition. The researcher observed: "When Mee Hang has difficulty with an alphabetization lesson, Pang Lor explains, in Hmong, how to proceed. Chia Ying listens in to Pang's explanation and nods her head. Pang goes back to work on her own paper, keeping an eye on Mee Hang. When she sees Mee looking confused, Pang leaves her seat and leans over Mee's shoulder. She writes the first letter of each word on the line, indicating to Mee that these letters are in alphabetical order and that Mee should fill in the rest of each word. This gives Mee the help she needs and she is able to finish on her own. Mee, in turn, writes the first letter of each word on the line for Chia Yang, passing on Pang Lor's explanation."[11]

THINKING THROUGH DIVERSITY:

journal entry

When is diversity within a team an asset? When is it a liability?

Diversity is only an asset when team members develop skills to manage the assets and challenges of diversity. By becoming more conscious of diversity, you will improve those skills that are essential for true teamwork; these include communication, conflict management, empathy, self-evaluation, and leadership.

1. *Communication.* Since people process information in different ways, it is important to utilize a variety of communication styles (see Chapter 5). For example, team members may be more productive and creative if they constantly combine visual, verbal, and experiential modes of communication.

2. *Conflict management.* Dealing effectively with conflict requires fundamental skills in interpersonal relations. These skills, which include showing empathy and listening actively, can help team members work through and benefit from conflict. Conflict in groups is discussed in more detail toward the end of this chapter.

3. *Empathy.* Author Stephen Covey views empathy as the most important skill we need for teamwork He argues that all members of a team must really listen and "put themselves in other people's shoes."[12] This skill creates the openness that allows creativity to flourish. It also helps us realize that there is more than one way to accomplish a task.

4. *Self-evaluation.* As a team member, you need to evaluate your performance continually. This is particularly important in self-managed work teams. To use Langer's terminology, replace mindlessness with mindfulness. *Mindlessness* blots out intuition and much of the world around us. *Mindfulness* raises our consciousness and awareness.[13] Although total self-awareness is virtually impossible, ask yourself questions that focus on how you see yourself and others. Such questions might include:

- ❍ Are there parts of myself that I do not share with others?
- ❍ Am I comfortable with myself and other team members?
- ❍ What do I know, think, and feel about team members?
- ❍ How do my emotions, values, and experiences affect my ability to work *with* other team members?
- ❍ How do I handle conflict and change?

5. *Leadership.* **Leadership** refers to the ability to influence group members and enable them to work together and achieve their goals. Increasingly, leadership is expected of all group members rather than a select few. When we learn to accept and share leadership, we are able to facilitate, empower, and bring out the best in everyone. For example, you may show leadership when you fill a particular role in a group. Perhaps you take on an assignment that no one wants. Or maybe you help other members work through conflict that threatens your ability to function as a team.

◼ TEAM LEADERSHIP

As work teams become more global and heterogeneous, leaders will need to develop their diversity consciousness. Moreover, leadership skills are becoming increasingly important for everyone. Employers typically expect workers with widely different job functions and levels of authority to assume leadership roles. As an example, it is not unusual for management to delegate responsibilities to workers, who then organize teams and get the job done with little if any supervision. These are sometimes referred to as *self-managed work teams.*

Many companies have found that self-managed work teams raise product quality and lower employee absenteeism. Suarez Electric Company, one of the fastest-growing Latino-owned companies in the United States, illustrates this kind of shared, team leadership. The owner, David Suarez, divides his workforce into teams. Each team is delegated the responsibility of doing their jobs and *not* accepting mediocrity. At each job site, there are usually one or two leaders. Although Suarez provides minimal supervision, he is always accessible through his pager and cellular phone.

Like other skills related to diversity consciousness, we can learn and develop leadership skills. John Kotter's *The General Managers* is based on his study of the traits of top executives. The author, a professor at Harvard Business School, found that effective leaders are trained and learn to develop their own potential. According to Kotter, the careers of effective general managers are distinguished by almost constant growth in their interpersonal and intellectual skills and in their relationships with "relevant others."[14]

What qualities do you think make a leader effective? This question was asked of a wide cross section of employees in public, private, and academic institutions. Their answers point to specific attitudes and behaviors each of us can develop over time. Based on responses from these employees, a model of effective leadership emerges. In this study, effective leaders are described as "pluralistic" because they are adept at working with many, diverse populations. As pluralistic leaders, they:

- *Are open to change based on input and feedback from the team.* In particular, they are open to diverse views and encourage others to disagree. They value feedback and are not defensive when their opinions are challenged.
- *Empower others.* They have a coaching style that is encouraging rather than conforming. Moreover, they give timely, constructive, and honest feedback.
- *Have a broad knowledge and awareness regarding diversity issues.* They do not wait for others to educate them; rather, they seek out information from a variety of sources. Those surveyed often point to a leader's language as a gauge of personal understanding.
- *"Walk the talk" when it comes to diversity issues.* It is not enough just to say the right thing, they lead by example. A pluralistic leader shows that he or she values diversity by taking a stand and being a catalyst for change.[15]

There is more than one way to be an effective team leader. **Instrumental leaders** tend to focus more on the task at hand and less on how group members get along. **Expressive leaders** take a different approach. Their primary concern is the well-being of group members and their ability to work as a unit. Some leaders are both instrumental and expressive or find that different situations require different approaches.

For example, imagine that you are asked to lead a task force at work. You are given a relatively short period of time to gather information, analyze it, and submit a report to your supervisor. Seven other employees whom you hardly know have also been appointed to work with you. Which type of leader are you going to be in this situation? Given the fact that you need to produce a report quickly, you might prefer to focus on making sure that your team completes its job. However, what if the people on the task force find it difficult to get along with each other? Is this something you can afford to ignore? What about your own personality? Do you feel equally comfortable as an instrumental or an expressive leader?

journal entry

Leadership Strategies

One of the major challenges that team leaders face today is how to manage and utilize the creative power of diverse work teams. Leaders in business, government, education, health care, and the entertainment industry adopt a variety of leadership techniques to cope with this challenge.

1. A top-ranking government official manages her team by hiring "top-notch" people from all walks of life. She then gives them a great deal of freedom and support. By discussing issues and problems one-on-one with as many people as possible, she gets more input. The result is that she can choose from more varied and creative solutions. Additionally, more people buy into the solutions since they are part of the decision-making process.

2. Leaders of one large corporation now refer to employees as associates. This new terminology was partly in response to data collected from a survey of its employees. Findings from the survey indicated that many employees did not feel they were part of any group. Consequently, they were not inclined to think in terms of the company's welfare. Both employees and management view the term *associate* positively because it makes titles unimportant. Treating each other as associates symbolizes a willingness to work together as equals.

3. A few years ago, a multicultural executive team was assembled to build a record company. With most record labels, white and black employees have traditionally been segregated into different music departments. At this company, the leadership seeks to diversify the racial and cultural composition of work teams. These teams market and promote pop, rock, rap, and rhythm and blues records. The result is phenomenal. Not long ago, this company had a greater market share than such established labels as Capitol and Motown Records.

4. One of the first actions taken by the president of a newly formed multi-national organization was to restructure the organizational chart. He now refers to it as a "pizza chart" because it resembles a pizza covered with many pieces of pepperoni. The circular shape of the pizza shows the sharing of leadership in this organization as well as the inclusiveness. Pepperoni represents self-directed work teams and the role they play in carrying out key business functions. According to the president of this organization, the pizza chart "makes people take off their organizational hats and put on their team hats. It gives people a much broader perspective and forces decision making down at least another level."[16]

Leadership has become a necessary skill for everyone. Our diversity consciousness will enhance our ability to lead all types of people in all kinds of situations. We will be better able to relate to others and if necessary, mobilize them in order to get things done. Similarly, we are much more likely to be successful if we look to others to challenge and complement our thinking and come up with new ideas. Conversely, we severely compromise our effectiveness if we can relate only to people who think and act like us. Research shows that one of the primary reasons that managers and executives fail is their inability to build teams with colleagues. Regardless of our job function and position, our ability to lead and work with others will be tested.

HIGH-PERFORMANCE TEAMS

Working Together Works

Working together can never be a policy.
It can only be an idea.
It can never be a code of rules.
It can only be a way of looking at the world.
We can say, "This is mine," and be good,
or we can add, "This is ours" and become better.
We can think, "I do my share," and be satisfied,
or we can ask, "Can I do more?" and become prosperous.
We can work along side each other and function,
or we can work with each other and grow.

—Author Unknown[17]

High performance teams do not just happen. They evolve over time and require people who possess certain talents, a wide range of diversity skills, and a common vision. Try to recollect some of the teams to which you have belonged in school or at work. On which teams did people work well together? Which teams did the best job of making people feel included? Which teams got the most accomplished? High-performance teams are not necessarily made up of the most talented individuals. In sports, it is not uncommon for a team of

Figure 6.3: *A study group of students can develop into a high-performance team over time.*

superstars to get beaten by a team with much less individual talent. Things such as team togetherness, commitment, and communication can be as, if not more, important than raw talent (see Fig. 6.3).

journal entry

THINKING THROUGH DIVERSITY:
More often than not, teams operate at less than peak efficiency. Why?

Research has shown that it is not enough simply to include diverse and capable people on a team. High-performance and low-performance teams differ in how they manage diversity. "When well-managed, diversity becomes a productive resource to the team....When ignored, diversity causes process problems that diminish the team's productivity."[18] For a moment, think of the storyline from *The Wizard of Oz*. In a training video marketed to business, a management expert analyzes the team that Dorothy built. Her team consists of a scarecrow, a lion, and a tin man. Each character has a different talent. Together they delegate tasks, take risks, establish trust among themselves, and pursue a common goal. When managed effectively over a period of time, their diversity allows them to empower each other.

In real life, team members need to come together, coalesce, and realize their common purpose in much the same way. According to Tuchman, periods of conflict (called *storming*) will occur. Often, it will take considerable time and effort to develop a sense of trust and cohesiveness, as well as a common understanding regarding the norms or rules of the team and its mission (called *norming*).[19] Although the development of each high-performance team is unique, there are nine proven strategies to keep in mind.

Nine Proven Strategies for Building High-Performance Teams

1. Get to know each other first.
2. Make sure that you understand your role and the team's goal(s).
3. Respect the ideas and feelings of other team members.
4. Keep your word.
5. Continue to build relations with other members of the team.
6. Think and act like a team.
7. Decenter and recenter.
8. Avoid groupthink.
9. Be flexible.

With each of these guidelines, what is involved, and why is it important? A brief explanation follows.

1. *Get to know each other first.* Before you start focusing on the task at hand, take some time to learn about group members. What are your interests at home and at work? What special talents do each of you have? What is distinctive about your personal and professional backgrounds? Sharing a part of yourself with the group initiates the process of establishing and nourishing a comfort zone in which to operate. It brings out individual differences and similarities and uncovers team members' skills. Although becoming acquainted takes time, it is worth it. If you ignore this step, there is a good chance that you will encounter problems later.

2. *Make sure that you understand the goal(s) of your team as well as the role of each person.* High-performance teams unite around a common vision. Team goals, team knowledge, team skills, and even team problems should be your focus. Also, everybody needs to understand what part they play and how every part is vital to their success as a group. If certain people feel that others do not want or value their input, commitment to the group is likely to be weak.

3. *Respect the ideas and feelings of other team members.* This helps to create an open, supportive environment that allows team members to feel comfortable and express themselves uniquely. Building diversity consciousness in yourself enhances your ability to value what each member brings to the team.

4. *Keep your word.* If you agree to take on a task, make sure that you do it. Your team has to be able to rely on you.

5. *Continue to build relations with other team members.* Sometimes, high-functioning teams are described as having the right "chemistry." Typically, this is something that evolves over time. To complement others, you need to know something about them. Over time, for example, my wife and I have learned to work as a team. When it comes to computer technology and anything of a mechanical nature, I tend to look to her for help. If we need groceries, she invariably seeks my advice. I cut out the coupons, read the ads, and buy virtually all of the food for our family. With other tasks, our skills are more similar than complementary. It is important to remember that utilizing our respective strengths does not just happen magically. It requires hard work, mutual respect, and continual learning about each other and ourselves.

6. *Think and act like a team.* Put your attitudes and egos aside. For many students, athletic teams provide excellent examples of teamwork. You can nourish the team concept in a variety of ways. One student recalls how members of his basketball team decided not to put their individual names on the backs of their jerseys. In the case of another student, her track coach is instrumental in building unity. "We all have talent but we have to learn to work together. We run everybody's event at practice—hurdles, sprints, long distance. You run it, we do it. We have rules. We have to be at practice on time, warm up together, stretch together, work out together, and cheer each other on to finish the workout. When we go to meets, we go there as a team and leave as a team."

7. *Decenter and recenter.* As discussed earlier, synergy occurs when the sum total of a group is greater than its parts. Decentering and recentering represent two techniques for achieving synergy in a diverse team. When you decenter, you and other team members shift your perspective and adopt multiple points of view. Recentering allows each member to identify and construct a common vision. Both are critically important and interconnected.

8. *Avoid groupthink.* As mentioned earlier, groupthink is the tendency to go along with a group and discourage differences of opinion. When this happens, every voice is not heard and teamwork suffers. Part of the lure of groupthink is that decisions can be made quickly. This often becomes an overriding concern in a society such as ours which revolves around deadlines and emphasizes immediate results. In a high-performance team, the mindset of the group does not constrain or stifle you. Rather, you are comfortable raising issues, challenging others, and being yourself.

9. *Be flexible.* Exercise "give and take" as needed. For example, be willing to give help and receive help. When necessary, assume the role of a leader in order to mobilize the team for high performance. Similarly, there are situations that require you to be a good follower. This might mean taking directions and accepting criticism from someone who thinks differently than you.

Realize the process of building a high-performance team is not linear. It has its ups and downs. Reaching decisions may take longer. You can do your part to construct a high-performance team by keeping track of where you are and where you are going. Are you helping to create a climate of trust, commitment, cooperation, and flexibility? When you assume leadership, is it empowering or conforming? Finally, do you really believe in the value of diversity and what each member brings to the group?

When spider webs unite, they can tie up a lion.

—Ethiopian proverb

OBSTACLES TO TEAMWORK

Numerous obstacles can detract from the synergy of a team. Some can be traced to the thinking and behaviors of individual members; others originate outside the team. Obstacles, such as those that follow, compromise a team's potential.

1. *Social values.* Teamwork can be difficult in a society that stresses the importance of individualism and competition. Common sayings in the United States, such as "make your own breaks' and "look out for number one" support values that may undermine teamwork. As an example, U.S. workers are sometimes reluctant to share their ideas because they fear that someone else might get the credit. Contrast this kind of thinking with the African saying: "One finger cannot pick up a grain."

▨ MUSICAL CHAIRS

Susan Takata, a professor at the University of Wisconsin, uses the game of musical chairs to teach students the value of cooperation. The game, as it is traditionally played, teaches the value of competition and "going for yourself." Participants walk around a number of empty chairs while music is being played. When the music stops, they scramble to find a seat. Because there are not enough chairs for everyone, one person is left standing. It is a win–lose situation.

After playing this game by the traditional rules, Takata introduces a twist. The chairs are reset, the music begins, and Takata tells the students to find either a lap or a chair to sit on. As she gradually removes chairs one by one, students must become more creative and cooperative. Afterward, students analyze how they feel about the two games and why they reacted the way they did.

2. *Stereotypes.* One popular exercise used in diversity training illustrates the negative effect of stereotypical images on teamwork. A label is placed on each person in a small group, such as leader, secretary, newcomer, and idealist. Participants are instructed to treat each other according to his or her label. Then they are assigned a task. What evolves during this role playing is typical of what takes place in teams on a daily basis. If we let stereotypes cloud our thinking, it becomes difficult to move beyond these labels and interact with each other as individuals.

3. *Unequal distribution of power.* In the context of teamwork, power affords you the opportunity to participate in decision making, access resources, make yourself heard, and make things happen. In some cases, an imbalance of power or a lack of understanding regarding the implications of power can sabotage team goals. As an example, it may be difficult for supervisors and their subordinates to work together as a team. A subordinate may be afraid to talk openly and honestly to his supervisors because of the power they hold. A supervisor may perceive her subordinates as rebellious or militant when they speak out or resist going along with the group. Because of their relative lack of power, subordinates may be expected to keep a lower profile.

4. *Disagreement over the roles of team members or the team's mission.* Think of a team as an interlocking set of gears on a machine. Each gear needs to do its part and work together in order for the machine to run smoothly and efficiently. This same set of dynamics governs a team. Team members need to agree and be clear regarding their individual responsibilities and collective goal or goals. If not, roles will overlap and time as well as effort will be wasted.

5. *Unequal treatment or the perception of unequal treatment.* Discrimination is one of the surest, quickest ways to sabotage teamwork. It undermines trust and cohesiveness. It arouses anger and makes it more difficult to focus on the task at hand. Excessive avoidance or acquiescence replaces genuine interaction. Psychologically speaking, the group mentality shifts to "us" versus "them."

6. *Lack of communication or miscommunication.* Communication is the "glue" that holds a team together. It is the vehicle by which people come together, share, and learn from each other. Unfortunately, open, honest, and clear communication is a rarity on many teams. As teams get larger and more heterogeneous, communication styles and skills tend to become more numerous and differentiated. This makes it difficult for a team to develop a common language.

7. *Lack of outside support.* Teams do not operate in a vacuum. They connect to other teams, organizations, and the larger community. External support can take many forms, including funding, volunteer help, and commitments from organizational and community leaders. A team that feels cut off from the outside world will probably find it difficult to sustain any amount of synergy.

As you develop diversity consciousness, these obstacles to teamwork will become more visible. Furthermore, you will have a vast array of skills at your disposal to possibly prevent, minimize, or overcome such obstacles.

CONFLICT

Absolute calm is not the law of the ocean. And it is the same with the ocean of life.

—Gandhi

Conflict is the struggle that results when two or more parties perceive a difference or incompatibility in their interests, values, or goals. It can occur between individuals as well as among and within groups, communities, and societies. Every time we interact with someone, there is the potential for conflict.

A variety of individual, group, and cultural differences may give rise to conflict. More specifically, it may stem from misunderstandings as well as different interests, values, and needs. Within a team, potential sources of conflict include stereotypical assumptions, discriminatory behavior, and disagreements regarding the roles of team members and the team's mission.

What comes to your mind when you hear the word *conflict?* When I pose this question to college students, the answers I get typically portray conflict as problematic or negative. Some of the terms that students use are *disagreement, "attitude," problems, trouble, fighting, frustration, anger,* and *tension.*

Traditionally, conflict has been viewed as a negative in the United States. It is seen as something that stands in the way of communication and teamwork. Therefore, some people assume that we should avoid conflict at all costs. Although conflict can have negative consequences, it can have positive outcomes as well. At school, conflict can increase your achievement by motivating you to work harder. It can also be a learning experience that deepens your understanding of a problem. Conflict in your personal life can make you stronger and strengthen your relationships with others. In the workplace, conflict can bring certain issues out into the open and in some cases bring people closer together. It can stimulate creativity and signal a need for change.

In Chinese, the word *crisis* is created by using two characters, representing both danger and opportunity (see Fig. 6.4). Without a crisis or conflict of some sort, personal growth is often impossible. For example, take the smallest and most intimate of all teams—a marriage. Many of us grow up with the belief that a perfect relationship is one in which conflict is avoided or absent. However, that kind of relationship is not realistic or productive. Two people have different needs, values, and priorities. These differences often result in conflict. Although conflict may be emotionally difficult and painful, it needs to be addressed for growth to occur.

In my marriage, I am often the one who is wrong in the conflict. It hurts, it's not pretty, but that is where the real growth starts and I am better for it. Even with all the affirming, it still is an uncomfortable experience.

—A student's perspective

危機

Figure 6.4: *Chinese characters for the word* crisis.

Without struggle there is no progress.

—Frederick Douglass

Conflict Management

The effect that conflict has on us depends largely on how well we manage it. **Conflict management**, the process by which conflict is dealt with in an effective and constructive manner, is a key diversity skill. To develop this skill and understand the causes and consequences of conflict, we need some knowledge of subjects such as history, sociology, economics, and psychology. Of equal importance are basic interpersonal skills. In some cases the management of conflict results in resolving or eliminating conflict by changing how we relate to an issue and/or each other. There are other circumstances when it makes sense to avoid or smooth over conflict. Although this does not necessarily make the conflict go away, it might very well be the prudent thing to do in a particular situation. A variety of approaches to managing conflict are discussed later.

People who manage conflict well at school, work, and home have an advantage. The issue is not whether people experience conflict but how they experience it. While conflict frustrates and stymies some people, others seem to take it in stride and even thrive on it. The difference in how people react has a lot to do with their upbringing, cultural background, and people skills. In his book *Conflict: Resolution and Prevention*, John Burton argues that it is important to take a proactive approach to conflict.[20] Dealing with conflict proactively means that we prepare ourselves for conflict in advance. In other words, it is important to develop our conflict management skills continuously.

Learning to deal effectively with conflict is a skill that expands both your diversity consciousness and your chances for success. It builds your self-respect and increases your confidence in yourself. Your interpersonal relationship skills benefit as well. These include your ability to communicate, cooperate, negotiate, manage your anger, and exercise self-control. In addition, working through conflict in a constructive way helps you to develop your cognitive skills. You will become a better problem solver by developing your understanding of the sources, dynamics, and effects of conflict.

Approaches to Conflict Management

Different situations may require different approaches. Flexibility is key. Sometimes, situations call for strong responses, and sometimes the response needs to be more gentle. The setting, as well as the people and their relationships to each other, need to be taken into consideration. If your boss at work comments "You're so articulate for a foreigner," you might feel rage, hurt, or a mix of positive and negative feelings. Depending on how you feel, you might want to hit her or him over the head, ignore it, or explain why you find this "compliment" offensive. Your ability to control your feelings, consider the consequences of your actions, and act accordingly will be pivotal to your success on the job.

Cultural differences need to be taken into consideration. Although we should not jump to conclusions about people because of their cultural backgrounds, it is important to be sensitive to the impact that culture might have on managing conflict. For example, what do you assume about people who disagree on important issues? Can they work through their differences and interact effectively? When confronted with an argument, do you look at all sides or presume automatically that there are only two sides? Do you assume that if people think differently, they must be opposed to each other? Your responses to these questions have a lot to do with your cultural background. For example, in many Native American and Asian cultures, people view differences or opposites existing in harmony. People or things are not either this *or* that; rather, they overlap and interconnect. The ancient Chinese concepts of yin and yang illustrate this kind of thinking. Differences can be interactive and even complementary. Instead of simply focusing on differences, the concept of yin–yang reminds us to search for common ground.

⊠ YIN AND YANG ☯

The dark and light halves of the yin–yang symbol represent the two sides of a hill, one shadowy and one sunny. Although the outer circle of the symbol shows that yin and yang are not two separate things, the small black and white dots in the symbol show that yin and yang contain the seed of its opposite. Like day and night, one cannot exist without the other. Viewing conflict in terms of yin and yang helps us realize that sometimes there are more than two sides to an issue. Similarly, differences do not necessarily have to result in opposition.

According to Deborah Tannen, author of *The Argument Culture*, Americans traditionally assume that opposition is the best way to get things done. As a result, people are inclined to settle their differences by resorting to debate, fighting, and lawsuits. There is an emphasis on finding fault rather than solving a problem, having an argument rather than making an argument, and winning the argument rather than understanding another point of view.[21] We can find evidence of this emphasis in the metaphors we use. Examples include phrases such as the "battle of the sexes" and the "war on drugs." The power of words to shape perceptions has been substantiated by research. Phrasing a conflict as "Black" versus "White," "rich" versus "poor," or "old" versus "young" is counterproductive. It not only forces people into two artificial, opposing camps, but it may also alienate or exclude many people.

journal entry

What is one issue that elicits considerable disagreement among college students? Can you think of more than two sides to this issue?

Approaches to Conflict Management: The 6 C's

When you encounter conflict, you may choose to communicate, circumvent, confront, conform, compromise, or collaborate.

Approach 1: Communicate. With dialogue, people who hold conflicting views on divisive and emotional issues are brought together to talk, listen, and learn. Unlike a debate, the goal is not to score points. As an example, the Public Conversations Project is an initiative that has brought people with strong differences together to converse on such potentially volatile topics as sexual orientation, abortion, and the environment. The project team establishes certain guidelines to ensure that conversations are respectful and constructive. Project leaders encourage participants to avoid name-calling, stay on task, and give everyone "a home in the conversation." Dialogues do not necessarily resolve the conflict or significantly change people's positions on an issue. However, they can open up lines of communication and help people see each other as people rather than enemies. When this happens, people's views can shift ever so slightly and new options may emerge.

▦ CONFLICT AND COMMUNICATION

Conflict can make person-to-person communication particularly difficult. Anger and ill feelings can easily get in the way of meaningful dialogue. One way to work through conflict is to view communication as a building process, Breaking the process

down into steps can help you take advantage of the opportunities conflict affords.

1. Share information. Use the "I feel formula." Each person should state the problem clearly. Try not

to blame. Rather, focus on how you feel as a result of what happened. For example,
I feel _____ when you _____ because _____. In stating how you feel, try to avoid words such as *angry* or *mad.* Be more specific, such as I feel "left out" or "embarrassed."

2. Explore differences and similarities in your assumptions.
3. Try to understand the perspectives of others.
4. Brainstorm possible solutions. Determine the advantages and disadvantages of each.
5. Try to agree on a solution that is fair to all.

Approach 2: Circumvent. There are times when it is necessary to avoid or get around conflict in some way. Sometimes, you may feel as though you want to "fight the world." Everything seems to be a source of potential conflict. To keep from being overwhelmed, you may find it necessary to "pick your battles." In other words, choose what to fight and what to avoid. Sometimes the situation might be too volatile. Maybe the timing is bad and people need to "cool off." After thinking it through for a while, you may even discover that you are at fault or overreacting.

Some students encounter the possibility of conflict on an everyday basis. A gay woman comments: "I unfortunately very often feel different from my fellow students and instructors. Working in the dental hygiene clinic, I have heard negative comments regarding gay people. They come from department coordinators, instructors, and students. The interesting aspect of it is they include me in these discussions, never thinking for a moment that I might be gay. It is funny how people just assume that sometimes. I know in these situations I just have to play the game. There are too many people to deal with, and I know it would not be in my best interest to come out. I have also been warned by other gay women who have graduated from this program to remain discrete. The program is tough enough as it is. I think it is better in this case to avoid unnecessary emotional turmoil."

Approach 3: Confront. In some instances it is necessary to be assertive and take action immediately. Maybe it is a matter of speaking up for yourself or someone else. A person's safety may be an issue. Certain conflicts may result in people being denied respect or even basic human rights. For example, what if a co-worker or your boss tells you the latest "Polish joke?" You might respond by informing the co-worker that you find this joke offensive. With your boss, you might simply not laugh and walk away. Remember: Confrontation need not be overtly challenging to be effective.

Confrontation may also be necessary when people show a lack of respect for certain cultural traditions. Put yourself in the position of a person who has to take time off from work or school to observe a religious holiday. If you are denied this opportunity or penalized in some way because of your religious beliefs, you have the right to take whatever action is necessary to ensure that your rights are not being violated.

Approach 4: Conform. There may be times when you feel that you have to smooth over conflict or simply "give in" because you do not want to upset or jeopardize your relationship with others. The people may be more important than the issue. In some instances, conformity is a short-term solution. For example, you may find yourself in a no-win situation with your parents. They make it clear to you that they do not approve of the fact that you are unmarried and living in a co-ed apartment. Consequently, they have asked you to avoid talking about your living arrangement when other people are present. Although you may disagree with your parents and even think of them as old-fashioned, you respect their strong feelings on this issue and conform to their expectations.

Approach 5: Compromise. With this approach, all the parties feel they can give a little. A typical example is what happens when students reside in a college living unit. Students living in close quarters are likely to prefer different kinds of music. Chances are they will play it softly or loudly at different times of the day and night. Given these differences, compromise is often necessary.

A widely used program that teaches students the need for compromise is the "Model United Nations." Using a realistic simulation of the actual United Nations, its purpose is to bring students together to discuss real-world issues. During these discussions, conflicts arise that students need to resolve. A student UN delegate comments: "My experiences as a delegate allow me to see the world through others' eyes. Passing substantive resolutions is extremely difficult. Many end up being watered down to make them agreeable to countries."

Approach 6: Collaborate. Rather than taking sides or compromising, we may reach agreement by finding some common ground. Collaboration requires creativity and "buy in" from everyone. Maybe you remember a time when you were part of a group that was trying to solve a problem of some sort. No one could agree on a solution. Each person felt strongly that his or her approach was right. Nevertheless, all of you were determined to find a solution that was satisfactory to everyone. After brainstorming for a while, someone came up with a great idea that was surprisingly simple. Everyone immediately felt a collective sense of relief.

There is no one correct approach to conflict management. An approach that works for you in one situation might backfire on someone else. Sometimes, we can use a combination of approaches. As an example, confrontation may lead to communication and even collaboration. The situation as well as your own comfort level with various approaches are factors you need to consider. You may feel more at ease being confrontational at times, while someone else may prefer to avoid this approach at all costs. Remember that you will make mistakes. You might not control your anger, or perhaps you will avoid a situation you need to confront. Simply learn from your mistakes. Like team building, conflict management is a continual growth process.

⌘ MULTICULTURAL MEDIATION TEAM

Mediation is a give-and-take process in which a neutral third person (the mediator) helps disputing parties reach an agreement. Since mediators lack authority or power, their decision is not binding. This distinguishes it from **arbitration**, in that an arbitrator has the power to render a binding decision. Mediation is used in a wide variety of settings, including international conflicts, workplace and public policy disputes, and divorce proceedings. A skilled mediator may employ one or more approaches to conflict.

In recent years, a growing number of programs at all levels of schooling

have initiated peer mediation. One such example is the Multicultural Mediation Team at the University of Massachusetts. The team hears disputes that revolve around such issues as race, gender, sexual orientation, and disabilities. The team is made up of 24 undergraduate and graduate students from extremely diverse backgrounds. As part of their training, they study mediation techniques, engage in case discussions, and role play. The emphasis is on student mediators being able to understand themselves and others from a variety of perspectives.

The Ten Principles of Conflict Management

Regardless of your approach to conflict management, you may not always be able to control your emotions. This makes it more difficult to compromise, collaborate, or even communicate. The following principles of conflict management will help you manage your emotions, relate to others, and maintain your focus.

1. *Manage conflict in the early stages.* Do not wait for it to explode. Conflict that we allow to build up, especially when communicating across a distance, is more difficult to resolve.

2. *Think through conflict.* In other words, what is the conflict about, why does it concern you, and what would be a satisfactory solution for you and the other parties involved? Additionally, what do I need to learn and do to deal more effectively with conflict of this nature?

3. *Take enough time to get your emotions under control and gather your thoughts.* When you are angry, it is difficult to evaluate the situation from different perspectives. Ask yourself "Is this the best time and place to resolve this?" "Are my feelings under control?" "Is there enough privacy?" As you deal with conflict, be constantly aware of your own thoughts and feelings. This can help you avoid a destructive power struggle.

*As a child, people picked on me because I was the quiet one, the "nerd."
I took martial arts. It gave me discipline, self-motivation. It taught me not to
resort to violence every time a problem arises. It taught me to tone down my
temper, keep it under control.*

—A student's perspective

4. *Listen actively.* Pay careful attention to what you and others are saying and feeling. Listen to the total message rather than what you want to hear. Try restating what you think the other person is saying before responding. Active listening coupled with good feedback promotes understanding.

5. *Watch your body language.* Most certainly, there are times when you share something very personal and important to you. If the person with whom you are talking appears disinterested, how does that make you feel? How does it affect your communication? As you interact, be aware of your body language. For instance, nodding your head and leaning forward while seated in a chair shows your interest. Leaning back, crossing your arms, pointing your finger, or smiling during a heated discussion might put others on the defensive. Keep your nonverbal language consistent with your verbal message.

6. *Be open-minded.* Realize that your view is just one way of looking at things. Instead of asking yourself how you can win, ask yourself what you can learn.

7. *Criticize ideas, not people.* Keep your focus on the issue or issues. Insulting or blaming people blocks communication and results in destructive conflict.

8. *Ask questions rather than assume.* You can only guess what another person is thinking. Keep checking out your assumptions. Accept and respect corrections from others.

9. *Try to put yourself in the other person's place.* Guerney states: "Once you have placed yourself 'inside' the other person, 'walk around' in there. Ask yourself: If I were this person, what would I be thinking?…How would I be feeling? What would I be wishing for?"[22] This does two things. First, it helps you get a better idea of someone else's perceptions, beliefs, and wishes. Second, it helps you react in a way that is respectful and caring.

10. *Be willing to change.* You are at a severe disadvantage if you are extremely rigid in your thinking and locked into your approaches or solutions to conflict. A willingness to change allows you to turn conflict into opportunity.

Like many other diversity skills, the management of conflict is a critical component of teamwork. Although teamwork is not necessarily one long-drawn-out battle, there will be times when conflict occurs. Conflict can tear a team apart and waste human potential. As a team member, you can help make conflict a growth experience. This is clearly not easy. It takes knowledge, skills, and commitment on your part. How well you and your team work together in the face of conflict will have a significant impact on your individual and collective success.

Throughout this chapter we have explored a variety of issues and concepts related to teamwork. We examined how teams are changing and why employers attach so much importance to teamwork. Additionally, we focused on the relationship between teamwork and diversity. Finally, we addressed a variety of obstacles that can make teamwork difficult, if not impossible. Developing and refining diversity skills, such as communication, conflict management, and leadership, makes it possible to recognize and overcome these obstacles.

Exercises

IN-CLASS

Exercise 1: Obstacles to Teamwork

Directions for Instructor.
Arrange five chairs in a semicircle at the front of the classroom. Ask five students to be *role-players*. Instruct them to sit in the chairs. Randomly, put a label on each one. Instruct the five students *not* to read their own labels. (*Note:* You might place the label on a hat or hang it around the person's neck.) The labels might read "smart and helpful," "knows a lot," "asks stupid questions," "idealistic," and "talks too much." Remember to position the label so that it can be seen by everybody except for the student wearing it. Position the other students in class so that they can see and hear the students in the semicircle. These other students will act as *observers*.

Role-Playing: Next, the five students will create and act out a scenario that takes place at school or in the workplace. For instance, students might imagine that they are members of a student committee discussing an issue of concern to the student body. Another possible situation might relate to work. Perhaps they are members of a task force looking into some aspect of employer–employee relations. The role-players have approximately 5 to 10 minutes to perform the scenario, treating each other according to her or his label. During this time, the observers will closely examine how the role-players interact. In particular, observers should focus on any obstacles that get in the way of teamwork. Observers should not interrupt.

Analysis: Finally, provide time to analyze what took place.

1. Ask each of the five role-players to try to figure out what is written on his or her label.

2. Ask the role-players:

   ○ How did it feel to be treated according to your label?

   ○ How did the way you were treated affect your behavior? How did it affect the team?

3. Ask the observers:

   ○ Do you see this kind of thing happening at school or at work?

   ○ How can we create teams where labels like these do not operate?

Exercise 2: Putting the Pieces Together

Directions for Instructor

Purchase puzzles for your class (one puzzle for every four or five students). The puzzles may be different or the same, but they should all be equally difficult and have the same number of pieces (preferably 25 to 50). Randomly divide students into groups of four or five. Give each group the unassembled puzzle. Then place each group in a different area of the classroom. Instruct each group to put the puzzle together. Record how long it takes each group to finish the puzzle.

Analysis

1. Ask members of each group to (a) explain how teamwork was or was not evident while putting the puzzle together and (b) describe the roles assumed by each of the group members (e.g., leader, co-leader, icebreaker, follower, rebel, mediator, facilitator, outsider).

2. Ask students about the diversity in their group. For example, did group members have different talents? Did they take different approaches to solving the puzzle? Was the diversity of the individuals in the group a help or a hindrance? Why?

3. Ask groups what they might have done differently to make better use of the talents of *all* group members.

Exercise 3: Cooperative Controversy

This group exercise is modeled after "cooperative controversy," a cooperative learning method that we can use to study an issue that generates a lot of disagreement.[23] When using this method, there are seven rules to follow.

1. I am critical of ideas, not people.

2. I remember that we are all in this together.

3. I encourage everyone to participate.

4. I listen to everyone's ideas even if I do not agree with them.

5. I restate what someone says if it is not clear to me.

6. I try to understand both (all) sides of the issue.

7. We first bring out all the ideas, then we put them together.

Directions for Instructor

Divide the class into groups of four. Each group will examine the following statement: "Students who dine solely with members of their own ethnic group and participate in ethnic student organizations and activities contribute to a decline of ethnic relations on campus." In each group, students should follow these steps:

1. Two students should argue in support of this statement and two students should disagree.
2. Switch sides and argue the opposite position.
3. Try to reach some consensus regarding the statement.
4. Have groups share their conclusions with the class.

OUT-OF-CLASS

Exercise 1: Conflict Management

1. Describe one example of conflict you encounter at work or school.
2. Explain how you manage the conflict.
3. Which of the 6 C's of conflict management (communicate, circumvent, confront, conform, compromise, collaborate) do you use, and why? Do you feel that you manage the conflict effectively? Why?

Exercise 2: High-Performance Teams

Form a team with other students in your class. Team members agree to use the "Nine Proven Strategies for Building High-Performance Teams" (see page 175). You will use these strategies throughout this exercise.

Task. Find a high-performance team in your community. Write a report on this team that addresses the following:

1. Briefly describe the team: who they are and what they do.
2. Explain why you think members of this team work so well together and utilize everybody's talents.
3. Explain how members of this team promote teamwork. In other words, what things do they do to make sure that everyone is working together toward a common goal? What obstacles to teamwork do they encounter? How do they deal with these obstacles?
4. The last section of your report should focus on *your* team of students. How effectively did you work together? Of the nine strategies, which seemed to help the most?

Exercise 3: Team Journal

Select a team to which you currently belong. Keep a journal of this team for a week or more during the semester. Record your thoughts about any of the following:

- Conflict and how you as well as other team members manage it
- Assignment of tasks and roles

- ○ Ability of the team to think and act as one
- ○ Team leadership
- ○ Communication among team members
- ○ Ability of the team to utilize its diversity

Note: You may want to bring your team journal to class. As you discuss communication, diversity consciousness, and other concepts related to teamwork, refer to your team journal entries.

✷ INTERNET ASSIGNMENT

Find Web sites that address the concept of teamwork *or* virtual teaming. In particular, search until you find at least three sites that discuss the relationship between one of these concepts (teamwork, virtual teaming) and diversity. Write a one-page paper that summarizes what you found. Include the Web addresses in your paper.

NOTES

[1] Jerome Dancis, "Group Learning Helps Minority Students Excel at University," *Cooperative Learning*, 12(1), Oct. 1991, 26–27.

[2] Abby Karp, "Working Together: Innovative Programs Promote Tolerance in Schools," *The Sun*, Oct. 17, 1989, 1C.

[3] Elliot Aronson and Neal Osherow, "Cooperation, Prosocial Behavior, and Academic Performance: Experiments in the Desegregated Classroom," *Applied Social Psychology Annual*, 1, 1980, 174–175.

[4] Sherry Silver, "Advice for Adjusting to the World of Work," *Washington Post Advertising Supplement*, Oct. 19, 1997, 60, 65.

[5] Faye Rice, "How to Make Diversity Pay," *Fortune*, Aug. 8, 1994, 79.

[6] Stephen Covey, *The Seven Habits of Highly Effective People* (New York: Simon & Schuster, 1989).

[7] Jessica Lipnack and Jeffrey Stamps, *Virtual Teams* (New York: Wiley, 1997).

[8] L. Sproull and S. Kiesler, *Connections: New Ways of Working in the Networked Organization* (Cambridge, MA: MIT Press, 1991).

[9] Mark Mehler, "AMS Centers Deliver Global Information Access," *Integration Management: The Newspaper for Global Integrators*, 1(8), Sept. 18, 1997, 1.

[10] Sue Hanley, letter to the author, Dec. 22, 1997.

[11] Christina Hvitfeldt, "Traditional Culture, Perceptual Style, and Learning: The Classroom Behavior of Hmong Adults," *Adult Education Quarterly*, 36(2), Winter 1986, 70.

[12] Stephen Covey, "How to Succeed in Today's Workplace," *USA Weekend*, Aug. 29–31, 1997, 5.

[13] E. J. Langer, *Mindfulness* (Reading, MA: Addison-Wesley, 1989).

[14] John Kotter, *The General Managers* (New York: Free Press, 1982).

[15] Marilyn Loden and Judy Rosener, *Workforce America: Managing Employee Diversity as a Vital Resource* (Homewood, IL: Business One Irwin, 1991), 180–195.

[16]D. Sullivan, "Organization Structure in Multinational Corporations," in *International Encyclopedia of Business and Management*, M. Warner (ed.) (London: Routledge, 1996), 3595.

[17]"Working Together Works," Online, World Wide Web, Nov. 28, 1998. Available: http://www.diversitydtg.com/thoughts/thought_mnu.html.

[18]N. Adler, *International Dimensions of Organization Behavior* (Boston: Kent, 1986), 111.

[19]B. W. Tuchman, "Developmental Sequences in Small Groups," *Psychological Bulletin*, 63, 1965, 384–399.

[20]John Burton, *Conflict: Resolution and Prevention* (New York: St. Martin's Press, 1990).

[21]Deborah Tannen, *The Argument Culture: Moving from Debate to Dialogue* (New York: Random House, 1998).

[22]Bernard Guerney, *Relationship Enhancement Program*, 2nd ed. (Bethesda, MD: Ideals, 1997), 4.

[23]K. A. Smith, D. W. Johnson, and R. T. Johnson, "Can Conflict Be Constructive? Controversy versus Concurrence Seeking in Learning Groups," *Journal of Educational Psychology*, 75, 1983, 654.

7 CONCLUSION

chapter objectives

Upon completion of this chapter, you will be able to:

○ Explain the value of diversity education.

○ Explain why diversity consciousness will expand your opportunities for success in the future.

○ Discuss three future challenges that will test your diversity skills.

The scene: As you walk down the halls, you hear many different languages. Flags hang in the front lobby of the school designating each student's country of origin. The principal can say "welcome" in a dozen languages. In her office, she makes a habit of displaying and rotating dolls and other cultural gifts she has received from students over the years. The school's philosophy is simply "the best way to learn about diversity is to live it." Thirty nine countries are represented at Wellwood International Elementary School.

Wellwood International School provides us with one effective form of diversity education. In the process of working and learning together, Wellwood students develop diversity awareness and skills at an early age. They learn that people look different and may act different...and that is "OK." Students learn to help each other. For example, children who do not speak English are assigned a buddy. This type of buddy system challenges children to be creative. They have to figure out a way to communicate. At a very young age, these students are gaining skills that many adults lack.

The best education for this world is one that gives students first-hand experience of diversity during their college years and includes multicultural fluency as a skill graduates are expected to acquire.

—Karen Kennelly, President, Mt. St. Mary's College

Diversity education extends over a lifetime. It involves much more than books, workshops, and dialogues about diversity issues. Indeed, some argue that one of the best ways to learn about diversity is through life experiences that *involve* diversity but are not *about* diversity (see Fig. 7.1). Former U.S. Senator Bill Bradley wrote: "Only through doing things together that have nothing to do with race will people break down the racial barriers...in a way that conversation cannot."[1]

Although Bradley focuses on the issue of race, what he says applies to all facets of diversity. One highly effective diversity education program cited by Bradley is Common Ground, held annually at Western Maryland College. This community program for people of all ages offers a wide variety of hands-on activities with master musicians, artists, and craftspeople. The thinking behind Common Ground is that the arts allow us to experience each other as artists, as human beings. Walt Michael, Director of Common Ground, expands on this idea. "You learn about yourself when you paint, play music or engage in some other art form. In the process of self discovery, a lot of stereotypes go out the window. As an example, our expectations about who prefers what kind of music might be reversed...maybe a black student becomes fascinated by blue grass music while a white student gets into the blues."[2]

Figure 7.1: College dance workshop. The arts provide us with a basis for engaging and communicating with each other, as well as the opportunity to discover "common ground." (Courtesy of the Office of Communications, Colgate University, Hamilton, N.Y.)

■■■ OPENING YOUR MIND TO OPPORTUNITIES

Through perpetual learning, we become more conscious of diversity. Too often, we think learning about diversity is a single learning experience rather than something that is ongoing and lifelong. Learning of this nature is a multifaceted process that requires our commitment, time, and energy. It reaches far beyond what takes place in a formal educational setting. Moreover, there is no acceptable level of diversity consciousness where you can stop. The more conscious of diversity you become, the more you realize how much more you have to learn and grow.

The skills we acquire through this process, such as communication, teamwork, flexible thinking, and conflict management, will become even more important in the future. As change in our lives becomes even more rapid, we will need skills such as these to adjust. Viewing each new situation as one more opportunity to expand our diversity consciousness will ensure that we will not get left behind.

Education is our passport to the future, for tomorrow belongs to the people who prepare for it today.

—Malcolm X

In the future, diversity consciousness will open your mind to new and exciting opportunities for a number of reasons.

1. *Diversity consciousness prepares you for life.* The more prepared you are for life, the greater your opportunities. The benefits of diversity consciousness extend far beyond a particular job or field of employment. By developing diversity consciousness, you have fundamental skills you need for *any* job. As more and more people find themselves working a number of jobs over the course of their lifetime, diversity consciousness takes on added importance.

It is very important for students to become not only knowledgeable in diversity but skilled as well. Valuing and understanding diversity allows students to handle themselves adeptly in a heterogeneous society.

—Andrea-Teresa "Tess" Arenas, Assistant to the President for Multicultural Affairs, University of Wisconsin System Administration

2. *Diversity consciousness empowers you and others.* It gives you skills that enable you to capitalize on your own potential and the potential of others. By way of illustration, learning about sociocultural theory (see Chapter 2) helps you recognize that which you can or cannot change in your life. A case in point is a heated discussion about social inequality that took place in one of my classes. Samuel, a student who has served time in prison, laments the lack of opportunities "out there." "All I see is negative," he says. "I see brothers on the corner selling drugs. I see prostitutes. I go back to my old neighborhood in L.A. Some of my friends went to jail, some got shot, and some are incoherent." From his point of view, he has few if any choices.

Other students take issue with what Samuel is saying. They argue that despite all the barriers—where he was born, who his friends are, his criminal background—he does have important choices to make. One student, who describes herself as a poor single parent, feels that Samuel is confusing "insurmountable barriers" with "stumbling blocks." She elaborates: "People who tell me I cannot do it or I am crazy for going to school and raising a child are stumbling blocks. They are easy to overcome because I do not let them mentally become a barrier. If I let these same people mentally debilitate me, then they become a barrier. They make me unable to use the one thing that could help me overcome them. That is my mind." This student was clearly empowered by her ability to make sense of the relationship between her environment and her choices in life.

If you can't see the top, how are you going to make it to the top?

Each person, whatever their diversity, needs to accept themselves and feel proud even in the face of oppression. Change takes time. But with education and understanding, piece by piece, the world can become a better place.

—Students' perspectives

Often we look so long at the closed door that we do not see the one which has been opened for us.

—Helen Keller

3. *Diversity consciousness changes the way you view differences.* Throughout this book, we examine how people view and react to diversity. Diversity consciousness gives us the awareness and understanding we need to embrace, value, and enjoy differences. If we only learned to appreciate one type of food, one type of music, or one type of recreational activity, think of all we would miss. American Express Financial Advisors, one of the largest financial planning companies in the United States, expands on this idea. "Our differences are what make us strong…How dull to live in a world where everyone is the same. After all, it's our differences that make us learn and grow. It's our differences that shape who we are, who we love, and what we believe. At American Express Financial Advisors, we encourage diversity in our workplace and we celebrate it wherever we find it."[3]

◼ FUTURE CHALLENGES

The day on which one starts out is not the time to start one's preparations.

—A Nigerian proverb

The relevance of diversity consciousness takes on additional significance when we examine future challenges. Because we do not anticipate or react quickly enough to change, many of us are not in a position to compete in the twenty-first century. Therefore, it is important to assess whether a gap exists between the skills we have now and those we need in the years ahead.

The changes taking place around us are causing us to reevaluate how we view diversity. The elasticity of the term *diversity* makes it possible to constantly redefine and broaden what we know about human differences. Gradually, the term has become more inclusive and multidimensional. Our differences extend far beyond race, ethnicity, and gender. We are single and multiple jobholders, computer whizzes and phobics, auditory and visual learners, and so much more. Indeed, when we consider our inner dimensions of diversity, there are an infinite variety of possibilities. This is important to remember, especially as we learn more and more about ourselves and others.

Organizations have traditionally invested most of their time and money in training directed at technical skills rather than what has been termed "soft stuff" such as interpersonal skills. Nevertheless, in many cases it will be the breadth and depth of one's diversity skills that can either create problems or lead to success. Consider the advice given by Yvonne Chang, the Director of Corporate Affairs for American Telephone and Telegraph (AT&T) in Basking Ridge, New Jersey. She points out that you have to "be flexible and have many different skills" to succeed in corporate America. "You can't be very good at one thing; you have to be good at a lot of different things. The most important things to have are diversity of knowledge, interpersonal skills, and an understanding of technology."[4]

The relevance of diversity skills becomes even more apparent when we examine the social, technological, and economic changes that are occurring all around us. In the United States, knowledge workers and service workers continue to replace laborers. Consequently, different skills are needed. For most jobs, skills that enable us to absorb and share information are more important than mechanical or physical abilities. The frequency of interpersonal, intergroup, and cross-cultural interactions is increasing as well. These changes, along with growing global competition, make diversity a business issue (see Fig. 7.2).

Figure 7.2: The ability to recognize the power and possibilities of diversity has increasingly become a requirement for success in today's competitive business environment. (Photo by Regina Bryan.)

The days of people staying and working within a few miles of where they grew up is long gone. The norm is becoming two or three jobs in ten years with significant geographic moves to secure those jobs. And country boundaries are no longer a barrier as well. I looked around a recent meeting in our corporate headquarters and saw our female IT [information technology] specialist, executive vice president, a programmer from India, a division head from Italy, and a marketing manager from Ohio. It's people who are comfortable in this type of environment that will be successful. The stars of this new workforce will be those who can mediate these widely different working styles and get the most out of a broadly diverse group of people.

—Carl T. Camden, Executive Vice President for Field Operations, Sales, and Marketing, Kelly Services, a Fortune 500 staffing services company

A number of notable challenges lie ahead. Three in particular will test our diversity skills: technological change and globalization, changing demographics, and the potential for divisiveness. These challenges will have implications for each of us.

Technological Change and Globalization

According to *Workforce 2020*, technological advances will be one of the major forces shaping our lives in the early twenty-first century.[5] This report states that the pace of technological change has never been greater, and it will only accelerate in the future. The best jobs in the Innovation Age will be filled by those who possess the necessary skills. These skills will increasingly rely on brains rather than brawn. As "knowledge organizations" continue to proliferate, workers will have to keep pace with the need for continual learning and growth. If workers with a certain skill level cannot be found in the United States, companies will continue to look elsewhere.

Due to this change, the rest of the world will become more fused with our immediate world in the years ahead. James Becker, senior consultant at the Social Studies Development Center at Indiana University, states: "We don't look at the world as separate pieces of real estate, but as a society in which people interact in different ways."[6] The increased flow of communications, goods, and people will make distance less important. However, cultural barriers will be much more difficult to overcome than geographical barriers. It will be increasingly necessary to look at the "big picture" (see Fig. 7.3).

For those innovative, flexible thinkers who can adopt a multicultural perspective, globalization will open up opportunities. Conversely, ethnocentric thinking will be a liability to an even greater degree than it has been in the past. In a booklet titled *Transforming Higher Education: A Vision for Learning in the 21st Century*, Donald Norris and Michael Dolence state that tomorrow's student,

Figure 7.3: *Students, representing different regions of the world, work in teams to solve complex problems. This global simulation requires them to see across geographical and cultural boundaries. (Courtesy of the Office of Communications, Colgate University, Hamilton, N.Y.)*

teacher, and worker need to move beyond thinking "out of the box." Rather, they will need to see "around the curvature of the earth."[7]

> *It is imperative that I develop a global perspective in order to attain a more definitive and unbiased perception of who I am, and not just who they say I am. If given the choice between the fish bowl and the ocean, I for one choose the ocean. To first understand it will make it easier for me to embrace it.*
>
> —A student's perspective

As technology grows, globalization envelopes our lives. As one business consultant points out, the global marketplace is not only the Pacific Rim or faraway places. It includes downtown Toronto, Phoenix, Spokane, and lesser known places. In short, "the global marketplace is wherever organizations do business."[8] According to experts, U.S. companies that cannot understand what is going on around the world will not be successful at home or abroad.

Consider a company such as Bank of America. Their employees work in 37 countries. Staff at their California customer service center can communicate in at least 13 different languages. This allows them to accommodate millions of customers who speak a language other than English.

THINKING THROUGH DIVERSITY:

In what ways will an increasingly global environment alter the skills required by your chosen career?

In an environment becoming more global each day, it is absolutely essential to think and act inclusively. If our thoughts and actions are too restricted, we waste human resources and miss opportunities. Coopers and Lybrand, a professional services firm, captures this idea in one of their advertisements. The advertisement poses the question: "Who would you exclude from the future? Your choices include 730,000,000 people in the world with ideas to share; 4,000 languages in which to communicate; 255 nationalities with different perspectives and goals; 20 major religions with unique beliefs and customs; and 1 belief that everyone has something to contribute." The advertisement ends by stating: "You never know from where the next great idea will come."

LEARNING TO MANAGE GLOBALLY

Do today's leaders have the skills they need in a global marketplace? According to a survey of 108 executives, 75 percent feel that their companies do not have nearly enough global leaders. Moreover, only a handful (8 percent) have programs in place to address this shortage. Data from the survey, which appear in the book *Global Explorers: The Next Generation of Leaders*, show about 80 percent of the executives feel overseas assignments are critically important.[9]

One example of diversity education which incorporates experiences overseas is the Fluor program. Participants in this program spend 12 to 18 months "living out of their suitcase" overseas. Their work on consulting teams assigned to operations worldwide means that they have to deal with numerous languages and complex cultural issues. They learn to think flexibly, process a large amount of information, and do their homework. Laws, government regulations, currency, transportation, credit systems, and political conditions are just some of the issues they must study.

One corporate leader, with multiple assignments throughout Asia, spends an inordinate amount of time learning how to conduct business in "Thailand versus Malaysia, or in the Philippines versus Japan." He adds that his overseas experiences sharpen his listening skills. By learning to ask more questions, he ensures that he and colleagues from other countries will understand each other.[10]

Changing Demographics in the United States

At present, we are in the midst of a rapid demographic shift. As the U.S. population grows more diverse and inclusive, a number of trends are increasingly evident:

- ○ People of color are a growing percentage of the workforce
- ○ Whites are a decreasing percentage of the workforce.
- ○ More women are working.
- ○ People with disabilities are gaining more access to the workplace.
- ○ Workers are increasingly from "nontraditional" families (single parents, dual wage earners).
- ○ The average age of workers is increasing.
- ○ The religious diversity of workers is increasing.

Within the lifetime of today's teens, population changes will significantly alter how we conceptualize age, race, and ethnicity in this country. According to the authors of *Workforce 2020*, "the American labor force will become somewhat more brown and black in the next 20 years, but its most pervasive new tint will be gray."[11] People over 85 are presently the fastest-growing segment of the U.S. population. America's aging baby boomers, those born between 1945 and 1965, will stay on the job longer and seek more flexible work options. Social institutions, such as the family, economy, education, and medicine, will have to adapt.

With regard to racial and ethnic diversification, Census data indicate a much greater percentage of the U.S. population (approximately 33 percent) will be Latino, Asian/Pacific American, and Native American by the year 2050. Many of today's youth will see the day when no one ethnic group—including Whites of European descent—makes up more than 50 percent of the nation's population.

If Census Bureau projections are on target, religious diversity will become even more noticeable. At present, Protestants account for roughly 56 percent of the total population, followed by Catholics (26 percent), Jews (2 percent), and Muslims slightly less than 2 percent. If projections hold true, by the year 2050 no religious faith will constitute a majority. Two religious groups, Catholics and Muslims, are likely to experience the most growth during the next 50 years.[12]

My family looks like the U.N. It ranges from Jews to Buddhists. We have East Indians. We have a couple of American Indians, a couple of Europeans. My husband is from Lima, Peru. And it's great...The fights we have in our family are not about color. They're about religion.

—A student's perspective

Migration within the United States will continue to affect specific regions. For instance, in 1940, nearly 90 percent of Asian-Americans lived in the Western United States. A study by Sharon Lee based on U.S. Census data and published by the Population Reference Bureau reveals only about 54 percent live in this region today.[13] Other factors, such as immigration and intermarriage, will continue to make the racial and cultural mix that much more blurred and complex.

No matter what occupations or activities students pursue in the future, individual interaction will be more diverse than ever before in the history of this country. Most dramatic is skin color, culture/background and gender, but it will include many other differences and attributes.

—Frank Blethen, CEO of the Seattle Times Company

Continuing Potential for Divisiveness

Numerous surveys in recent years reveal that the growing diversity in the United States is giving rise to a sense of pessimism about the future. This pessimism is fueled by what many perceive as the downsides of diversity and change. People are skeptical about whether the motto *e pluribus unum* (out of many one) can become a reality. Does the emphasis on diversity weaken our sense of oneness?

In the workplace, initiatives aimed at recognizing diversity can have unintended effects. For example, misunderstanding and intolerance can become more of a problem if we do not handle diversity education with care. Some well-intentioned programs actually teach people to stereotype by ignoring the diversity within groups. Also, programs that focus exclusively on human differences may reinforce ignorance of our many similarities.

I have learned pain has no color; disappointment has no color; abuse has no color; caring, joy, hope, and happiness have no color; and above all, love has no color.

—Arnette Scott Ward, President, Chandler-Gilbert Community College

In all likelihood, hatred and hostility will continue to be a major social problem as our world changes. W. E. B. Dubois, civil rights leader and author as well as the first African-American to earn a doctorate from Harvard University, foresaw the potential divisiveness of diversity years ago. Dubois stated that the problem of the twentieth century would be the problem of the color line. In the 1960s, the historic Kerner Commission provided a similar warning. The Commission warned: "Our nation is moving toward two societies, one black, one white—separate and unequal."[14] Since that time, the lines or divides have been transformed. There are more divisions and inequality is more complex. While the race divide is still a central issue, it is one of many. A growing number of divides are economic as well as cultural.

⊠ A SHIFT IN ATTITUDES AMONG YOUTH?

While some assume that divisiveness is on the increase, recent surveys of youth show a willingness to bridge at least some of our differences. One poll by *USA Weekend* magazine examines the attitudes of nearly a quarter of a million teenagers. Of those teens surveyed, nearly three out of four say that they have a close friend of another race. Another *USA Today*/Gallup survey of teens throughout the country reveals a similar trend. A majority of teens who report going out on dates say that they have been out with someone of another race or ethnic group. Findings such as these may signal an important shift in attitudes and behavior in the future. Other surveys conducted in 1997 by MTV and *Time*/CNN show that young people tend to be more optimistic than adults. They generally see less divisiveness, fewer barriers, and more tolerance.

journal entry

THINKING THROUGH DIVERSITY:
Where is the hostility in your life? Where is the hope?

As we examine the negatives associated with diversity, it is important to remember how far we have come, both individually and collectively. William Raspberry, the noted journalist, says: "All of us are capable of getting so caught up in the distance that remains to be run that we forget to give ourselves full credit for the distance we've come."[15] It is all too easy to focus solely on our shortcomings and the social problems that have seemingly become a permanent fixture in our communities. We tend to do this because much of the change in the area of diversity is incremental and hardly noticeable. Additionally, what we read and see in the media often emphasizes the negative.

To focus only on the progress we have *not* made is to ignore reality. In your own life, think of the times when somebody was "hurting" and people helped. The fact that they did not share the same skin color, background, or values did not matter. What about the great relationships that you see among your friends and co-workers of various races and cultures?

On a broader level, it is important to remember the barriers of discrimination, segregation, and bigotry that have fallen. Alice Moy keeps her perspective by remembering her past. "It's like fifth heaven today I would say, for people who come over now. Opportunities galore. It wasn't available to us at that time, even though we were born here and we went to school here. Now I remember I had friends who attended and graduated from MIT, attended and graduated from Harvard—no one would hire them. Where did they end up? They ended up working for Chinese restaurants. No American firm would hire them."[16]

Change is one of the few things we can count on as we peer into the future. Technology, globalization, changing demographics, and the continuing potential for divisiveness will challenge our adaptability and our ability to get along with each other. If we can develop diversity consciousness in ourselves, we will be ready to meet these challenges and open our minds to many more people, cultures, and opportunities.

The need for developing diversity skills on the part of our students extends well beyond their success in school and in the workplace. If our increasingly diverse society is to achieve its fullest potential, it will be because we collectively have made a deep and personal commitment to understanding 'the other,' to caring about 'the other,' and to having the skills to work together to shape a just and effective society.

—Lou Albert, Vice Chancellor of Educational Services,
San Jose Evergreen Community College District

Exercises

IN-CLASS

Exercise 1: Checking Up on Yourself

Directions for Instructor.
Randomly assign students to groups. Ask students in each group to:
1. Explain how their diversity skills (i.e., communication, teamwork, conflict management, flexible thinking, etc.) will affect their plans for the future.
2. Discuss how their perceptions of diversity have changed during the course of the semester, and what might have precipitated this change.

Exercise 2: A Look Back

Directions for Instructor.

Ask students to:

1. Write down *one* thing they will remember most about this class in the future. It can be anything—an important concept, a funny story, someone's comment, an assignment, discussion, or something else that relates to the class.

2. Share what they wrote with the entire class. Consider forming a circle and using a pencil or some other object as a "talking stick." Traditionally, in decision making meetings, Native Americans sometimes pass around such a stick to show whose turn it is to talk. Only the person holding the stick can talk. All others should actively listen and express their desire to participate nonverbally.

OUT-OF-CLASS

Exercise 1: The Transformation of Barbie

The Barbie doll is the world's best-selling toy. Two Barbies are sold every second. Sales each year exceed $2 billion. In recent years, Barbie has undergone significant changes in order to broaden her appeal. According to one toy analyst, Barbie is like Betty Crocker. Her looks get updated to keep up with the times. Answer the following questions regarding Barbie and her transformation.

1. Find someone who remembers what Barbie dolls looked like 20 to 30 years ago. Ask this person the following questions. How did Barbie look years ago? Describe her physical appearance. What about her occupations? Could you choose the race or ethnicity of Barbie? Was it different from today's Barbies?

2. Visit a local toy store and see what kinds of Barbie dolls are for sale. Do you think the image of Barbie has been altered? Why? Is the change driven by financial and/or social concerns? Explain. Finally, what do you think of the changes?

Exercise 2: Stretch Targets

Situation: You are a city employee. As one of five employees in the Department of Tourism, you are responsible for finding new and innovative ways of increasing the number of tourists visiting your city. Recently, the mayor attended a conference in which he learned about using *stretch targets* to increase worker productivity. Stretch targets are "gigantic, seemingly unreachable milestones…which require big, athletic leaps of progress."[17] The mayor has sent out a memo asking all employees to establish one stretch target in the area of diversity.

Directive: Specifically, you are to write a memo to the mayor and clearly explain (1) your chosen stretch target, (2) how it relates to your job, and (3) how you will evaluate your progress in reaching the goal or target. The memo states that your response to the mayor should be no more than one typewritten page.

Exercise 3: A Classroom for All

Situation: You have been appointed to serve on a statewide task force on higher education. Your work on the task force requires you to create an orientation course at the college level for incoming freshmen. The purpose of this course is to acquaint students with the skills they need to be successful. Your responsibility focuses on the part of the course that deals with diversity skills.

Directive: Submit an outline of the diversity skills to be taught. Briefly describe:
- Each skill.
- The connection between the skill and student success.
- Ten specific resources that students will use. These may include videos, books, journal articles, and Web sites. List the skill or skills *each* resource addresses.

✿ INTERNET EXERCISE

Using the Internet, find two diversity training programs. These programs should approach diversity training differently. What are the major differences and similarities in the programs? Based on the information available, which of the two do you think would be more effective? Why? Support your answer and be as specific as possible. Include the URL for each Web site.

NOTES

[1] Bill Bradley, "How America Can Make Brotherhood Work," *Reader's Digest 75th Anniversary Issue*, 1997, 96–101.

[2] Walt Michael, letter to the author, Jan. 9, 1998.

[3] Richard Gaskins, letter to the author (attachment), Nov. 9,1997.

[4] Jerry Berrios, "A Balancing Act," *LATINA Style*, 3(2), 1997, 24–28.

[5] Richard W. Judy and Carol D'Amico, *Workforce 2020: Executive Summary* (Indianapolis, IN: Hudson Institute, 1997).

[6] Karen Rasmussen, "Gaining Perspective on Global Education," *ASCD (Association for Supervision and Curriculum Development) Curriculum Update*, Summer 1998, 3.

[7] Donald Norris and Michael Dolence, *Transforming Higher Education: A Vision for Learning in the 21st Century* (Ann Arbor, MI: Society for College and University Planning, 1995), 3.

[8] Trevor Hitner, letter to the author, Mar. 15, 1998.

[9] Hal Lancaster, "Learning to Manage in a Global Workplace," *The Wall Street Journal*, June 2, 1998, B1.

[10] Ibid.

[11]Frank Swoboda, "Study: Many in Graying Work Force May Not Have the Green to Retire," *The Washington Post*, Apr. 18, 1997, G3.

[12]U.S. Bureau of the Census, *Statistical Abstract of the United States*, 1994 (Washington, DC: U.S. Government Printing Office, 1994).

[13]Nicole Koch, "Asian-Americans Have Become Fastest-Growing Ethnic Group," *The Dallas Morning News*, June 9, 1998, 4A.

[14]National Advisory Commission on Civil Disorders, *Report of the National Advisory Commission on Civil Disorders* (New York: Bantam, 1968) 1.

[15]William Raspberry, from a lecture at Kansas State University, *Vital Speeches of the Day*, June 1, 1995, 493–496.

[16]Alice Moy, as found in Balch Institute of Ethnic Studies, "The Bachelor Society," *Perspective*, Spring/Summer 1998, 4.

[17]Sharon Tully, "Why to Go for Stretch Targets," *Fortune*, Nov. 14, 1994, 145–158.

BIBLIOGRAPHY

ABC News. *The Eye of the Storm* (video). Mount Kisco, NY: Guidance Associates, 1981.

Abraham, Ansley. *Racial Issues on Campus: How Students View Them.* Atlanta, GA: Southern Regional Education Board, 1990.

Adler, N. *International Dimensions of Organization Behavior.* Boston: Kent, 1986.

Alvarez, Rafael, and Dan Thanh Dang. "Embracing the New, Preserving the Old," *The Sun,* Apr. 27, 1995, 1A+.

American Management Association. "What Do Organizations Really Want?" *AMA Catalog of Seminars,* Oct. 1997.

Angelou, Maya. *I Know Why The Caged Bird Sings.* New York: Bantam Books, 1993.

Appel, Morgan, David Cartwright, Daryl Smith, and Lisa Wolf. *The Impact of Diversity on Students.* Washington, DC: Association of American Colleges and Universities, 1996.

Aronson, Elliot, and Neal Osherow. "Cooperation, Prosocial Behavior, and Academic Performance: Experiments in the Desegregated Classroom," *Applied Social Psychology Annual,* 1, 1980, 174–175.

Associated Press. "More Women Finish College Than Men," *The Sun,* June 29, 1998, 3A.

Associated Press. "Number Living in Poverty Drops for 3rd Year in a Row, U.S. Says," *The Sun,* Sept. 25, 1998, 3A.

Astin, Alexander. "Diversity and Multiculturalism on the Campus: How Are Students Affected?" *Change,* Mar./Apr., 1993, 44–49.

Astin, Alexander. *What Matters in College? Four Critical Years Revisited.* San Francisco: Jossey-Bass, 1993.

Axtell, Roger E. *Gestures: The Do's and Taboos of Body Language around the World.* New York: Wiley, 1991.

Balch Institute of Ethnic Studies. "The Bachelor Society," *Perspective*, Spring/Summer 1998.

Bates, Karen G., and Karen E. Hudson. *Basic Black: Home Training for Modern Times*. New York: Doubleday, 1996.

Belenky, Mary, Blythe Clinchy, Nancy Goldberger, and Jill Tarule. *Women's Ways of Knowing*. New York: Basic Books, 1986.

Bellarosa, James M. *A Problem of Plumbing and Other Stories*. Santa Barbara, CA: J. Daniel, 1989.

Berrios, Jerry. "A Balancing Act," *LATINA Style* 3(2), 1997, 24–28.

Berscheid, E., and E. Walster. "Beauty and the Beast," *Psychology Today*, Mar. 1972, 42–46, 74.

Bingham, Raymond. "Leaving Prejudice Behind," *The Washington Post Health Section*, Sept. 6, 1994, 9.

Black, J. Stewart, Allen Morrison and Hal Gregersen. *Global Explorers: The Next Generation of Leaders*. New York: Routledge, 1999.

Blauner, Bob. *Black Lives, White Lives*. Berkeley, CA: University of California Press, 1989.

Block, J. Richard, and Harold Yuker. *Can You Believe Your Eyes?* New York: Brunner/Mazel, 1992.

Bodenhausen, Galen V. "Stereotypic Biases in Social Decision Making and Memory: Testing Process Models of Stereotype Use," *Journal of Personality and Social Psychology*, 55, 1988, 726–737.

Bogardus, Emory. "Measuring Social Distance," *Journal of Applied Sociology*, 9, Mar./Apr. 1925, 299–308.

Bradley, Bill. "How America Can Make Brotherhood Work," *Reader's Digest 75th Anniversary Issue*, 1997, 96–101.

Bridge, M. Junior. "Marginalizing Women," *Women, Men, and Media*. Unabridged Communications, 1996.

Brown, David (ed.). *Higher Education Exchange*. Dayton, OH: Kettering Foundation, 1995.

Burton, John. *Conflict: Resolution and Provention*. New York: St. Martin's Press, 1990.

Butterfield, Bruce. "Xerox Makes It Work," *Boston Globe*, Oct. 20, 1991, 33–37.

Carson, Benjamin. "Carson Philosophy Is 'Think Big,'" *The Sun*, Aug. 24, 1997, 6H.

Carson, Benjamin. *Gifted Hands*. Washington, DC: Review and Herald Publishing Association, 1990.

Carter, Carol, Joyce Bishop and Sarah Lyman Kravits. *Keys to Success*. Upper Saddle River, NJ: Prentice Hall, 1998.

210

Checkley, Kathy. "The First Seven…and the Eighth: A Conversation with Howard Gardner," *Educational Leadership*, 55(1), Sept. 1997, 8–13.

Chemers, Martin M., Stuart Oskamp and Mark A. Costanzo (eds.). *Diversity in Organizations*. Thousand Oaks, CA: Sage, 1995.

Clemens, Lynda P., and Andrea T. Dolph. *How to Hit the Ground Running in Your New Job*. Lincolnwood, IL: VGM Career Horizons, 1995.

The Color of Fear (video). Oakland, CA: Stir Fry Productions, 1994.

Cortës, Carlos E. "The Societal Curriculum: Implications for Multiethnic Education," in *Education in the 80's: Multiethnic Education*, James Banks (cd.). Washington, DC: National Education Association, 1981.

Cose, Ellis. *The Rage of a Privileged Class*. New York: HarperCollins, 1993.

Covcy, Stephen. "How to Succeed in Today's Workplace," *USA Weekend*, Aug. 29–31, 1997, 4–5.

Covey, Stephen. *The Seven Habits of Highly Effective People*. New York: Simon & Schuster, 1989.

Cox, T. *Cultural Diversity in Organizations: Theory, Research, and Practice*. San Francisco: Berrett-Koehler Publishers, 1993.

Cox, T., and S. Blake. "Managing Cultural Diversity: Implications for Organizational Competitiveness," *The Executive*, 5(3), 1991, 45–56.

Cullen, Countee (ed.). *Caroling Dusk*. Secaucus, NJ: Carol Publishing Group, 1993.

Dancis, Jerome. "Group Learning Helps Minority Students Excel at University," *Cooperative Learning*, 12(1), Oct. 1991, 26–27.

DeSantis, Andrea, and Wesley Kayson. "Defendants' Characteristics of Attractiveness, Race, and Sex and Sentencing Decisions," *Psychological Reports*, 81, 1997, 679–683.

Disch, Estelle. *Reconstructing Gender: A Multicultural Anthology*. Mountain View, CA: Mayfield Publishing, 1997.

"Diversity: Making the Business Case," *Business Week Special Advertising Section*, Dec. 9, 1996, 83+.

Dowd, Karen, and Jeanne Liedtka. "What Corporations Seek in MBA Hires: A Survey," *The Magazine of the Graduate Management Admission Council*, Winter, 1994, 34–39.

Dubois, W. E. B. *The Souls of Black Folk*. New York: Fawcett, 1961.

Ehrlich, Howard J. *Campus Ethnoviolence: A Research Review*, Institute Report 5. Baltimore: National Institute Against Prejudice and Violence, 1992.

Enayati, Amanda. "Not Black, Not White," *The Washington Post*, July 13, 1997, C1.

"Facts about Higher Education in the U.S.," *Chronicle of Higher Education Almanac Issue 1998/1999*, XLV(1), Aug. 28, 1998.

Feagin, Joe, and Melvin Sikes. *Living with Racism: The Black Middle Class Experience.* Boston: Beacon Press, 1994.

Federal Glass Ceiling Commission. *A Solid Investment: Making Full Use of the Nation's Human Capital.* Washington, DC: U.S. Department of Labor, 1995.

Fernandez, John P. *Managing a Diverse Work Force: Regaining the Competitive Edge.* Lexington, MA: Lexington Books, 1991.

Fine, Marlene G. *Building Successful Multicultural Organizations: Challenges and Opportunities.* Westport, CT: Quorum Books, 1995.

Fine, Michelle, and Adrienne Asch (eds.). *Women with Disabilities: Essays in Psychology, Culture, and Politics.* Philadelphia: Temple University Press, 1988.

Fletcher, Michael. "Crazy Horse Again Sounds Battle Cry," *The Washington Post,* Feb. 18, 1997, A03.

Ford, Clyde W. *We Can All Get Along.* New York: Dell Publishing, 1994.

Frankenburg, Ruth. *White Women, Race Matters: The Social Construction of Whiteness.* Minneapolis, MN: University of Minnesota Press, 1993.

Fraser, Barbara. "U.S. Colleges Step Up Recruiting in Latin America," *Chronicle of Higher Education*, XLIV(10), Oct. 31, 1997, A58–A59.

Frey, William. "The Diversity Myth," *American Demographics*, June 1998, 38–43.

Gallagher, Charles. "White Reconstruction in the University," *Socialist Review,* 24, 1994, 165.

Gang, Philip. *Rethinking Education.* Atlanta, GA: Dagaz Press, 1989.

Gardner, Howard. *Frames of Mind: The Theory of Multiple Intelligences.* New York: Basic Books, 1983.

Gaskins, Richard. Letter to the author (attachment), Nov. 9, 1997.

Gibson, M. A. "Parental Support for Schooling." Paper presented at the annual meeting of the American Anthropological Association, Dec. 1986.

Gilens, Martin. "Race and Poverty in America: Public Misperceptions and the American News Media," *Public Opinion Quarterly,* 60, 1996, 515–541.

Goldsmith, Charles. "Look See! Anyone Do Read This and It Will Make You Laughable," *The Wall Street Journal,* Nov. 19, 1992, B1.

Goleman, Daniel. *Working with Emotional Intelligence.* New York: Bantam Books, 1998.

Gonzales, Juan L., Jr. *The Lives of Ethnic Americans,* 2nd ed. Dubuque, IA: Kendall/Hunt, 1994.

Granrose, Cherlyn S., and Stuart Oskamp (eds.). *Cross-Cultural Work Groups.* Thousand Oaks, CA: Sage Publications, 1997.

Graves, Earl. "On Financial Hurdles Facing African Americans," *The Washington Post*, May 4, 1997, H4.

Greissman, Eugene. *Diversity: Challenges and Opportunities*. New York: HarperCollins, 1993.

Griffin, John H. *Black Like Me*. New York: NAL/Dutton, 1999.

Griggs, Lewis Brown, and Lente-Louise Louw (eds.). *Valuing Diversity: New Tools for a New Reality*. New York: McGraw-Hill, 1995.

Grimsley, Kristen Downey. "Training in the Theater of the Real," *The Washington Post Business Section*, Mar. 24, 1997, 12–14.

Guerney, Bernard, Jr. *Relationship Enhancement Program*, 2nd ed. Bethesda, MD: Ideals, 1997.

Hacker, Andrew. *Two Nations*. New York: Ballantine Books, 1995.

Hall, Roberta M., and Bernice Sandler. *The Classroom Climate: A Chilly One for Women*. Washington, DC: Association of American Colleges, 1982.

Hall, Roberta M., and Bernice Sandler. *Out of the Classroom: A Chilly Campus Climate for Women?* Washington, DC: Project on the Status and Education of Women, Association of American Colleges, 1984.

Hanley, Sue. Letter to the author, Dec. 22, 1997.

Harvey, Carol, and M. June Allard. *Understanding Diversity: Readings, Cases, and Exercises*. New York: HarperCollins, 1995.

Heath, Shirley Brice. *Ways with Words*. Cambridge: Cambridge University Press, 1983.

Hegi, Ursula. *Tearing the Silence*. New York: Simon & Schuster, 1997.

Henderson, George. *Cultural Diversity in the Workplace: Issues and Strategies*. Westport, CT: Praeger Publishers, 1994.

Higginbotham, E. *Integrating All Women into the Curriculum*. Memphis, TN: Memphis State University Center for Research on Women, 1988

Hitner, Trevor. Letter to the author, Mar. 15, 1998.

Huffman, Terry. "The Transculturation of Native American College Students," in *American Mosaic: Selected Readings on America's Multicultural Heritage*, Young I. Song and Eugene C. Kim (eds.). Englewood Cliffs, NJ: Prentice Hall, 1993, 211–219.

Huffman, Terry, Maurice Sill and Martin Brokenleg. "College Achievement among Sioux and White South Dakota Students," *Journal of American Indian Education*, Jan. 1986, 32–38.

Hvitfeldt, Christina. "Traditional Culture, Perceptual Style, and Learning: The Classroom Behavior of Hmong Adults," *Adult Education Quarterly*, 36(2) Winter 1986, 65–77.

"Inclusion," *Book and Video Catalog*. Manhattan, KS: The MASTER Teacher, 1999.

"Inclusion, Not Rejection Will Spur Racial Harmony," *USA Today*, June 16, 1997, 18A.

Jackson, Susan, and Marian Ruderman (eds.). *Diversity in Work Teams: Research Paradigms for a Changing Workplace*. Washington, DC: American Psychological Association, 1996.

Jamieson, Daniel, and Julie O'Mara. *Managing Workforce 2000*. San Francisco: Jossey-Bass, 1991.

Johnston, William B., and Arnold Parker. *Workforce 2000: Work and Workers for the 21st Century*. Indianapolis, IN: Hudson Institute, 1987.

Judy, Richard W., and Carol D'Amico. *Workforce 2020: Executive Summary*. Indianapolis, IN: Hudson Institute, 1997.

Kabagarama, Daisy. *Breaking the Ice: A Guide to Understanding People from Other Cultures*. Boston: Allyn & Bacon, 1997.

Karp, Abby. "Working Together: Innovative Programs Promote Tolerance in Schools," *The Sun*, Oct. 17, 1989, 1C.

Katz, Neil H., and John Lawyer. *Communication and Conflict Resolution Skills*. Dubuque, IA: Kendall/Hunt, 1992.

Kauffman, L. A. "The Diversity Game," *Voice*, Aug. 31, 1993, 29–33.

Kendall, Diana. *Race, Class, and Gender in a Diverse Society*. Boston: Allyn & Bacon, 1997.

Kenton, Sherron, and Deborah Valentine. *CrossTalk: Communicating in a Multicultural Workplace*. Upper Saddle River, NJ: Prentice Hall, 1997.

King, Martin Luther, Jr. *Where Do We Go from Here: Chaos or Community?* Boston: Beacon Press, 1968.

Koch, Nicole. "Asian-Americans Have Become Fastest-Growing Ethnic Group," *The Dallas Morning News*, June 9, 1998, 4A.

Knox, D., and C. Schacht. *Choices in Relationships*. Belmont, CA: Wadsworth, 1997.

Kochman, Thomas. *Black and White Styles in Conflict*. Chicago: The University of Chicago Press, 1981.

Kotter, John. *The General Managers*. New York: Free Press, 1982.

Kramer, Martin, and Stephen Weiner. *The Project on Campus Community and Diversity*. Phoenix, AZ: Oryx Press, 1994.

Kuntz, Gabriela. "My Spanish Standoff," *Newsweek*, May 4, 1998, 22.

Labaton, Stephen. "Denny's Gets a Bill for the Side Orders of Bigotry," *The New York Times*, May 29, 1994, E4.

Lahr, John. "Speaking across the Divide," *The New Yorker*, Jan. 27, 1997, 41–42.

Lancaster, Hal. "Learning to Manage in a Global Workplace, *The Wall Street Journal*, June 2, 1998, B1.

Langer, E. J. *Mindfulness.* Reading, MA: Addison-Wesley, 1989.

LeBeau, Christina. "Attitude Adjustment," *Rochester Democrat and Chronicle*, Oct. 19, 1997, 1e+.

Levinson, Wendy, Debra Roter, John Mullooly, Valerie Dull, and Richard Frankel. "Physician-Patient Communication: The Relationship with Malpractice Claims Among Primary Care Physicians and Surgeons," *Journal of the American Medical Association*, February 19, 1997, 553–559.

Lipnack, Jessica, and Jeffrey Stamps. *Virtual Teams.* New York: Wiley, 1997.

Loden, Marilyn, and Judy Rosener. *Workforce America: Managing Employee Diversity as a Vital Resource.* Homewood, IL: Business One Irwin, 1991.

Longstreet, Wilma. *Aspects of Ethnicity: Understanding Differences in Pluralistic Classrooms.* Williston, VT: Teacher's College Press, 1978.

Maddox, Amy. "Underneath We're All the Same," *Teaching Tolerance*, Spring 1995, 65.

Massachusetts Commission Against Discrimination, as reported on "Age and Attitudes," *ABC News Primetime Live*, June 9, 1994.

McIntosh, Peggy. *White Privilege and Male Privilege.* Wellesley, MA: Wellesley College Center for Research on Women, 1988.

McLaughlin, Barry, and Beverly McLeod. "Educating All Our Students: Improving Education for Children from Culturally and Linguistically Diverse Backgrounds." Online. World Wide Web. June 1996. Available: http://www.ncbe.gwu.edu/miscpubs/ncrcdsll/edall.htm.

McLuhan, Marshall. *The Mechanical Bride: Folklore of Industrial Man.* Boston: Beacon Press, 1967.

McNatt, Glenn. "Instant Communication Is Changing Our Very Form of Government," *The Sun*, Feb. 9, 1997, 5E.

Mehler, Mark. "AMS Centers Deliver Global Information Access," *Integration Management: The Newspaper for Global Integrators*, 1(8), Sept. 18, 1997.

Merton, Robert. "Discrimination and the American Creed," in *Sociological Ambivalence and Other Essays*, New York: Free Press, 1976, 189–216.

Michael, Walt. Letter to the author, Jan. 9, 1998.

Montagu, Ashley. *Man's Most Dangerous Myth: The Fallacy of Race.* Cleveland, OH: World Publishing, 1964.

Moremen, Robin. "A Multicultural Framework: Transforming Curriculum, Transforming Students," *Teaching Sociology*, 25(2), Apr. 1997, 107–119.

Morgan, Appel, David Cartwright, Daryl Smith and Lisa Wolf. *The Impact of Diversity on Students: A Preliminary Review of the Research Literature.* Washington, DC: Association of American Colleges and Universities, 1996.

Morrison, Toni. *Playing in the Dark*. Cambridge, MA: Harvard University Press, 1992.

National Advisory Commission on Civil Disorders. *Report of the National Advisory Commission on Civil Disorders*. New York: Bantam, 1968.

National Center for Education Statistics. *Digest of Education Statistics, 1997*. NCES 98-015. Washington, DC: U.S. Department of Education, 1997.

National Council of La Raza. *Don't Blink: Hispanics in Television Entertainment*. Washington, DC: Center for Media and Public Affairs, 1996.

National Institute of Education. "Involvement in Learning: Realizing the Potential of American Higher Education," *Report of the Study Group on the Conditions of Excellence in American Higher Education*. Washington, DC: U.S. Department of Education, 1984.

Nelton, Sharon. "Meet Your New Workforce," *Nation's Business*, July 1988, 15.

Nieto, Sonia. *Affirming Diversity: The Sociopolitical Context of Multicultural Education*. White Plains, NY: Longman, 1996.

Norris, Donald, and Michael Dolence. *Transforming Higher Education: A Vision for Learning in the 21st Century*. Ann Arbor, MI: Society for College and University Planning, 1995.

O'Hanlon, Ann. "Lost in the Translation," *The Washington Post*, May 24, 1998, D1+.

Parillo, Vincent. *Diversity in America*. Thousand Oaks, CA: Pine Forge Press, 1996.

Parker, Pat. *Movement in Black*. Ithaca, NY: Firebrand Books, 1978.

Pitts, Leonard. "Watching Whites Struggle to Understand Their Whiteness," *The Sun*, Apr. 21, 1997, 9A.

Proctor, Samuel D., and William Watley. *Sermons from the Black Pulpit*. Valley Forge, PA: Judson Press, 1984.

Rasmussen, Karen. "Gaining Perspective on Global Education," *ASCD (Association for Supervision and Curriculum Development) Curriculum Update,"* Summer 1998.

Raspberry, William. Quote from a lecture at Kansas State University, *Vital Speeches of the Day*, 61(16), June 1, 1995, 493–496.

Reid, Alice. "Mosque's Children Await Playground," *The Washington Post*, Nov. 22, 1998, B4.

Rice, Fay. "How to Make Diversity Pay," *Fortune*, Aug. 8, 1994, 79–86.

Riley, Dorothy Winbush (ed.). *My Soul Looks Back, 'Less I Forget: A Collection of Quotations by People of Color*. New York: HarperCollins, 1995.

Rodriguez, Richard. *Hunger of Memory: The Education of Richard Rodriguez.* Boston: David R. Godine, 1982.

Rubinstein, Moshe. *Patterns of Problem Solving.* Englewood Cliffs, NJ: Prentice Hall, 1975.

Ruderman, Marian, Martha Hughes-James, and Susan Jackson. *Selected Research on Work Team Diversity.* Washinton, DC: American Psychological Association, 1996.

Rush, Sheila, and Chris Clark. *How to Get Along with Black People.* New Rochelle, NY: Third Press-Joseph Okpaku Publishing Co., Inc., 1972.

Ryan, Michael. "If You Can't Teach Me, Don't Criticize Me," *Parade Magazine,* May 11, 1997, 6–7.

Sacks, Oliver. *Seeing Voices: A Journey into the World of the Deaf.* Berkeley, CA: University of California Press, 1989.

Schuman, David, and Dick Olufs. *Diversity on Campus.* Boston: Allyn & Bacon, 1995.

Schwartz, Howard. "Further Thoughts on a 'Sociology of Acceptance' for Disabled People," *Social Policy,* Fall 1988, 36–39.

Scripps Howard News Service, "White Men Still at Top of the Business Heap, Study Finds," *Carroll County Times,* Mar. 16, 1995, A7.

Sedgwick, John. *Rich Kids.* New York: William Morrow, 1985.

Servaes, J. "Cultural Identity in East and West," *Howard Journal of Communications,* 1(2), 1988, 58–71.

Shipler, David. *A Country of Strangers.* New York: Alfred A. Knopf, 1997.

Silver, Sheryl. "Advice for Adjusting to the World of Work," *Washington Post Advertising Supplement,* Oct. 19, 1997, 60, 65.

Silver, Sheryl. "New Grads: Make the Most of Your First Job," *The Washington Post High Tech Horizons,* Aug. 3, 1997, M19.

Slavin, Robert. "Synthesis of Research on Cooperative Learning," *Educational Leadership,* 48, 1991, 71–82.

Slepper, Jim. "Liberal Racism," *The New Democrat,* July/Aug. 1997, 8–12.

Smith, K. A., D. W. Johnson, and R. T. Johnson. "Can Conflict Be Constructive? Controversy versus Concurrence Seeking in Learning Groups," *Journal of Educational Psychology,* 75, 1983, 651–663.

Solomon, Joshua. "Skin Deep: Reliving *Black Like Me:* My Own Journey into the Heart of Race Conscious America," *The Washington Post,* Oct. 30, 1994, C01.

Southern Poverty Law Center. "E-mail on Trial," *Intelligence Report,* Winter 1998, 5.

Southern Poverty Law Center. "163 and Counting…Hate Groups Find Home on the Net," *Intelligence Report,* Winter 1998, 24.

Sproull, L., and S. Kiesler. *Connections: New Ways of Working in the Networked Organization.* Cambridge, MA: MIT Press, 1991.

Steele, Claude. "Twenty-First Century Program and Stereotype Vulnerability." Unpublished study and program, Stanford University, Stanford, CA, 1995.

Strait, George. "Health Care's Racial Divide" [online]. Available: http://more.abc-news.go.com/sections/living/DailyNews/racial_healthcare990224.html (March 7, 1999).

Sullivan, D. "Organization Structure in Multinational Corporations," in *International Encyclopedia of Business and Management*, M. Warner (ed.). London: Routledge, 1996, 3573–3597.

Swoboda, Frank. "Study: Many in Graying Work Force May Not Have the Green to Retire," *The Washington Post*, Apr. 18, 1997, G3.

Takaki, Ronald. *A Different Mirror: A History of Multicultural America*. Boston: Little, Brown, 1993.

Takata, Susan R. "The Chairs Game—Competition versus Cooperation: The Sociological Uses of Musical Chairs," *Teaching Sociology*, 25(3), July 1997, 200–206.

Tan, Cheryl. "For College Students, Degrees of Ethnicity," *The Washington Post*, Sept. 3, 1996, B1.

Tannen, Deborah. *The Argument Culture: Moving from Debate to Dialogue*. New York: Random House, 1998.

Tannen, Deborah. *Talking from 9 to 5: How Women's and Men's Conversational Styles Affect Who Gets Heard, Who Gets Credit, and What Gets Done at Work*. New York: William Morrow, 1994.

Tannen, Deborah. *That's Not What I Meant*. New York: Ballantine Books, 1992.

Tannen, Deborah. *You Just Don't Understand: Men and Women in Conversation*. New York: William Morrow, 1990.

Terkel, Studs. *Race: How Blacks and Whites Think and Feel about the American Obsession*. New York: New Press, 1992.

Tharp, Roland. "Psychocultural Variables and Constants: Effects on Teaching and Learning in Schools," *American Psychologist*, 44(2), Feb. 1989, 349–359.

Thiederman, Sondra. *Bridging Cultural Barriers for Corporate Success: How to Manage the Multicultural Workforce*. New York: Lexington Books, 1991.

Thomas, Roosevelt. *Beyond Race and Gender: Unleashing the Power of Your Total Work Force by Managing Diversity*. New York: American Management Association, 1991.

Tuchman, B. W. "Developmental Sequences in Small Groups," *Psychological Bulletin*, 63, 1965, 384–399.

Tully, Sharon. "Why to Go for Stretch Targets," *Fortune*, Nov. 14, 1994, 145–158.

U. S. Bureau of the Census. *Historical Statistics of the United States, Part II*. Washington, DC: U.S. Government Printing Office, 1976.

U.S. Bureau of the Census. *Historical Statistics of the United States, Part II.* Series Z 20-132. Washington, DC: U.S. Government Printing Office, 1993.

U.S. Bureau of the Census. *Statistical Abstract of the United States: 1994.* Washington, DC: U.S. Government Printing Office, 1994.

U.S. Bureau of the Census. *Statistical Abstract of the United States: 1997*, 117th edition. Washington, DC: U.S. Government Printing Office, 1997.

Verville, Anne-Lee. "What Business Needs from Higher Education," *Educational Record*, 76(4), Fall 1995, 46–50.

von Oech, Roger. *A Kick in the Seat of the Pants.* New York: Harper & Row, 1986.

West, Cornel. *Race Matters.* New York: Random House, 1993.

Whiting, Robert. "You Gotta Have 'Wa,'" *Sports Illustrated*, Sept. 24, 1979, 60+.

Wilson, Angus. *The Strange Ride of Rudyard Kipling: His Life and Works.* New York: Viking Press, 1978, 290.

Winkler, Karen. "While Concern over Race Relations Has Lessened among Whites, Sociologists Say Racism Is Taking New Forms, Not Disappearing," *Chronicle of Higher Education*, Sept. 11, 1991, A10–A11.

Wood, Donna. *Business and Society*, 2nd ed. New York: HarperCollins, 1994.

Wood, Julia T. (ed.). *Gendered Relationships.* Mountain View, CA: Mayfield Publishing, 1996.

"Working Together Works" [online]. World Wide Web. Nov. 28, 1998. Available: http://www.diversitydtg.com/thoughts/thought_mnu.html.

X, Malcolm. *The Autobiography of Malcolm X.* New York: Ballantine Books, 1965.

Yardley, Jonathan. "Coping with History," *The Washington Post: Book World*, July 6, 1997, 3.

Young, Whitney. *To Be Equal.* New York: McGraw-Hill, 1966.

Zangwill, Israel. *The Melting Pot.* New York: The Jewish Publication Society of America, 1909.

SUGGESTED READINGS

Developing our diversity consciousness requires continual learning. Reading is one important means of challenging and expanding our thinking in the area of diversity. The following books, many of which have been recommended by students as well as educators, deal with a wide range of diversity issues.

Alvarez, Julia. *Something to Declare*. Chapel Hill, NC: Algonquin Books, 1998.

Andersen, Margaret, and Patricia Hill Collins. *Race, Class, and Gender: An Anthology*. Belmont, CA: Wadsworth, 1997.

Banks, James A., and Cherry A. McGee Banks (eds.). *Handbook of Research on Multicultural Education*. New York: Macmillan, 1995.

Battle, Stafford, and Rey Harris. *The African-American Resource Guide to the Internet and Online Services*. New York: McGraw-Hill, 1996.

Belenky, Mary, Blythe Clinchy, Nancy Goldberger and Jill Tarule. *Women's Ways of Knowing*. New York: Basic Books, 1986.

Bellarosa, James M. *A Problem of Plumbing and Other Stories*. Santa Barbara, CA: John Daniel, 1989.

Bradley, Bill. *Time Present, Time Past*. New York: Vintage Books, 1996.

Bragg, Rick. *All Over but the Shoutin.'* New York: Vintage Books, 1998.

The Broad Minds Collective (eds.). *Ourselves as Students: Multicultural Voices in the Classroom*. Carbondale, IL: Southern Illinois University Press, 1996.

Bystydzienski, Jill M., and Estelle P. Resnik (eds.). *Women in Cross-Cultural Transitions*. Bloomington, IN: Phi Delta Kappa Educational Foundation, 1994.

Cadet, Jean-Robert. *Restavec: From Haitian Slave Child to Middle-Class American*. Austin, TX: University of Texas Press, 1998.

Canfield, Jack, Mark Hansen, Jennifer Hawthorne, and Marci Shimoff. *Chicken Soup for the Woman's Soul*. Deerfield Beach, FL: Health Communications, 1996.

Cisneros, S. *House on Mango Street*. New York: Random House, 1994.

Covey, Stephen. *The Seven Habits of Highly Effective People*. New York: Simon & Schuster, 1990.

Daloz, Laurent A. Parks, Cheryl H. Keen, James P. Keen, and Sharon Daloz Parks. *Common Fire: Lives of Commitment in an Complex World*. New York: Beacon Press, 1996.

Dees, M., with S. Fiffer. *A Season of Justice: A Lawyer's Own Story of Victory Over America's Hate Groups*. New York: Simon & Schuster, 1992.

Dog, Mary Crow. *Lakota Woman*. New York: HarperCollins, 1991.

Dresser, Norrine. *Multicultural Manners: New Rules of Etiquette for a Changing Society*. New York: Wiley, 1996.

Duneier, Mitchell. *Slim's Table: Race, Respectability, and Masculinity*. Chicago: The University of Chicago Press, 1994.

Essed, Philomena. *Understanding Everyday Racism*. Newbury Park, CA: Sage Publications, 1991.

Ford, Clyde W. *We Can All Get Along: 50 Steps You Can Take to Help End Racism*. New York: Dell Publishing, 1994.

Glusker, Susannah Joel. *Anita Brenner: A Mind of Her Own*. Austin, TX: University of Texas Press, 1998.

Golden, Kristen, and Barbara Findlen. *Making a Difference: 100 Remarkable Women of the Twentieth Century*. New York: Michael Friedman Publishing Group, 1998.

Goleman, Daniel. *Emotional Intelligence: Why It Can Matter More Than IQ*. New York: Bantam Books, 1995.

Gonzales, Juan L., Jr. *The Lives of Ethnic Americans*, 2nd ed. Dubuque, IA: Kendall/Hunt, 1994.

Henderson, George. *Cultural Diversity in the Workplace: Issues and Strategies*. Westport, CT: Greenwood Publishing Group, 1994.

Hockenberry, John. *Moving Violations: War Zones, Wheelchairs and Declarations of Independence*. New York: Hyperion, 1995.

Hull, Gloria, Patricia Bell Scott, and Barbara Smith (eds.). *All the Women Are White, All the Blacks Are Men, but Some of Us Are Brave*. Old Westbury, NY: Feminist Press, 1982.

Immerso, Michael. *Newark's Little Italy*. Piscataway, NJ: Rutgers University Press, 1997.

Jackson, Susan (ed.). *Diversity in Work Teams: Research Paradigms for a Changing Workplace*. Washington, DC: American Psychological Association, 1996.

Jennings, Kevin (ed.). *Becoming Visible: A Reader in Gay and Lesbian History for High School and College Students*. Los Angeles: Alyson Publications, 1994.

Jordan, Judith, Stephen Bergman, Cynthia Garcia Coll, Natalie Eldridge, Julie Mencher, and Jean Baker Miller. *Women's Growth in Diversity*. Wellesley, MA: Wellesley College Center for Research on Women, 1997.

Kaplan, Justin, and Anne Bernays. *The Language of Names: What We Call Ourselves and Why It Matters*. New York: Simon & Schuster, 1997.

Katz, Judith. *White Awareness: Handbook for Anti-racism Training*. Norman, OK: University of Oklahoma Press, 1978.

Katz, Neil H., and John W. Lawyer. *Communication and Conflict Resolution Skills*. Dubuque, IA: Kendall/Hunt, 1992.

Katz, Phyllis. *Towards the Elimination of Racism*. New York: Pergamon Press, 1976.

Kim, Elaine H., and Eui-Young Yu. *East to America: Korean American Life Stories*. New York: New Press, 1997.

Lewis, Reginald, and Blair S. Walker. *Why Should White Guys Have All the Fun?* New York: Wiley, 1995.

Linton, Simi. *Claiming Disability: Knowledge and Identity*. New York: New York University Press, 1998.

Liu, Eric. *The Accidental Asian*. New York: Random House, 1998.

McCall, Nathan. *Makes Me Wanna Holler*. New York: Vintage Books, 1995.

McIntosh, Peggy. *White Privilege and Male Privilege: A Personal Account of Coming to See Correspondences through Work in Women's Studies*. Working Paper 189. Wellesley, MA: Wellesley College Center for Research on Women, 1988.

Mfume, K., and R. Stodghill. *No Free Ride*. New York: Ballantine Books, 1996.

Mintz, Steven (ed.). *Native American Voices: A History and Anthology*. Saint James, NY: Brandywine Press, 1995.

Morrison, Toni. *The Bluest Eye*. New York: Holt, Rinehart & Winston, 1970.

Nieto, Sonia. *Affirming Diversity: The Sociopolitical Context of Multicultural Education*. White Plains, NY: Longman, 1992.

O'Hearn, Claudine Chiawei (ed.). *Half and Half: Writers On Growing Up Biracial and Bicultural.* New York: Pantheon Books, 1998.

Okwu, Julian C. R. *Face Forward: Young African American Men in a Critical Age.* San Francisco: Chronicle Books, 1997.

Parks, Gordon. *The Learning Tree.* New York: Harper & Row, 1963.

The Project on Campus Community and Diversity of the Accrediting Commission for Senior Colleges and Universities of the Western Association of Schools and Colleges. *Dialogues for Diversity: Community and Ethnicity on Campus.* Phoenix, AZ: Oryx Press, 1994.

Roberts, Bari-Ellen (with Jack E. White). *Roberts vs. Texaco: A True Story of Race and Corporate America.* New York: Avon Books, 1998.

Roberts, Ralph. *Genealogy via the Internet.* Alexander, NC: Alexander Books, 1997.

Rodriguez, Richard. *Days of Obligation: An Argument with My Mexican Father.* New York: Viking, 1992.

Santiago, Esmeralda. *Almost a Woman.* Reading, MA: Perseus Books, 1998.

Shinagawa, Larry Hajime, and Michael Jang. *Atlas of American Diversity.* Thousand Oaks, CA: Sage Publications, 1998.

Shorris, Earl. *Latinos: A Biography of the People.* New York: W.W. Norton, 1992.

Sims, Ronald R., and Robert F. Dennehy (eds.). *Diversity and Differences in Organizations: An Agenda for Answers and Questions.* Westport, CT: Quorum Books, 1993.

Sosa, Lionel. *The American Dream: How Latinos Can Achieve Success in Business and in Life.* New York: E.P. Dutton, 1998.

Stalvey, Lois. *The Education of a WASP.* Madison: University of Wisconsin Press, 1989.

Stavans, Ilan. *The Hispanic Condition: Reflections on Culture and Identity in America.* New York: HarperCollins, 1995.

Suro, Robert. *Strangers among Us: How Latino Immigration Is Transforming America.* New York: Alfred A. Knopf, 1998.

Suskind, Ron. *A Hope in the Unseen.* New York: Broadway Books, 1998.

Takaki, Ronald. *A Different Mirror: A History of Multicultural America.* Boston: Little, Brown. 1993.

Takaki, Ronald. *A Larger Memory: A History of Our Diversity, with Voices.* Boston: Little, Brown, 1998.

Tannen, Deborah. *You Just Don't Understand: Women and Men in Conversation.* New York: William Morrow, 1990.

Tatum, Beverly Daniel. *Why Are All the Black Kids Sitting Together in the Cafeteria? And Other Conversations about Racial Identity.* New York: HarperCollins, 1997.

Terkel, Studs. *Coming of Age: The Story of Our Century by Those Who've Lived It.* New York: New Press, 1995.

Terkel, Studs. *Race.* New York: New Press, 1992.

Thomas, Roosevelt. *Beyond Race and Gender.* New York: American Management Association, 1991.

Verburg, Carol. *Making Contact: Readings from Home and Abroad.* Boston: Bedford Books, 1997.

Walters, Mary. *Ethnic Options: Choosing Identities in America.* Berkeley, CA: University of California Press, 1990.

West, Cornel. *Race Matters.* New York: Vintage Books, 1993.

Wiesel, Elie. *Night.* New York: Bantam Books, 1987.

Williams, Gregory. *Life on the Color Line: The True Story of a White Boy Who Discovered He Was Black.* New York: NAL/Dutton, 1996.

Wiseman, Richard, and Robert Shuter (eds.). *Communicating in Multinational Organanizations.* Thousand Oaks, CA: Sage Publications, 1994.

Wood, Julia. *Gendered Lives: Communication, Gender, and Culture.* Belmont, CA: Wadsworth, 1998.

X, Malcolm. *The Autobiography of Malcolm X.* New York: Ballantine Books, 1992.

Zuckerman, Amy J., and George Simons. *Sexual Orientation in the Workplace: Gay Men, Lesbians, Bisexuals, and Heterosexuals Working Together.* Thousand Oaks, CA: Sage Publications, 1996.

INDEX

A

Active listening:
    checklist, 152
    discussed, 118, 151
Adaptability, in organizations, 49
Ageism:
    defined, 112
    study of, 79
Albert, Lou, 204
Americans, defined, 12
Angelou, Maya, 138
Arbitration, 185
Arenas, Andrea-Teresa, 195
Aronson, Elliot, 161–62
Arreola, José, 48
Assimilation, theories of, 10–11
Astin, Alexander, 19, 37, 120
Axtell, Roger, 129

B

Barriers:
    acknowledging and overcoming, 37,
        83–88
    to effective communication, 144–46

    examples of, 59–83
    personal, defined, 58
    social, defined, 59
    See also Social barriers.
Bates, Karen, 86
Becker, James, 198
Bingham, Raymond, 135
Blair, Judy, 163
Blauner, Bob, 78
Blethen, Frank, 45, 202
Bodenhausen, Galen, 62
Bogardus, Emory, 108
Box, James, 67, 117
Bradley, Bill, 193
Burton, John, 180

C

Camden, Carl T., 198
Campus climate, effects of, 100–101
Carson, Benjamin, 21
Census:
    changes in, 2–6
    data
        on education, 99
        on poverty, 97

Census *(continued)*:
  first, 2–3
  projections from, 3–4, 21, 201
  racial categories in, 5
Chang, Yvonne, 197
Classism, defined, 115
Cognitive flexibility, defined, 132
College students:
  diversity of, 6
  intolerance among, 9–10
  isolation of, 100–101
  misconceptions about, 97, 98–99
Common ground, 193
Communication:
  barriers to, 144–46
  cultural differences and, 136–37
  and culture, 128–32
  difficult, 149–51
  and diversity consciousness, 134–42
  electronic, 132–34
  "I feel" formula, 85, 182–83
  importance of, 142–43
  inclusive, 151–53
  intercultural, 129–30
  multicultural, 141–42
  in organizations, 49
  rate of, 153
  styles, 136–37, 141, 152–53
  and teamwork, 165–66, 169, 178
  wait time in, 141
  See also Kinesics; Language.
Computers:
  communication through, 132–34
  virtual teamwork on, 165–66
Conflict:
  and communication, 182–83
  discussed, 179–87
  management of, 180, 181–87
    approaches to, 181–84
    defined, 180
    discussed, 158, 169, 180, 181–187
    the six C's of, 182–85
    ten principles of, 185–86
  yin-yang in, 181
Cosby, Bill, 119

Cose, Ellis, 84
Covey, Stephen, 45, 164
Co-victimization, 149
Critical thinking, 116
Cullen, Countee, 143
Cultural awareness workshops, 120
Cultural diffusion, 133
Cultural encapsulation, 108
Cultural immersion, 101
Cultural lag, 8–9
Cultural landscape, 2–10
Cultural pride, 8, 36–37, 85, 95
Cultural separation, 8–10
Culturally specific, 129
Culture:
  affirming, 36–37, 39, 104–106
  and communication, 128–32, 135–37
  defined, 2
  material, 135
Cummings, Elijah, 141

D

Decentering, 176
Demographics:
  changes in, 2–4, 201–202
  urban vs. rural, 2–3
DeSantis, Andrea, 67
Dialogues, difficult:
  explained, 149
  ground rules of, 150–51
Disabled:
  discussed, 20, 32, 88, 108, 201
  entering workforce, 6
  perceptions of, 61, 67, 70
Discrimination:
  blatant vs. subtle, 80–81
  costs of, 49, 52, 82–83
  defined, 79
  extent of, 81
  individual vs. institutional, 81–82
  intragroup vs.intergroup, 82
  and prejudice, 79–80

Diversity:
    awareness of, 7–8
    between and within groups, 17–18
    defined, 2, 15–16
    dimensions of, 13–16
    education, 21–23
    linguistic, 132
    managing, 15, 49
    myths about, 18–19
    religious, 201
Diversity consciousness:
    and communication, 134–42
    as a continuing process, 122
    defined, 20–21
    developing, 33, 101–22, 193
    and teamwork, 168–70
    value of, 95–96, 194–97
Diversity education:
    defined, 21
    forms of, 22, 193
    opportunities for, 120–22
Diversity skills:
    benefits for individual, 45–47
    benefits for organization, 48–50
    defined, 32
    and globalization, 198–200
    importance of, 32–45
    inadequate, costs of, 50–52, 65
    list of, 95
    at school, 33–39
    and technological change, 198–200
    at work, 40–45
Divisiveness, potential for, 202–203
Dolph, Andrea, 44
"Double consciousness," 111–12
Dowd, Karen, 41
Dubois, W.E.B., 111, 202

E

Erlich, Howard, 75
Elderly, 21, 79
Elizondo, Pat, 50

Elliott, Jane, 75–76
Ellison, Ralph, 122
Empathy, 43, 169
Ethnic humor, 152, 155–56
Ethnicity, defined, 13
Ethnocentrism:
    corporate, 65
    defined, 63
    discussed, 63–66, 146
Ethnographer, 135

F

Feagin, Joe, 81
Feedback, defined, 140
Flixible thinking, 21, 33, 43–44, 95
Frey, William, 9

G

Gardner, Howard, 34–35
Gaskins, Richard, 48
Gender:
    and campus climate, 100–101
    defined, 13
    differences in communication, 130, 137
    media coverage of, 97
    and social inequality, 113
Gilens, Martin, 97
Glass ceiling, 9, 49
Glass walls, 9
Global village, 7
Globalization, effects of, 7–8, 198–200
Goleman, Daniel, 43
Gregorian, Vartan, 133
Griffin, John Howard, 111
Groupthink:
    avoiding, 175, 176
    disadvantages of, 49
Guerney, Jr., Bernard, 186

H

Hacker, Andrew, 82
Hate crimes, on Internet, 10
Heath, Shirley Brice, 135
Hegi, Ursula, 104
Henderson, George, 145
Hot buttons, 142, 146–148
Huffman, Terry, 39
Hurston, Zora Neale, 84, 102

I

"I feel" formula, 85, 182–83
Immigrants, 7, 10, 38, 74–75, 96, 104,
　　132, 168–69, 202
Inactive listening, 146
Individualism, 105
Inequality:
　　and communication, 139–140
　　costs of, 82–83
　　defined, 112
　　experiencing, 112
　　explanations of, 58–59
　　perceptions of, 114–16, 195–96
　　and privilege, 113–14
　　seeing, 113–16
　　and social class, 13
　　and teamwork, 178
　　See also Social inequality
Intelligence:
　　critical thinking, 116
　　emotional, 42, 43
　　multiple, 34–35
Interpersonal skills, 41–43
Isms, defined, 76
Isolation:
　　at college, 100–101
　　development of, 99–100
　　and perceptions of college students,
　　　96, 97–99

J

Jefferson, Carl, 45, 50
Jigsaw method, 161–62

K

Keller, Helen, 196
Kennedy, John Fitzgerald, 122
Kennelly, Karen, 193
Kinesics, defined, 129
King, Martin Luther, 9, 112, 151
Kipling, Rudyard, 63
Kotter, John, 170–71

L

Language:
　　culturally specific, 129
　　differences, 145–46
　　diversity of, 132
　　"hot buttons" in, 142, 146–48
　　men's vs. women's styles, 130, 137
　　political correctness in, 147
　　sign, 131
　　and silence, 145
　　speed of, 153
　　in translation, 145–46, 152
　　See also Communication, Kenesics
Leadership:
　　defined, 170
　　expressive vs. instrumental, 171
　　global, 200
　　pluralistic, 171
　　strategies of, 172–73
Learning styles, 33–34
Linguicism, defined, 132
Linguistic diversity, 132

Lipnack, Jessica, 165
Listening:
    active, 118, 151–52
    inactive, 146
Longstreet, Wilma, 145

M

Maddox, Amy, 109
Majority, defined, 116
Mankiller, Wilma, 66
Maps, projections in, 63, 64
McIntosh, Peggy, 113–14
McLuhan, Marshall, 7
Media, influence of, 61, 71, 77–78, 97,
        99–100
Mediation, 185
Melting pot: *See* Assimilation.
Mercator Projection, 63–64
Meritocracy, defined, 115
Messmer, Max, 40
Mfume, Kweisi, 12
Michaelsen, Larry K., 163
Migration, 202; *See also* Demographics
Mindfulness, 170
Mindlessness, 170
Minorities:
    defined, 116
    and diversity myths, 18
    entering workforce, 6
    glass ceilings and, 9, 49
    glass walls and, 9
    marketing and, 44, 49
    and population trends, 3, 7
    and racism, 77
    and scapegoating, 87
    students as, 75, 150
Montagu, Ashley, 16
Morrison, Toni, 12
Moy, Alice, 203–204

N

Nature, influence of, 103
Networking, 37, 95, 96, 118
Nieto, Sonja, 36
Norming, 175
Norris, Donald, 198–99
Nurture, influence of, 103

O

Octoroon, 5
Olmeda, Rafael, 73
Organization, 48–50

P

Parker, Pat, 153
Perception:
    limited, 59–62
    selective, 62
Peterson, Ron, 40
Pillsbury, George, 112
Pitts, Leonard, 20
Pluralism, theory of, 13
Polisseni, Gene, 43
Porter, David H., 21
Poussaint, Alvin, 87
Power:
    and communication, 139–40
    defined, 76
    discussed, 115–16
    and prejudice, 76–78
    and teamwork, 178
Prejudice:
    defined, 71
    and discrimination, 79–80
    learning of, 72
    one's own, 72–76, 116–17
    and power, 76–78

Prejudice *(continued)*:
   results of, 74–75
   and studying, 149
Privilege, 113–14, 115
Problem solving, 35, 46
Proctor, Samuel, 31
Pulley, Tegwin Dyer, 46

Q

Quadroon, 5

R

Race:
   and communication, 149, 150
   defined, 13, 16
   and demographics, 2–6, 201–202
   and discrimination, 81–83
   discussed, 19, 74, 107, 111–12, 139,
       193, 203
   and hot buttons, 146–48
   and inequality, 58, 113–15
   as master status, 15–16
   and prejudice, 73, 74
   and stereotypes, 69
   See also Racism
Racial profiling, 74
Racism
   defined, 76–77
   discussed, 111
   institutional, 78
   and O.J. Simpson trial, 77–78
   See also Race, Social barriers
Recentering, 176
Religion:
   and discrimination, 52, 183–84
   discussed, 106, 108
   and diversity, 201
   pride in, 36
   and segregation, 9
Robinson Projection, 63–64

Robinson, Arthur, 63
Roosevelt, Eleanor, 84
Rubinstein, Moshe, 105–106
Rush, Sheila, 148

S

Sacks, Oliver, 131
Satir, Virginia, 143
Scapegoating, defined, 87
Schulman, Kevin, 75
Segregation,
   discussed, 9, 22, 99, 172, 203
   self- 100
Self-evaluation, 45, 95, 170
Sexism, defined, 115. *See also* Gender
Sexual orientation:
   and discrimination, 80, 83, 183
   discussed, 72, 86, 87, 147
   and marketing, 49
Shaw, George Bernard, 140
Shipler, David, 77
Simpson, O.J., trial of, 77–78
Social barriers:
   coping with, 84–88
   ethnocentrism as, 63–66
   perception as
      limited, 59–62
      selective, 62
   stereotypes as, 66–71
Social class:
   and cultural adjustment, 39
   defined, 13, 112
   and residential segregation, 8–9
   See also Inequality
Socialization, defined, 99
Sociocultural theory, 30–32
Solomon, Joshua, 111
Sproull, L., 134
Status:
   and communication, 139–40
   defined, 139
   master, 15–16
Steele, Claude, 69–70

Stereotypes:
  attractiveness, 67–68
  discussed, 66–71
  in teamwork, 177–78
  vulnerability, 69–70
Stohl, Ellen, 67
Storming, 174
Stretch targets, 205
Study circles, 22, 122
Success:
  barriers to, 59–83
  defined, 27–30
  at school, 33–39
  sociocultural theory of, 30–32
  at work, 40–45
  See also Communication, Diversity
       Consciousness, Teamwork
Symbols, defined, 129
Synergy:
  defined, 164
  in teamwork, 166, 176–178
  and total quality management (TQM),
       163

T

Takaki, Ronald, 12
Tannen, Deborah, 130
Teams:
  defined, 160
  high-performance, 173–76
  leadership in, 170–73
  self-managed work, 170
  strategies for building, 175–76
  virtual, 165–66
  See also Teamwork
Teamwork:
  and communication, 165–66, 169, 178
  and conflict, 179–87
  defined, 160
  development of skills, 167–68
  and diversity consciousness, 168–70
  vs. individualism, 177
  jigsaw setup of, 161–62
  obstacles to, 177–78

  predominance of, 159–60
  at school, 160–62
  synergy of, 164, 166, 176–78
  in the workplace, 162–65
  See also Teams
Terkel, Studs, 74
Thinking Outside of the Box, 44, 55
Thomas, Roosevelt, 15
Total quality management (TQM), 163
Transculturation, 39
Treisman, Uri, 161
Tschechtelin, James, 48

V

Victimization, 116
Victimization, co-, 149
von Oech, Roger, 44

W

Ward, Arnette Scott, 202
Washington, Booker T., 30
West, Cornel, 58, 149
Winfrey, Oprah, 31
Woodson, Carter, 108

X

X, Malcolm, 15–16, 107, 195
Xenophobia, 74–75

Y

Yin and Yang, 181
Young, Whitney, 117
Youth, attitudes among, 203

Z

Zangwill, Israel, 10